HOLINE

By the same author:

The Chronicles of the White Horse (Findhorn Press)
Uffington (Plantlife)
Children's Gardening (Horticultural Therapy)
The Little Big Step (Away Publications)
Able To Garden (Batsford)

HOLINE
A BRITISH JOURNEY

Bulletins from the Wayside (1950–1997)

by

PETER ALFRED PLEASE

Illustrated by

Sean Borodale

A W A Y
publications

1997

First published in 1997
by Away Publications
P.O. Box 2173, Bath BA2 3YN

Special thanks to Palden Jenkins, Annie Hunt and Martin Cox.

Cover by Alan Peacock.
Illustrations by Sean Borodale.

British Library Cataloguing-in-Production Data

ISBN 0 9530330 1 5

Typesetting by Robert W. Palmer at
Tuff Talk Press, Bath.

Printed and bound by
Antony Rowe Ltd.
Bumper's Farm, Chippenham,
Wiltshire SN14 6LH
England.

To my grandparents

HOLINE (1)

When I look through my journals of the late eighties I am confronted by pages of squiggly patterns drawn in ink. They are simple marks repeated, alternated or touching each other. I put them inside circles or shapes like sculptures I had never seen. Then one day I saw them on an Indian coin, a hand-made coin from the 14th century, a currency I did not understand, yet I felt it perfectly as a soul language, the native movements in my heart. Every little bit, twist and squiggle, when looked at as a whole, had a place, some meaning. But by themselves they appeared lost, nebulous, without real life. They resembled germs, pictures under a microscope. The squiggly lines always seemed to be swimming somewhere purposefully. But where?

I remembered the words 'germs', 'germane' and 'germinal', and 'semen' and 'seminal'; the primal fear that I was falling apart hugged them, and I liked that tender embrace. I collected old Indian coins: sometimes I arranged them on the floor around me and handled them one by one. They soothed this new-born place in me.

I never had any intention to compose this book, this holine – this bringing together of ordinary things, people, intimacies, places that have touched me on my British journey. I had written nearly all of it in my journals before the idea jumped out in the early nineties. I set to with a passion: for most of my life I have lived on a cultural wayside, and I wanted to make sense of that. The only way into my kingdom is through the shit-house door. I had to eliminate things. Look at the wayside – and it's full of debris, tenacity and insects. I always felt there was a dream there. It's in the world now. It's a common journey.

I have grouped the entries around the seasons, for the book is also a gardening odyssey, a techno-peasant dream. The italicised pieces are taken directly from my journals. I have edited out repetitions and changed them, on occasion, to make the sense clearer, or to respect privacy.

AUTUMN

A CIRCULAR WALK AROUND FROME

Beginnings are always difficult, especially finding a way on this sodden November day with a tarmacadam sky. I wanted to make a journey, anything I had not done before, so this is what I did: I walked in a circular fashion around Frome, no more than three miles. What am I doing? What am I looking for? The suburban homes, lego palaces with the omnipresent tablecloth lawns, were unlit and I felt on the outside on the street, emphasising my alone-ness. I glimpsed the subterranean reefs of compressed leaves in puddles and this warmed me with its childhood associations. I hung onto the umbrella with grim determination, refusing to be drawn in by the sombre, brooding conifers matching perfectly the uniformity of the estate houses, their shapes (like their gardens) predetermined by the shapes of bricks, the fenced boundaries. I noticed the leaves floating on puddles but I wanted to keep walking as it was so wet. Nothing is happening, just as I thought.

Children with sodden white shirts clinging to the skin passed by; others waved goodbye to each other from bicycles. I remembered the day that I walked at Christmas (after a family row) and the houses were lit with coloured lights and I felt utterly alone. A ginger cat stepped into the road and greeted me by flicking its jaw as if it were winking. I felt blank most of the time, my feet and trousers getting steadily wet.

Walking into the old part of Frome was a walk into sound, warmth and people, away from the unlit residential world with the combat weary honeysuckle hedges. 'This place is dead,' said a schoolgirl on the street. I said hello to the street cleaner; his face smoothed by the outdoors quickly relaxed: 'I'm working by six every morning.' He runs on the spot looking at me. 'When your feet get wet there's nothing you can do about it.' The rubbish, he says, has changed over the years. 'Once it was only leaves but now it's take-aways.' I walk astride the puddle flowing along the shopping arcade. The ducks on the River Frome face the current nosing the leaves. I catch nobody's eyes. I don't really want to see anything. I am content to get from A to B. I am withdrawn into my world. What am I doing in Frome? I don't know.

I see a row of derelict houses in Castle Street, all for sale and I think: I could buy this cheaply and... I'm mad! I don't want to go through this reconstruction again. I have done it. I want to move on and make contact with the BIG world again. I finished this

11

circular walk with the rain rushing down drainpipes, overflowing the kerbstones. I did not collapse. I sat by this one-bar fire and remembered this meaningless walk where nothing has been gained except this soaking and this page of words. Later, an old friend appears crying and distraught. She kneels and rests her head on my knee. I rock her gently. Her cat sits beside her, leaning against the window and the splatter of neon-lit raindrops. Beginnings and endings; this business of love is a tragic game. We no longer live together as lovers.

I have made a circular walk around Frome not just today but for the past eighteen months. These things I found: a ginger cat saying hello; my old therapist saying hello; a girl saying this place is dead; the centre of the town is alive; the friendly rubbish man; the beauty of changing autumn leaves; the pain of parting. I am back in my home again and wondering what's next.
(November 9, 1992)

STAG AND HIS BENDER

Stag Bidmead has changed his name to Peter. He lives in the bender he made, tarpaulin and hazel wands intricately woven into a huge eel trap, on the edge of the mill stream at Dunsford. He is a friend from the first Glastonbury Dance camp in 1984, and later we pushed our children in prams around Victoria Park, Bath, talking of our marriage problems. He was there at my first venture into independence, Cockmill signal box; he gravitated to the Rainbow Orchard at Pilton. Inside his bender is a cracked earthen floor, the outside coming in he says, creasing his greying, stubbly beard. His short hair, short beard, matches his stocky build with a slightly shallow chest. In the hurricane light dangling from a hook, his eyes glisten and I see both the dignity and tenderness of an older man, in his sixties, say. I am surprised and touched by the absence of forlorn Stag, now Peter, and then he laughs cocking his head and is suddenly boyish again. We talked for five hours, eight in the evening to one in the morning. He said the evening reminded him of a part of himself that he had forgotten, that he did not know; just sharing space, steaming buttercup squash in the skillet, puffing the embers in the stove, the one made by Brian Monger and Keith Nagle. It was enough.

Peter has had his heart broken in many places. He commutes between his two daughters in Bristol and his daughter Ash in

North Wales; on Tuesdays, he runs the organic vegetable stall in Glastonbury, the rest of the time he works on his well-being, going to healing classes in Bristol... A copy of my novel, The Chronicles of the White Horse, sits on a pile of clothes; inside the pages are notes on the Medicine Wheel and healing spirituality. An astrological ephemeris, a copy of Despair and Empowerment by Joanna Macey, and Understanding Key Lines in Your Life are in the bender. He leans against the peeled pole with natural crescent moons poking above a circular woven shield with a picture of a wolf on it: trust your instincts, it says. His chest wheezes a little as he speaks as if he still struggles to find the wolf in his belly.

I show him my sculptures - 'Love Me Do' - 'Stand By Me' - 'My Beautiful Anger'... I wanted to share my journey with Peter. Keeping boundaries (especially with women) is a common theme between us and we talked about the patterns in the soap opera of our lives. I like the contained feeling of the bender, the privacy, the absence of services, the space for conversation. I stitched the calico binding for the sculptures. 'No-one is fulfilled at the farm,' he says. 'The lack of proper tenancy agreements puts too much uncertainty into people's lives.' He trudges from day to day, but his dream is to journey about Britain going where his spirit takes him, taking part in the healing of the land. I say I can only make journeys when I have a settled base. Stag muses incredulously at the words a grandmother told him at a medicine wheel gathering in Wales: 'You have unconditional love for all beings.' He shakes his head and laughs boyishly. 'She said that...about me!' I go to sleep with a recurring question: Who is my family? I sleep fitfully, listening to the mill stream. I dream of a great wind blowing. I am hanging onto some house foundations but futilely. I see the underground home of a book artist and it is full of food to eat. I dance for Stag in the morning when he has gone. I wish him wholeness and the cutting edge. (Dunsford Farm, November 11, 1992)

MUD POOL AT SUNSET

I stop by the straight-line thistles, pappus mopheads drooping on single stems; the prevailing wind has carried them to the bottom of this slope, crowding the hazel margins with stillness and dry, faded browns, with leaves bent down crackly to the touch. These woolly thistles cannot move; they appear resigned, stuck to the ground, waiting for the wind's touch. Their grave stillness is the opposite of the incessant slippery ice slide movements of crane flies, searching searching and never appearing to find it. A pointed-eared fox stares hard at me, moves silently off along the sheep track, then stops and risks another stare. I stop by the cauldron; the trickle of the stream, the sticks crossing each other, the banks of moss and rust excite my attention for detail. The cool misty air beside the pool surprises me. I am alarmed by waving branches, isolated cracks and creaks, and then I see the squirrel collecting the nuts. I am relieved. I keep looking around. This pool is a hidden bowl with margins of mud as flat as the water. Out of both come sturdy bulrushes, spear-like leaves taller than the brown fruiting shafts, at once so near, bold and striking. I look for the words and they do not appear easily. Goat willow, in dense, arched stands, rise first from the mud: they are dwarfed by sombre-green alder, with ash, oak and pine rising higher on all sides in the distance. This mud is fertile. I see the grey-world shadows of trees in the water. I listen. I am very receptive, and I am going too fast for this quiet place.

Circular ripples cross the still water. A lone gnat patrols the edges, moving up and down, up and down. I am blank. I notice more gnats, the way they free-fall and flick themselves up, giving the impression of ever moving and always staying still. The mare's tail thronging the boundary of one side of the pool are keeling over, the ring of thread-like leaves blackening with bolts between them. I am drawn by the mud pool and the spear which quickens its depths. I am frightened of this deep down place. I hold onto too much, including this fear of being all of myself, enjoying myself. I glimpse a quiet, walking image, a man with a green-leafed coat, long-tongued hair and grinning eyes. I look up quickly towards the far bank. He isn't there. Rooks return raucously, singly, in pairs, droves against the sky. I try to name the colour for this pearly shade of blue and it eludes me. I am getting cold sitting here. The scolding wren is silent. Distance comes closer in this thinning light. I think: I am always alone with my pen yet rarely am I lonely. Bored sometimes. Why do I do it? The thought arrives: I see and feel things more sharply; it brings my world into focus, just as the branches jump out at me in this half-light. I literally jump! A sharply moving hum like an arrow (except it looked more like a disc) passed rapidly over my head. I shuddered. I could not believe it, or move, and then I did, retreating ignominiously the way I had come and frightened by something nameless. I did not look back. A bird? I think not. It could not have landed safely at that speed in

the *undergrowth, literally a few feet away. The way my psychic
hairs bristled I felt I had received a warning shot. Time to leave
and so I did, grateful to climb into this warmer air and see the
peach melba sky over Wellow.* (September 26, South Stoke, 1990)

LAST DANCE

Little historical connections fascinate me, especially when they
spring out of nowhere, from the trampled blades of couch grass
on the wayside. I stopped on a narrow track behind the Cluny
Hill Hotel, Forres, and let the autumnal, stone-clear air embrace
me. I heard the chirrupings of a grasshopper, then another
calling nearby at my feet, picking its way awkwardly through the
grass and stepping into a small, earthen depression. Something
made me crouch, stay silent. It turned around slowly as if trying
to see its back legs, stopped and chirruped. Another one answered from the long grass, and another, both crawling carefully to
the mud arena. Within minutes, to my amazement, five grasshoppers stared across inches of silence at each other without
moving, as if they were eyeing each other up. Then one struck
its soundboard and spun on its heels. This set them all going
and they twirled, chirruping loudly, waving their antennae, and
I fancied they stamped the ground, getting excited by the dance,
for what else could it be. Two minutes later they left as they had
come, one by one. A day passed and I remembered Aesop, the
Greek storyteller, and how he described over two thousand years
ago grasshoppers dancing wildly while the industrious ants
stored food to survive the winter. (October 19, 1976)

IONA

I string together three memories and each has a little of the
miraculous in it, a feature of this Hebridean island.
On autumn days the Sound of Iona glows red from the reflections of the rosy granite cliffs of Mull. The colours float on the
water as if some big hand has painted them there. In a corn
stubble field, above the wee harbour opposite Fionnphort on
Mull, I hoped to see some unusual bird visitors, the twites. A
flock of these small, streaky brown birds gusted into the beach
end of the field. I stepped towards them and the wind lifted
them in its arms and threw the birds to the far end of the field. I
walked slowly towards them and they shifted over my head and

15

far away. I stood in the middle of the field not knowing what to do – suddenly it rained twites, the entire flock landed hopping around me, twittering noisily.

* * * *

The autumn gales hum violently in the telegraph wires, spinning the sand up from the salt-lean grazing pastures in the west of the island. In the teeth of a gale, a shepherd and his dog herded sheep into a sheltered valley, and they did their work well, keeping them bunched and moving, the dog weaving behind the flock, worrying their heels. Then one got stuck in a fence and the more it struggled the more the wires tightened their grip. Its forlorn cries sped through the storm like arrows. The main flock, now farther on, stopped and looked back. The dog stopped and looked at the sheep, looking back. The shepherd stopped and looked at the dog looking back at the sheep, looking at the one that was stuck. I stopped and looked at the shepherd, looking at the dog, looking at the sheep, looking at the one that was stuck. At that point I looked over my shoulder.

* * * *

A Dutch visitor to the island said his name was Oak and told me this story. There once was a man with a green complexion, greener in fact than the grass growing around his ears, much taller than a sparrow but considerably smaller than a marrow. He wore a silver axe on his back, a sharp little thing which he kept in leather skin. One day, he was walking in the oak forest when he heard the crash crash crash of a lumberjack. So Tom, that was his name, pulled out his little silver axe, swished round his head and cried: I'm a lumberjack. Well, their terrible laughter echoed among the trees; it was picked up by the birds and hummed by the bees. 'YOU A LUMBERJACK? IMPOSSIBLE.' So all that day, and the ones following it, Tom was climbing up the trees and felling them like fleas. A great fat hairy man came up to Tom and wanted to know where he learnt to cut trees like THAT. They had never seen anything like THAT before. 'In the desert', said Tom. 'The desert?' said the lumberjacks, 'But there aren't any trees in the desert.'
'Not any more,' said Tom. (Iona, autumn 1975)

THE DOORKEEPER

Michael Forsyth, the old gardener at Iona Abbey, lies under a small tombstone in that hallowed ground near The Reilig Orain where ancient kings of Scotland and Norway are said to be buried. He was my first gardening teacher, and back in the 1970's, while puffing on his full-strength Capstan cigarettes, he showed me how to cut straight lines in turf, how to prune the towering fuchsia hedges and to recognise my first garden plant, red valerian (*Centranthus ruber*) sprouting from walls at The Nunnery. I pieced together a little of his life, a thick-skinned, black sheep of man. He had worked in the engineering and construction industry building dams, discovered an illicit fur trade in cats in London during the Second World War, and what with coming and going through three marriages he gravitated to Iona in the 1960's where he worked as one of a group of crafts-men restoring the Abbey with the Reverend George MacLeod, the practical Scottish visionary. I suspect his proudest moment was putting up the mahogany roof for St. Michael's Chapel. He went away, came back, went away and finally stayed on, finding a place as a gardener. When the spiritual demands became a burden he disappeared to Oban on the mainland and drowned them with whisky. He always returned, picking up his spade and wheelbarrow and continuing as normal. I met him shortly before he died. I worked with him, cutting new edges to The Street of The Dead, and, twice a day, he brewed very strong tea and talked of his favourite subjects: sailing, the direction of the wind, the army, the building business, women ('can't live with them or without them'). I don't know what impulse drew me back, with affection, to light some sage on his grave. The gesture pleased me though I knew he would have laughed at it. The familiarity would have embarrassed him. The truth is I hardly knew him. Perhaps I knew dimly that this man who lived as the doorkeeper to the abbey, half-in, half-out, half sinner, half saint, had started me off in a direction from which I have never turned back. (Iona, 1990)

IONA PATCHWORK

I feel brave on Iona walking by myself. The chatter dies down bit by bit. There is no way to get lost here; all ways lead back home. The salt-lean Machair in the west, the earth stones under my feet; the ravens peeping over the cliff at the marble quarry, their eyes following me across each block of white stone. The beginnings of stone are smooth and hummocky as sand dunes. The little white-washed houses appear as specks of sand. I close my eyes: the greyness of not-knowing and questions questions questions. I have no answers. I am astounded by seaweed, it glistens, bends, glides out of the water the tips of islands under the sea. I feel safer on land doing amazing rock traverses four feet off the ground. I am stalked by a feeling of inadequacy this day. I see the Northern divers, ducks with eel bodies. How brave they are! Citrine and olivine I pick lightly from the Bay of the Coracle. They call me stranger. They are strange and beautiful. I want them. I return easily to this jewel day, sunrise to sunset, all the blues, reds and mauves. I lose my way, I find myself, I lose myself. I am stronger when I fight for what I value. What do I value?

The manoeuvres of the black Dor beetle confounds these thoughts. It is solid, scarab-like and a lover of sheep dung. The concrete eclipses all these words, makes shadows of things. I know nothing at the moment. I feel better when I acknowledge this. I picture the Englishman in an Arab's costume, the doves coming from his heart. I saw that first on Iona...the island of the kelp flies, scuttling out of seaweed ready made. A single bee startled me in the gulf of the Deep Valley; Lotta and her black dog appeared at The Machair; a buzzard mewing under the telegraph pole – these are pieces from this Iona patchwork, a lifetime in one day. Tranquillity touched me and made me speechless. I am none the wiser for coming here. I have made no decisions or given myself under-takings. The greyness remains; the questions are not so import-ant... I feel brave on Iona walking with myself. The chitter chatter dies down, flares up, goes away. There is no way to get lost here. All ways lead back home. Iona, I take you with me.

(Sithean House, Iona, November 7, 1990)

TRAVELLER

The word is from the French 'travail' and denotes the pain of a journey as well as the pain of birth, a labour that has been chosen. I cannot be sure when this idea of journeys announced itself. Two pictures appear: sitting in the back seat of my father's car and suddenly plunging into the Thames valley and a vast connected pattern of fields and river stretching into the water colour sunset. I remember thinking: I want to go down there as far as I can, to see what's on the other side. I was four-years-old. Another fragment: a boy running along a dirt track which leads to a garden I cannot see but I know is there. That is all. The dirt track, the unmade road without signposts, are significant for these are the ways I went as a child looking for sharp-teethed mice under corrugated iron, collecting dirty Tizer bottles (with threepenny refunds) from ditches, saving discarded cigarette packets with colourful pictures of ships, castles and bearded men, collecting baskets of buttercup flowers for sixpenny bits – a world of small things from the wayside.

I made my first garden in a barrel, a rocky landscape with stone houses for stag beetles, piping and grass for field mice, a plastic tub for tadpoles, a cave of bricks for the slow-worms I plucked from the sunny churchyard tombstones. This garden belonged to the creatures as well as me. It was not a prison. They could leave and they did. But it was *my* place, in a way that home and school belonged to somebody else. Here I had my first taste of being me. This garden was the outward sign, fruits as it were, of my private journeys between the fields, ditches and hedgerows, streams and housing estates around my home. I especially liked walking at dusk when the winter trees glittered with gold and blacks. Being alone, I could be me. This child is hard to see ferreting under hedgerows to find sleeping hedgehogs, coating branches with sticky condensed milk to catch small birds, sitting on ivy banks to hear squeaking voles. For this six-year-old the wayside was freedom, a natural world, uncultivated. It belonged to everybody. I did not know the word 'native' then. While the world moved (and going as fast as they could about it) I stood still, going nowhere in particular. I lived on the edge of the unknown and thought of it as home. I devoured books about animals (like the Tasmanian Devil); I dreamed of going port-knocking in Brazil, painting myself as an aboriginal. I made igloos, a wigwam and dressed as an Indian. I was always going to a new country and finding something precious. I lost this world, of course, because I could never name it and give it value. How can you name the contentment when the day sinks into the inky hedgerows, or the sun floats in the middle of a wood? At school I gave my hands away and a grimacing face peers out of the school photographs in mute disapproval. I did not like this sign-posted world.

Twenty years later I returned by accident to that wayside, still

19

oblivious of the accumulated floodwaters of woe and anger within me. I loved wandering on the Downs (ostensibly to write a series of walks for the *Berkshire Mercury*). I bought myself *The Oxford Book of Wild Flowers* and identified by colour the verge-side cow parsley, eggs-and-bacon, wild marjoram, six-spotted burnet moths, pygmy shrews. I opened a small, disused window and glimpsed a tense twine of yearning, frustration and uncertainty. I walked the back roads between Reading and Wokingham, soaking up the wayside smells, watching tadpoles by the River Loddon at Sindlesham, remembering names that I had forgotten for twenty years. I glimpsed that child again. The wayside listened to me like a grandparent without judgement, helping me without coercion to find my voice. I resolved to quit. Many years later I reconciled myself with journalism as an important stepping stone.

AUTUMN CROCUS

The back road ran within sight of the Findhorn estuary, behind the marshy headlands where sheep grazed the corn stubble. Once I had seen an osprey pluck a salmon from these waters but that day the sky was empty, and I was disappointed that the council had cut the wayside verges and the flowers had withered to a dry patchwork – except for a single bloom of the meadow saffron (*Colchicum autumnale*) swaying with the breeze. A faint buzzing sound came from the delicate, purplish flower. I squatted and saw a fat red-tailed bumblebee inside. It looked dead. I tickled its furry abdomen with a blade of grass until it hummed, turned around buzzing, and dragged itself up one of the milky petals, transparent in the biting northern light. The back legs stretched and combed the sides; the wings lifted it clear, steering a wobbly course before crash-landing on the road. The flower continued to buzz, for deep inside a second red-tailed bumblebee stirred on the cushion of orange anthers. The bee regained its senses in the sea air, except a sense of direction for it, too, nose-dived into the grass. Both these bees looked drugged as if they had succumbed to the narcotic alkaloid, colchicine, derived from this plant. Had these two bees, barely fitting inside that single bloom, fallen there by mistake or had they chosen it to ease their journey to wherever they go when they die? (Autumn, 1976)

THE ROAD TO GLASTONBURY

One strand in my life at the moment is my sculpture, exima, which I worked with at Dragon Hill, Glastonbury, and here at Urzulei, a Sardinian mountain village. Exima, blessing or curse, being held, loved by an older man and encouraged by the big eyes of a girl. I can see myself carving the germinal head inside the bender, the spiritual headquarters of Zeb and his followers, playing their didgees and talking of time portals in the Mayan calendar. I felt like an old man to their intoxicated youthful zeal. Outside, the juniper and pine scents the mountain air; thunder rolls across the valley and lightning vividly brightens the dark windowpanes. I wanted to write this beside the brooding giant holm oaks at the ruins of the Nuraghe, the Sardinian Bronze Age culture, on the white rugged mountain plateau above the village. But I would lose my way with this full-blown romanticism...

I met the old man – his name, significantly, I do not know – an old man almost anywhere, long-drawn weathered face and a honk of a nose, with a beret crowning his head which appeared to lean backwards, broad across the cheekbones, then narrow. He looked familiar, and then I recalled the Nuraghe bronze figures of the shepherds with cloaks and scabbards, bows or headgear sprouting horns, except this old man is a pastoralist in the mountains, likes his sixteen per-cent red wine he makes, his own aqua-vitae, and, in the words of his son Francesco, a student at Milan University, is kaputt. They live in different worlds, the old father out of the Bronze Age, his son looking towards the West. I see the mother, black-shrouded, is proud of her son speaking a foreign language, French, with me. At the table, his father stares ahead, grunting and blowing his breath, resuming his stillness as if he is a statue, a relic himself. When he dies the old ways would go, the cattle grazing, the

21

peccorrino sheep cheese, the vegetable garden on the mountain – all gone, and they know it. I felt sad, they felt sad, and there was no point in talking about it. It would happen anyway. This gulf between father and son echoed something in Glastonbury, the near impossibility of bridging spiritual places between different generations. Each has something other to discover, perhaps. Does the shadow of one generation become the doorway for their brightest children? My exima sculpture is about embodying this lost, submerged person, the disclaimed son of our fathers, a dreaming son. I thought that Francesco was like the Indian son who left the reservation to study the white man's ways and perhaps returned to defend the tribe in a modern way...

Out of the village in the fields and lanes Susan Seymour and I were invited to lunch by a group of Urzulei males, and I was touched by the respectful friendship between them, ranging from early twenties to mid-fifties, and how freely this friendship had reached out to us... It belonged to no individual. I wander through these associations not quite knowing what they mean. There is incomprehension between the generations...of grandfather's dreams, lives unlived or lived by grandchildren, or lives that are lived by grandparents so that the grandchildren do not need to live them. It is recognition of this struggle, this passing on and freeing dependents that abides with this sculpture. I see this in Francesco and his Nuraghe father. I think this happens all over the world. Exima is about meeting without the desire to change. It is a road to Glastonbury, a place where the generations can be reconciled.

I liked the old Nuraghe man, his mute and gruff witness, his crusty style so rugged and archaic, his continuity in the face of chosen loneliness, his fondness for strong drink, his conservatism, appalling stubbornness, fortitude... In some ways he reminded me of my grandfather, distant, reliable, old-fashioned, taken for granted, even a cause of embarrassment, but always loved.

A great thundering rain still beats at the windows. The street dogs bark. The lights come on and off. Urzulei is touched by its storm. I have wandered a whole page, and I know not what really.
(Urzulei, All Souls day, 1993)

SEPTEMBER CHANGES

There's drama in the air. The black tidal skies are drenched with sunlight and rainbows; the mushroom rains arrive at the autumnal equinox. Underfoot are galaxies of microbes stirring the pot, the sweet smell of decay – comma butterfly with white legs inspects rotting apple; red admiral on black mulberry fruits – first ivy flowers – windfall apples, eight out of ten with codlin apple moth borings; eight out of ten on tree without – poplar leaves clatter – swan leads cygnets on training flight, their wings pedal the wind – hazelnuts fall into my hand – grasshoppers call to each other and tryst in the long grass – wasps hunt flies on sunny corrugated iron – conkers gleam chestnut under trees – as elderberries darken, the colour drains from leaves – the solid purple of dogwood (*Cornus sanguinea*) highlights the true golds of field maple (*Acer campestre*) – wasps first thing in the morning, daddy-longlegs last thing at night – first impression of leaves flying about – I notice oak galls. Are they acorns? – yew berries splat onto cars – wayside skeletons of docks, thistles, burdocks, mulleins, hogweed, ragwort – when the swallows go, the starlings congregate – tiny male hazel catkins appear as nuts ripen – fourteen small tortoiseshells snug on red valerian.

ROTTING FRUIT

Drawn, in spite of my inertia, I pick up this pen literally mesmer-ised by the fanned beauty of two red admirals, perfection in every detail, stepping daintily over the rotting plums; thick brown, luscious squelches at the foot of the tree. I am stunned by this perfection; the wings beat faster at the approach of a bluebottle and vigorously as a wasp crawls closer. Perfection at every stage, one of the signs of nature's beauty and economy. The butterflies transform the rotting plums into jewels, the one needing the other. The red admirable blends with the earth, its central soft velvet mimicking a shadow, so well matched it is; startling to see the flashing border of russet red with four black dots and the black and white outer semaphores to each wing. This one holds its ground despite the whirlwind buzz of blowflies and one angry wasp...it feeds in peace, wings shut, revealing the chain necklace of white crescent moons. Above, poplar leaves rattle, echoing the sound of heavy raindrops falling. I notice, with a smile, that I, too, fan an inquisitive wasp away with my hand. The top part of the wings can also retract into the white broken ground of the undersides; so for a moment the butterfly vanishes, at one with crumbs of soil, plant feeding roots, bits of snail shell and leaf twists. I look hard to find something interesting to say and so go further from myself. The plums catch my eye. I move and the red admiral is gone. The wasps don't give a hoot. They feast without moving, buried head first. The old menace of being stung agitates me and I automatically protect my crotch with my hands.

The hard clatter of leaves tells the turning of the seasons. I feel sad seeing such exquisite beauty, side by side with these dismembered thoughts of winter. The sun has brought them all out and the plum tree has spread the table. A bluebottle clasps the base of the tree, facing the earth two inches away, not moving except to massage its jaws and rub the back of its head; out of the wind seems to be the main priority. The wasps are kindly to one another and step aside to let one of their kind approach the feast. One suddenly clasps the abdomen of another and they tumble for a second and return to the plum together. It's like a little spontaneous act of joy confronted by this abundance. I look at my watch. Time. My thoughts vanish into black holes when I turn my attention to this. The wasps are like lions at their prey. The flies move freely among them while they are feasting. On a flower they would be fair game... Is this part of our necessity, to experience the jewelled facets of each moment, of different lives, and to give this back; to hold up a mirror to recognise ourselves? The red admiral is back! (Combe Down, September 7, 1990)

LAWRENCE AND CHERRY HILLS

I finish cutting the grass and introduce myself. A wet day and two gaunt figures; both their hands are cold and like sealing wax. First impressions − bags under the eyes, the dull clothes, her's a sort of Marks and Spencer's checked woollen coat, his a 40s-style trench-coat, a mole-skin type hat with a black bow, patent boots and ditch-coloured trousers. I think smugly: they're just ordinary people. I don't have to put on any airs of knowing a lot. At lunch, Dr Peter Thompson (my boss at Oldfield Nurseries) writes on his clipboard about the minor and major purposes of establishing seed guardians for rare vegetables. He is going to present the case for Lawrence Hills to try and secure grants. Cherry Hills sits at the back. 'I mustn't interrupt,' she says. Mr Hills is going full steam. When he discovers that I am a HDRA member he eyes me up. I say nothing. He weaves a thick weft of possibilities, mixing facts with little-known theories and speculations. Lunch! Cherry eats a

24

roast wild pigeon she has brought specially. They describe themselves as nutritional cripples. She can't eat anything that may contain antibiotics; he has to have a gluten-free diet. Apparently he was so sick as a child he hardly went to school. He stayed at home almost an invalid. His mother thought he would be a writer. His father had been an inventor. 'At the age of four,' he says, 'I made up my first poem: When it rains the puddles are filled with water.' When Cherry met him he was close to dying. She recognised his problem – a gluten allergy – and he turned the crossroads. They fell in love over their joint interest in ancient archaeology. They married, she said under her breath, in an Oxford registry office. Observation, she says, is at the root of it all. 'Observing God's works in humbleness.' They say this several times. But who has time to see? Apparently the amateur, and this is what Mr Hills is after to conduct his experiments. But how is it you have not got stuck? I ask. 'Because I take side roads and I have never had a job with a pension.' He says he never forces any organic theory or practice on anyone. He quotes many examples. He abhors mumbo-jumbo; stirring Steiner potions one way for an hour and then the other way for another hour. 'All unnecessary. Be down to earth.' Cherry grabs my arm. 'You are tense. Gardener's grip.' Apparently too much gripping creates tensions because it only works one set of muscles. 'It's important to stretch the hands to work the other pair.' She quotes the medical names. I tell her of my work with disturbed children and my writing. 'Dr Thompson, you had better watch out or you will lose your gardener,' laughs Mr Hills... She describes herself as a Jungian, but how, before she met Lawrence, she was on the other side – the mystical side – but now she had learnt to be practical. I am impressed by their characters – originals, energetic (she is 85, he a few years younger). The room smelt of new beginnings. They stirred me up. I caught it – whatever IT is. (Oldfield Nurseries, Godspieceleaze, September 30, 1981)

* * * *

PS: Five years later I watched them walk slowly around the National Organic Demonstration Garden they had founded, two frail figures, by far the oldest living things above ground in that field. Their cranky persistence realised a dream belonging to many. I felt a wave of affection for them. (1986)

GILES CHRISTIAN

He told me this dream: 'I am in a room with a single electric light and a black dog watches and bites the lead. It turns into cinders. A wild-looking traveller appears on the other side of the room, holding three dogs but they look like one dog with three heads.' Giles wrinkles his thinking furrows and gazes at me with wide open eyes. Their slight intensity is softened by the sadness tweaking his generous lips. I feel it, too. Yet again he rocks the see-saw in his life, burning himself out, his intellect disregarding his fine animal nature. 'I am numbed sexually,' he tells me simply. He breathes some of the golden air this early autumn day, a big man at war within himself. A buzzard circles above the wood at White Ox Mead making the blue sky come closer. The path across green meadows weaves in and out of the wood using old lanes forgotten except by tussocks of bent grass, a bolting rabbit. It's an unusual story: the discovery of Findhorn and its own world of light; the refined brilliant world terminated by a descent into the mutant strains of the Windsor free festivals, the precursors of the travellers; Mathematics at Oxford; the eventual resurrection with Cybernetics at Edinburgh University; database trouble-shooting; the clean break selling his home and chattels, the move to Rainbow Orchard at West Pennard. Giles showed me photographs of his bender, the silver snout from the stove, the moat dug around it to collect flood water. A bear's den, indeed. 'I felt sexy then,' he tells me smiling, his big eyes staring out, not from the thinker but from a lost or forgotten part of himself. He travelled the Rainbow Camps in south west England, wore his black boots, old combat clothes, parked up on hills doing nothing in particular. A hundred little things sucked dry the money he had saved. Winter arrived, teasing apart his ideas. I met him in Bath. He had put aside his temple building plans, his monumental gesture to the intangible realms, and was applying for a computing job with a government research body. I knew all this but not the Giles before me now – burnt-out and living as a recluse in his Wantage terraced home. The brambles grew around him but it was there he mended from his earlier wanderings.

Down the glowing, winding lane from Wellow to Stony Littleton, he talked about The Decision. He has decided to sell his house and study theology at Oxford; that will be in his fortieth year. 'It reconciles everything in me,' he says, gesticulating with his broad *hands, soft plump flesh, yet with the span of a labourer's. 'It will be a point of balance.' This word is important to him for he knows his mistakes. He envisages a flatlet, a modern hermit's cell, a desk for writing, a place to sleep, wash and cook, his place in the battle-field of theology, as he puts it. I say he might become a travelling theologian, a balm for those on the road. He laughs, gurgling from somewhere in his ample belly. Giles is an old friend from the early days of Findhorn and of Iona where he often stayed, the world of St. Columba; he remembers eccentric priests who saw fairies, his childhood and schooldays on the Malvern Hills, his initiation into dope, sex and earth mysteries. They chucked him out from Malvern – he shared this distinction with Aleister Crowley.*

Dancing, he would find himself, an original, letting his long arms hang low, stepping into some African part of himself, taking off his clothes one by one until the sweat gleamed on his domed head, ran in rivulets down his back. This Giles tapped the energy rising from the ground. We climbed up to the long barrow at Stony Littleton and slept on the chalk turf, the seagulls following the farmer ploughing; so quickly did they land they appeared to fly up from under the wheat. That mound of initiation worked some of its magic; we left in more buoyant spirits, less talk, more acceptance. I told Giles he walked flat-footedly. 'I always walk like this,' he retorted, raising his voice and arching his eyebrows. 'And I intend to continue it.' The lane strolled through Foxcote and into the sheep-fall meadows and billowing trees. At every farmhouse, I cautioned Giles: 'This looks like a good place for a rottweiler.' Giles picked up a mean stick. I told him the true story of a sufi who hated dogs, loathed their four-footed ways, for the Muslim calls them dirty. One day, he wandered by mistake into a rubbish dump on the outskirts of Cairo. In this no-man's-land, he noticed a dog, another and more until he was surrounded by a pack, and they were not friendly. No words could describe the fear in this would-be saint. He howled out a huge ferocious dog in him and scattered the lot.

By the paddling murmur of a brook Giles cheerfully shrugged off his burdened adult. He touched the red-tangled alder roots, dipped his hands into gaping pools. He waddled on his haunches. 'I loved these places as a child. I'd explore them for hours. ' He opened his big eyes. He told me about Muffin, the sixteen-year-old beauty on Iona and their skinny-dipping in the moon tracks in the bay of

The Machair. The happiest moment of his life was at the Rock of Manannan, the Irish sea god, on Iona. 'I watched the sun set and the moon rise at the same time. There was nothing else, just me, and I was supremely happy.' When he is an old man he wants to die there. I see so much of myself in Giles, and I want to protect him when people find it hard to understand his strange genius combining the rocky elemental world, the piety of wattle churches or simple bender, and the brilliantly lit world of Internet, a contemporary Indra's Web of co-creation and interdependence. No wonder we are all lost, we are all travellers, for only those who share the travail, the pain of this birth, deserve the name... I said to Giles that the three-headed dog in his dream reminded me of Cerberus, the guardian of the Underworld. He would have to befriend him if he wished to make progress. I hope the theologian is unconventional, lusty, with a heart and sharp-edged thoughts to defend it. By the quarry at Writhlington, the former carboniferous coal measures, I found a rock with the perfect imprint of cycad tree ferns. The pattern of little hearts, or tear drops or wiggling spermatozoa reminded me of a seminary, something still dark and hidden but struggling on an unknown journey. (September 3, 1994)

STOCKPORT

Every time I see Stockport on the map, a mizmaze of lines rubbing shoulders with Manchester, I hear the singing voices of four tinker children. One Hallowe'en, they knocked on my door opposite Bolton's Superheater and Pipe Works and sang me this song and I wouldn't pay them – Roger Brereton, Shiun Playt, David and Daniel Donalin, all six and seven-year-olds – until they wrote it down.

> Bun fayre nat, sason brat
> Three litre angls des in brat
> Won can etr a bisct, and won can smoc an pap
> Won can go hunting at ten oclock at nat.

I worked there as a community service volunteer for nine months. I was unprepared for the gritty harshness of people's lives, out of my depth with the isolation of dying old people, yet attracted by the stranger's willingness to talk, and a certain north-facing vitality. A spade was a bloody shovel here. Things come back, the sweet hoppy clouds enveloping the city from Robinson's Brewery, the rag and bone men and their horses, the vast mill-town terraced estates (in one of those houses an old man showed me the touchstone of his life: a musical certificate signed by Henry Irving in 1902); the macaw which spoke in a northern accent, the banks of the River Mersey scarlet with Himalayan balsam, all seen with the focus and helplessness of the visitor's eye. In my journal I wrote: 'I was born to live in the world but I don't understand it.' I have forgotten the Boddington talk of God but not the imagination of community building from the grass roots. Twelve out of ten for C.S.V. Their proud boast is still true: they never turn anybody away.

* * * *

In 1974 Gorsey Bank housing estate was literally at the end of the road, hemmed in by the London-Manchester main-line railway and the muddy Mersey on the other side. It was built after the Second World War and had won architectural awards. But that was another lifetime. Now its pavements were strewn with rubbish and rubble; fireweed and couch grass grew in the cracks; at night fires burned on lawns in front of derelict houses, the walls full of loose bricks; large signs warned of alsatian security patrols but the street mongrels took no notice. The Last Place in Stockport was populated by nine-year-olds like Karen who appeared from behind a hedge to say hello. 'I know everybody and everybody knows me.' The youth club, a square brick building splattered with multi-coloured graffiti, stood at the end of the road. On hot dog nights about fifty bodies stamped and yelled to, 'OOO OOO OOO I WANT YOU.' Inside, the air was heavy with fireworks and the children danced ankle deep in sweet papers, cartons and old newspapers. The older girls with high platform shoes danced in a line together, sticking to a rigid routine of shuffling backwards and forwards until the record stopped. They shuffled double fast to the chords of 'Kung Fu Fighting', danced slow to, 'I'm Nobody's Child.' Older boys didn't dance. They lined the wall, eyeing up each other or the girls, or using the special boards for graffiti: 'If yer wanna scrap come to us'; 'Even Hitler's army ran away from the Gorsey Bank aggro.' The tots mimicked their elders dancing, passing cigarette butts around like seasoned campaigners. The evening wore on to its climax, a multi-piggy-back fight. The Gorsey Bank security guard tied up his alsatian and joined in, about six pairs battling it out to everyone's delight. The night finished with twizzles, holding children by their hands and spinning them around until their heads turned round by themselves. I had seen no demented kids, just children thirsting for contact.

* * * *

The old couple in Cherry Tree Road wanted someone to make them a hot drink each evening. The house, in a respectable semi-detached street, was dark on the outside, the curtains closed in every window. I knocked and waited, and knocked again. I was about to go when a crack of light appeared and a shadow climbed the frosty glass door. It loomed bigger, swaying from side to side and stopped short of the door. An old man appeared in the crack, raising his head slowly until he saw me. His pyjamas could not hide the emaciated legs and he wheezed for several seconds to catch his breath. 'I'm from the social services,' I said weakly. I followed him inside to the back room. An ancient woman, his wife, was squatting on a pot, her dress by her ankles. I pretended to ignore her. She finished as though I hadn't been there and asked: 'Is it Graham?' 'No,' replied her husband, dragging out the word. 'She's deaf, you know. Her mind's quite gone.' I told them about the evening drink. 'When can you do it from?'
'I can't promise anything but...'
'Promises,' he said, 'they're no good to us. We're just two old people. I come from a proud family. It took a lot of persuading before I would let the home help in.' He relaxed his back and rubbed slowly a roll of flesh above his upper waist. 'I would not have been like this six months ago but I was flattened and now you see us as we are. I expect we'll both die in this bed. They want us to go into a home. But you know what that's like. You got no independence. Don't you think so? The doctor said we should go into hospital but she'll be in one ward and me in another. It's no good.'
His wife started shivering. 'I'm cold,' she said. He put a coat over her shoulders and a jacket on for himself. 'If I didn't do this she'll only worry.' She wore an antique set of earphones which filled the room with irregular hissing sounds.
'Is it Graham?' she asked again. He shouted something into the earphone and then talked to me about his two sons, one in

Scotland, the other in the far south. He showed me a picture of them. 'But they can't leave their families to come here, can they?' He spoke louder. 'One's forty, the other over fifty. They would never be able to get a job, would they?'

I poured some tea and buttered the toast. 'You would never think we once had a house which was big enough to have two garages by the side.' He looked at me. 'Are you married?' 'Not yet,' I answered. He chuckled for the first time. 'It's got its ups and downs, good and bad points.' Inside his weathered skin, hanging loose in folds, keeping together his bamboo legs and arms, was a warm heart still beating. Later that evening, a mood of helplessness was dispelled when the doorbell rang and eight small faces, urchins every one, appeared in the hallway conducted by their ragged gaffer. They had sussed me as a soft touch and serenaded me like this:

Three little angels all dressed in white
Tried to get to heaven on the end of a kite.
But the kite end was broken, down they all fell
Instead of going to heaven they all went to hell.

Two little angels etc... (Stockport, 1974)

A BOTTLE STORY

In the early 1970s, my last staging post in journalism, I lived in a remote farmhouse up in the Moffat Hills of south west Scotland. On Sundays I walked into the cavernous conifer forests, either steering a compass course or keeping to the trails. I walked knowing that I would see nobody. One day I came to a part of the forest I did not know, off a path and hopelessly lost. I whittled a stick with my knife to clear a way through the nettles. I cut one of my fingers badly and needed to find water to clean the wound. Eventually I stepped out onto a track, walked three paces along it and saw a bottle lying on the wayside. A full bottle of TCP! (Dalbeattie, 1974)

DEATH

The air carries me in its arms – I am a flower on a tree, a splash at the river's edge, a firefly in a night wood. These images appear easily on this autumn day, cool air cut with bright edges and see-

through blue skies. Perhaps I indulge myself but these images of continuity and being held by a greater force, I suppose a sense of belonging to life even while the wheel is turning into night, I find comforting, satisfying a need to find a still, central point to all this change. I chose the black metal seat at the back of the garden, looking out onto the lawn and sunlight and the sprinkler fanning backwards and forwards over the shrubs. Decay is turning me inwards full of half-sweet, half-bitter thoughts. I think of Mary Nurse dying of cancer in Shepton Mallet hospital and the salute I gave her last autumn. Why don't I go and see her? I don't. God bless you Mary. The air carries me in its arms. I love that, at once so connected to a field of energy, life, intelligence, force. I am carried by something. Is it a dream? I sat under the apple tree, the one with masses of watery fruit and the apples spread on the lawn, singly, in groups, sprinkled along the outer edges; suddenly they appeared as stars and I played with naming the constellations. This is The Plough, that's Andromeda, this is the Milky Way and so on. I could look up and see the crossing lines of hedgerow tree clumps climbing up to the ridge of Lansdown, and the sky above that, and then I returned to the apples and imagined that a girl, perhaps Idun, had played with them arranging these patterns. As soon as I found the pattern, this parallel, and made it personal, familiar, I had entered, more correctly, stumbled into a mythic world of gods and goddesses, tamed the gigantic forces to a child's game of playing with apples on a lawn. I stayed crouched, imagining what it is like to be God, and everywhere I looked another world appeared before me. Even as God I couldn't take it all in and I wanted to know what was on the other side. It's impossible to force the lock on these gates; one can only enter as a spirit child...through wonder.

Autumn is descent. Old pains surface bringing me back to my body. Tragic scenarios unfold, wasting diseases of sweet and bitter pain. And I look for the stillpoint, the abiding image to carry me through this season. Is it the seed, the fruit, the berry? They will fall to earth, return, and like the flowers which made them they will crack, the colours fade, the rains and fungi will rot them, and only then, after time and frost has weathered them into skeletons, will they finally break and sprout some new life. These twin images of germ and dis-ease, side by side with fruitfulness and seeds, is a picture I do not understand.

I always find it hard to say goodbye. Autumn is such a leave-taking... In an actual way it is a dismembered land. When something is germane, it is a sprout, a birth, an origin. One day, I am sure, I will need to discover a new world in me, and it won't be on another planet, but it will be about living in this world now, participating more consciously in the actual workings of creation. The air carries me in its arms, and I do not know where. Autumn stirs the pot all right; it settles by Christmas. (September 13, Upton Cheney, 1990)

STORM PETREL

Old Willie Dawson, with his puckered cheeks, inch-long bristly eyebrows and his shock of grey hair topped by a battered leather trilby, was the character of the caravan park. He had lived there well before the New Age had arrived at Findhorn and had seen thousands of planetary travellers walk the sand tracks to their caravans scattered in the hollows of the dunes. What he thought of them I don't know but he had strong views on nearly everything else. While grubbing out daisies from the lawns he strolled over and said, without any introduction: 'When a nation's crafts are lost man will have no soul.' He had clear blue eyes and no teeth, so when he smiled he always appeared astonished. His Scottish accent was thick, canny and biting. I liked him. He thought most men were cowards. 'If they canna look at you in the eye they will tell you a lie.' I kept looking at his eyes. 'When they see someone lying on the ground they'll go and put the boot in. They're savages, but now...' he said, looking astonished again, 'they use their tongues.' He stuck his tongue out and pointed to it. 'These politicians are all tongues. There's nothing behind it.' There was a lot behind Willie but like many men of his generation he never showed it directly. I pieced this story together from two sources.

The healer in radionics, 'the art of the little black box', lived in one of the wooden chalets. She was slightly crippled and used sticks to get about. Her home faced south west in the teeth of the prevailing winds. She wanted a weather vane and asked Willie, who dabbled in metalwork, to make one for her. The months went by and nothing happened. She thought Willie had forgotten. Then he appeared one day with his ladder and mounted on her rooftop a little bird with funny outstretched wings and dabbling feet, made from scraps of metal. It wasn't a bird that she had seen before. It's a storm petrel, he told her, a wee little thing that lives at sea, treading the mighty rollers and braving the fiercest storms. It ventures onto land only to breed, and then, said Willie, its poor legs are so feeble it can only hobble and use its wings to stay upright. (Findhorn Bay Caravan Park, September, 1976)

DADDY-LONGLEGS

They are everywhere, always on the go, scrabbling over the short grass, slipping and sliding on the air as if they are treading ice. 'It must be here somewhere. I'll find it soon', they seem to say. Their heads are like horses, big jawboned with a tapering muzzle. The bulbous eyes glint emerald green in the sunlight. Their flimsy husky wings appear to grow out of their head; their long abdomens trail patiently behind them. Under the apple tree a wasp clings to one of their legs, then meanders among the rotting apples while a herd of craneflies pass by on all sides; it only attacks if it bumps into one. Hordes sun themselves on spreading junipers or peer through the opposite sides of windows. They are like flying spiders. A dismembered skeleton hangs from a single spider thread, while another rocks upside down, still alive, in the kitchen. One hangs from a wire by the hooks on its longest front legs. Then I make a discovery – a pair mating end to end, perfect calm between them, legs rock-still in this face away missionary position. From this coolness and precision comes a picture of stone-cut halls and insect gods as living sculptures, and a curious elation: can insects touch us with emotions completely out of proportion to their size? I like this way of being with the world. (Upton Cheney, September 27, 1990)

* * * *

The daddy-longlegs lurched drunkenly by the edge of the lawn. I was astonished to see a tiny wolf spider clinging to this heaving insect despite desperate efforts by the insect to fly away. It crawled into dense grass, thrashed its legs but could not shake off the spider. I looked closely. The spider absailed to the nearest grass blade, wrapped a loop of thread around it, and then scurried back up another leg to its perch. The great rolling movements continued but each time the spider darted to anchor another thread then scurry back, they became slower, more ponderous. I left this scene and returned twenty minutes later. The daddy-longlegs was not going anywhere. The spider had tied a thread to nearly all its legs, so no matter how hard it struggled, it couldn't move backwards or forwards. At last the wolf spider scaled a leg and sat behind the insect's head, a rider on a horse. It prodded around for a soft spot then attacked it with poisonous fangs. The daddy-longlegs quivered for a long time. I returned later. The insect was strung up, all his legs bundled into one, and secured to a grass tip. The spider, I presumed, was preparing for dinner. (Cuddesdon, 1977)

****

When I walked by the Greta river I noticed a large rock where the current divided and on it scrabbled a daddy-longlegs sliding down to the fast-flowing water. It vanished behind an outcrop, six inches above the water. The end, I thought. Then a leaf clattered out of a tree onto the water some feet upstream. It turned into a raft and landed against the rock beside the insect. Moments later the current pulled the leaf sharply downstream. I like to think the daddy-longlegs grabbed this opportunity. (Barnard Castle, October 13, 1994)

TREASURE

The three growers on the farm were the last to leave the annual barn dance, gone three in the morning and well oiled with the local cider. An almost physical camaraderie had rescued their shyness, unzipped their speech. Their natural warmth had started to glow. The last glass drained, they trudged across the muddy farmyard and past the barn door. They stopped and walked back. One turned the keys in the padlocks, another pulled back the bolts. The mounds of potatoes reared up in the torchlight... Cara, Sante, Remarka, Romano, Bailey. They looked, saying nothing. 'The rats wont get in,' said the tallest one. 'I cemented all the cracks.' The dark-haired one shone the torch in the windows. 'The nets will keep the birds out,' he said, 'I made sure of that.' The youngest had fixed the slats on the door. 'That will keep the rain off,' he said. They stared saying nothing for another whole minute. They closed and bolted the door, turned the keys and let the night swallow them up. (Dunsford Farm, October 31, 1994)

BLACKBERRY

Monica Vogel has a secret passion – blackberries. This woman from Bavaria, a big woman yet she walks lightly as a bird, picked the luscious berries one by one and couldn't stop until her mouth was full. Then characteristically she giggled and spluttered out this story: as a child on her home farm, both her mother and grandmother had forbidden her to eat blackberries growing in the Bavarian forest. She would catch fox tapeworm, she was told repeatedly, an incurable parasite. So she practised restraint until she encountered the spectacular crop of English blackberries in 1995. (Dunsford Farm)

JURASSIC STONE (1)

The story of stone touches an imaginative nerve in me – the fact that millions and millions of years can shrink to a few metres of rock. Then I start thinking that this life, everything I see, people talking, trees shedding leaves, the electricity of dragonfly wings will one day vanish into a centimetre of rock. For the next hour I find everything amazing, the smallest details of my everyday life shine against this geological anonymity. Will those two old people talking at the street corner be discovered as fossils, and how can the rock remember the sound of their voices and memories? Most of all I picture the people I love and this precious passing moment. This is the story of the oolitic limestone which underpins my homelands here in North Somerset.

Two hundred million years ago the sun rose on the heart of Pangea, the primal continent straddling the equator. The cold orange light illuminated the inland sea of sand waves stretching as far as the red mountains and forming the shorelines of the panned salt lakes. Already the blue light patterned the mountain slopes of scree debris washed down by the torrential flash floods. As the sun glistened on the salt rimes, high-lighted the mosaic reds on the sandstone, *kuehneosaurus*, the gliding lizard, lumbered slowly to the edge of the precipice and gazed into the vast Triassic silence. It did this every day and knew exactly the right place and the right time to do it: before the blistering heat haze had gained the ascendancy or the daily winds had scattered the sand across the ridges of the advancing dunes; and especially before its mortal foe, the lizard-hipped dinosaur, emerged to prowl along the salt-lake shores. Now, as the thermals shimmered, *kuehneosaurus* glided from the ledge to become a giant dragonfly, a blue dazzle air-borne among the desert-fringed hills of the Bath and Bristol region.

* * * *

One hundred and eighty million years ago, Pangea, the virgin landmass, gave birth to the continents of the modern world. The fragments, forty miles thick, navigated the currents of molten rock deep in the earth. Europe and the British Isles drifted away from the hot, arid interior of the southern Saharan latitudes. The Americas rifted from Africa and migrated westwards, allowing the sea to invade the heartland and create the Atlantic ocean. The sea bed rose, submerging the land into a series of constantly changing shallow basins, the warm waters supporting shoreline forests of horsetails, palm-like cycads and gingko trees. Here, the lizard-hipped dinosaur, *brachiosaurus*, gazed at her reflection in the water and saw the largest creature ever to walk on land. And *stegosaurus*, the bird-hipped dinosaur, trundled through the coastal heat haze arching its double shield of plates along its back and snapping its beak-like jaw. It had a brain the size of a walnut. Farther north, the first real bird, the *archaeopteryx*, navigated the tiny range of reddish islands, the

37

tips of the old red mountains, the future Mendip hills. It glided over the blue waters, luxuriating in the moist haze, oblivious to the sea bed far below one day to be named Aquae Sulis.

* * * *

Two miles east of the future site of Bath Abbey, *plesiosaurus*, the huge sea lizard, projected its twenty foot neck and watched the waves murmur on the great coral reef, white water around a lagoon of still turquoise (like the lagoons in the Bahamas today). It propelled itself with oar-shaped flippers and drifted over sea buds and sea lilies with waving armlets. It passed over the tracks of horse-shoe crabs, the hardened casts of sea worms and retreated momentarily from the giant squid emerging from the depths armed with long-hooked tentacles. The clear waters clouded as it squirted ink to escape. It paddled silently over ancient horn shells resembling ice-cream cones and entered warmer, shallower water where it sank slowly to the sand bed, balancing its streamlined body with its flippers. It felt the tidal turbulence around the reef, gently rolling shell and coral fragments along the sea bed. It watched the sun pattern swirling shadow clouds on the the surface, but it could not see the unicellular world of bacteria and plankton floating near the light. Nor did it see their limy secretions sinking through the waters like microscopic snow, invisible, falling down through the millennia, almost like snow...

TOTAL RECALL

In one of the clefts among the low, brooding hills of north Devon is Bradwell Mill, a smallholding with rich grazing and part of a hamlet known in bygone times as Buttercombe. I camped here one summer below Eight-Acre field beside a venerable ash tree, a sunny, well-drained place facing south. Each day brought fine rain with clanking, grey skies; each night, when I closed my eyes, brought pictures streaming out of the agricultural past: sheep droves, straw ricks, dusty tracks, gleaming shire horses, village streets without a car. Every night, just before sleep, I stepped into this past but one image kept recurring and impressed me: I saw a large gathering of people strangely dressed in antique clothes of Sunday best − starched white shirts, pleated skirts and voluminous bonnets. They were sitting in a sunny field against a blue sky, all looking the same way to someone or something out of the picture. I had the impression they were listening intently. The following morning I told my hosts, Bill Harvey and Gill Westcott about it...and none of us were any wiser. A month later Bill took down the old ceiling of their farmhouse and found newspaper clippings dating back to the 1880's. One clipping listed the local hamlets, and one ringed in ink was Bradwell Mill. There was a date and time on it, and at the top of the list were the words: Lay Preacher Meetings. (Devon, 1992)

* * * *

On another occasion a storm benighted me on a winter road beside Loch Lomond, not far from Inveruglas. I parked the van against the shelter of osiers and all night long I tossed and turned on the hard metal floor and I heard, or seemed to hear, loud metal clangings, a thunder of running feet or the yell of great crowds, and each time I surfaced I heard only the storm racking the osiers, the rain drumming on the roof or the waves buffeting the shoreline rocks. This coming and going went on all night so I emerged wrecked in the morning and could not tell what had been the storm or a dream. Then it occurred to me, looking at the autumnal loveliness of heathlands and colour-washed skies, that there may once have been a battle here, and the storm had stirred some memory in the land. Is this fancy? I don't know. (Autumn 1986)

OCTOBER CHANGES

A month dividing the living and the dead, all in tatters on their way to earth; leaves flame on trees or clatter on tarmac, a dance of death in the gutter. The shadows are drawn side by side with waterways of golden light; skies sombre grey and secretive in the drooling rain. Ghosts are everywhere, stiff and tilting above ground, a time of skeletons and seeds, debris dreams and intimations of journies to come. Winter gnats and gossamer sparkle above Mells Stream – ash keys are maroon brown with yellow-struck lightening leaves – bright pink reds of spindle fruits, chequered yellow greens of crab apple leaves – bloody-nosed beetles mating, males with rolled antennae cling upside down – the sweet stinkiness of ivy flowers – walking in Tellisford Wood I smell the aniseed fungi, (*Clitocybe odora*) – late autumnal

39

signs: beech leaves they flurry, ash keys do glow; leaves float in river; starlings scatter yew berries; horse chestnut leaves are green fingers in rusty gloves; fading russets of hawthorn – flies stream and teem on the sunny side of a telegraph pole oozing bitumen – dummy wasps chewing the inside of apples – thousands of yellow swarming flies on trunk of old cupressus – fists of mistletoe flowers are miniature gargoyles – chocolate eclair snails by every footstep across Wellow fields – gang of tired tomb-flesh flies on cat turd – dead flies on the inside of windows – red things in wood: berries of hawthorn, rowan, yew, gladdon, holly and rosehips, hibernating ladybird, stalks of sycamore, spindle and bramble leaf – black things in wood: stag beetle, badger shit, ivy berries, blackbird, bracket fungi, last year's poplar leaves, blackthorn.

GILES AND THE HAMMER

Do you give names to cars? Or talk to food mixers? Do atoms respond to your harsh word or soft caress? Giles Christian described this example of rare empathy and genuflected his hands to emphasise this point. He had been working on the candle studio at Findhorn, up a ladder banging tacks into elm cladding. He loved his hammer from the States, professional and sleek, all metal and with a leather finish. He held an open box of tacks, hundreds of them in one hand, the hammer in the other, and found a rhythm swinging his hammer, taking out a tack and banging it home. Somehow he dropped the box and instinctively looked down. The box was not on the ground. It was impaled on the hooks of his hammer. (1973)

* * * *

Another time, and another lucky escape. He was grape picking at Roquemaure, a small village near Avignon. One hot afternoon, he picnicked beside the Rhone river eating horse-meat sausages and drinking the local brew. He insisted he was not drunk, but the relentless sun and the cool waters turned his head a little. He dived into the river, upstream of the narrowing limestone gorge with cliffs soaring 300 ft and with steeply wooded sides. He intended to swim the 100ft to the other side and back. 'I swam most of the way and then had second thoughts. I turned round, facing downstream, and the current took me away. I went into white water, the river narrower and going faster. I tried to swim to the shore. The water ahead was rougher and full of rocks. I thought I was a goner. I was swept away for half a mile. Then I got my hands around a boulder. The sense of relief... The colours got brighter. I swam to the shore. I was bubble-headed and giggly the rest of the day.' (1976)

DARREN MILKING

Megan the labrador brushes my hand as I write this. 'She's around for the milk,' says Darren, finishing milking Honey, one of the five dairy cows at Dunsford Farm. Little black cats, members of the dairy posse – sit patiently in the corners of the stone barn awaiting their turn. Megan is already licking hers noisily . 'May I give you a prior warning,' says Darren, showing his teeth. 'Sometimes this lady gives a shit...' The milk spurts alternately into the plastic bucket. Darren asks to look at the previous page, the tight script flowing like timber rings from an old tree. He thinks it's from the 13th century. I say, maybe. I wanted to write about you milking, I tell him. 'Darren Gabriel Oak, there's a lot like me in that man...the man who walks the hills, big man, baggy trousers and big boots. He's a farmer and tends his sheep... inner strength, strong, distinguished features, a strong attitude but really soft inside.' I say that I have never done this before, sitting in front of someone and writing. 'Are you writing what you see?' Yes and no, it's my experience. Velvet is the nervous cow, always on the edge with a huge udder and volcanic orifice. Elfie, my daughter, laughs on my back as Darren tickles her. 'Only half a cow to go, then we're done.' Darren cleans the opposite pairs of teats otherwise dirt and dust finds its way into the milk. 'Milking is such a nice way to start the day, a good perspective on things.' There is a slow animal quality to Darren, lumbering lightly his sturdy frame across the yard; a large pear-shaped head, fine cropped hair in front, tailed by two long dreadlocks, hair wrapped in rainbow colours. I say that I feel awkward sitting here but it's fine as long as I am here and not just the observer.

The cows wait patiently, staring at the white-washed wall, turning their peachy russet flanks to the outside. I notice their tails, fat and arching over their pelvis, then smooth and tapering to long tresses almost touching their hooves. 'It's an accomplishment milking a cow first thing in the morning.' Stale cream, smell of silage, grass, urine are the smells of the byre. 'When the cows are fat they have a salty grass smell, quite sweet.' The repetitions of milk squirting milk is accompanied by a gurgling resonance, the occasional grunt. They smell of comfort. One teat sprays the milk in several directions. He gives Honey some alfalfa, homoeopathic medicine for an abscess in one of her teats. He puts comfrey ointment on any cuts to heal them and keep flies away. They are so patient, even tied to the standing bars with chains around their necks. 'COME ON, COME ON, COME ON.' He struggles to unloose the chains. The long tails swish and the shit starts to fly, plopping, splashing on the concrete floor. 'Come on Honey, just take this bloody tablet. It makes you better.' Wispy licks her sides. A faint heat wave touches me as Honey passes. The scrape and stony plod of hooves meander down the farmyard. Elfie is asleep. I blink my eyes outside. I am touched by this cow world. Darren touches me, too. His purposeful steps return. 'I have to wash this place, put out hay for the cows, feed the pigs... I like to push myself.' The little black cats appear in the cracks of the door. I go to my breakfast of pancakes thinking of the grandfather, the farmer in baggy trousers and boots, walking the hills. This man of earth, one who looks over, fathers, looks into the future... Who made this man? (Dunsford Farm, October 2, 1994)

RAINDROPS

The rain scatters seed lights over the windscreen, steamy on the inside. Here they go, staying the same size no matter how many others they swallow on the way down. I make this observation: they simply go faster. The first raindrops stick to the windscreen, fattening, shifting, wobbling before they're off! They avalanche, snaking erratically, making a path for others to follow. They quiver before they break. They are unpredictable. The other raindrops follow the pathfinders exactly: it's quicker, less fuss than finding another way down. I like the raindrops' progress, their hesitancy, their sense of timing. (Upton Cheney, 1991)

NOVEMBER CHANGES

The mud grows, the sunsets glow. The sun sits in the trees with cold cream outlines. Creation and elimination, a winter road, a long road going down alone, a month of epitaphs and gaps, a month of emergence: seeds from fruit flesh, bare branches from trees, single trees from the wood, skeletons from leaves. A trashing time, cutting things back and holding only pieces. November is a chasm to cross by foot – earth smells musty, worms wriggle and plug tunnels with leaves – subterranean reefs of leaves in puddles; leaves cartwheel alongside cars – the vanilla scent of sweet woodruff stalks me in Stoke Wood, Mendips – the tans and golds of oak, the opaque yellows of elm, the speckled yellows of blackthorn, quiet-washed yellows of silver birch, blood-red stems of dogwood with pink blancmange leaves – skeins of geese break their straight lines as they curve towards earth – the last crab apples on a tree are Christmas lights – bright orange cloaks of spindle berries on leafless trees – when the last crimson leaf of Prunus subhirtella 'Autumnalis' falls, the first almond scented flowers appear – one third of deciduous trees are bare by middle of month – two immobile bluebottles cling to sunnyside of windfall apple – when the leaves fall, the remaining ones appear purposeful, threaded and placed – ranks of starlings on telegraph wires in the country – hemlock stems streaked white and collapsing – rusty ash keys – spindle berries disgorge scarlet fruits by end of month.

TRAVELLER – THE FINDHORN GARDEN

I remember this November road well. The grass beside the Findhorn Bay crunched under my feet and the plangent geese calling to home encircled my senses with the physical premonition that something new was happening in my life. The bacon-and-eggs and restharrow of the wayside had led to the Findhorn garden and I worked there for the next fourteen months. Eighteen years ago! It seems inconceivable now that those strings of caravans, fragments of tarmac landing strips leading nowhere, shifting sand-dunes crowned with marram grass and rabbit-munched gorse could have held the hearts of so many flotsam travellers from the five continents. That it changed my life is beyond question. I left journalism for good. How it changed me is elusive. I see Ziggy, a Canadian believer in fairies, chalking the blackboard in the garden shed: 'All parts of the garden are connected. Here in the garden shed I'm standing at Pineridge.' I wanted to be connected again, especially to my cock. This shy Englishman used his hands pricking out heather cuttings, planting daffodil bulbs, sorting gloxinia bulbs for winter storage, spiking lawns and cutting and scarifying them, collecting seaweed after storms, turning tons of compost, cleaning tools; these became metaphors for self-care. The simple act of listening to each other extended out to the landscape around me, becoming another kind of touch.

At the end of the gardening day my pillow lit up with flowers and the tapestry of the hypnagogic world: horses with crocus horns and bulls with diamond patterns. I started to dream. Night after night they startled me with their intensity; dreams of healing brews, of being chased, crashes, murder, going through changing rooms, sex and more sex, dreams of the future. I wrote them down, drew them, became intoxicated by them. From nowhere appeared this strange intelligence on my side wanting me to change. The big ones are vivid now, landscapes of the past, present and future, and I'm walking through them along a road of longing, a road of joy. Such intense dreaming rarely visits me now. And sex and tenderness stirred my heart and lions (I meant to say loins!) in equal measure and they had nothing to do with time, confounding absolutely my Catholic guilt. The silent, sexual wasteland I lived in was awakened by the generosity of women; they warmed my life, rescued my desire.

In my hands is my journal from the Findhorn garden, a steaming heap of garden lore, confessions, Celtic yearnings for transformation, wine making, advice from ascended masters, how to shovel (clear a space at the bottom) or sharpen shears (on the sides only), creepy life in the soil, secrets of compost making, weird diets of waste and weeds. But what I let go of is equally significant. I went to Findhorn in a flooded vehicle, drowning in unknown emotions. There, in the company of love, I let some of it go, a good bit. I used to drag myself like a wounded animal to the pine woods to cry. There were so many tears. The first time I cried my heart out in a group, the sensation of lightness which followed overwhelmed me. Where did all this grief come from? I had no idea.

* * * *

Yet the real changes are carried by details. One day I noticed aphids clustering on bruised yarrow stems while avoiding healthy stems next to it. Instead of seeing the aphids as a pest I saw them as recycling a damaged plant. Then the whitefly in the greenhouse could be a sign of poor soil, waterlogged conditions... And there again, without the 'bad' pests what would the 'good' ones have left to eat? They were there for a reason. Like the 'bad' parts of me? I dimly asked myself. A talk by Lady Eve Balfour, the founder of the Soil Association, brought tears to everyone's eyes. This frail old lady with short-cropped silvery hair and brown tweeds, inspired us with her convictions that nature loves us, combining uniqueness with dependance and perfection at every stage. She exposed the two myths: survival of the fittest and that nature is wasteful. She said that whatever increases our reverence for life is the right way.

For years afterwards I would unwind back to that garden and think: did I walk around physical boundaries and imagine a light going into the ground with each footstep; did I ask moles to go from lawns by picturing a light wall around the garden with a door which only opens from the inside; did I place hands on trees or seeds and picture a healthy mature plant; did I maintain a conversation between force and cooperation, when to use it, when to relinquish it or welcome a storm as purification instead of simply destruction? Did I? I kept all this to myself. In the seventies if you asked the greengrocer for an organic lettuce he thought you came from Mars... I knew I had to leave Findhorn, discard my colourful, woolly clothes. The jargon had crept into my speech. I needed to return to the real world.

THANGOZ

I stopped at the brook, by the northern edge of Priston Wood, gazing up the field skating with daddy-longlegs towards the small crown of thorn trees. I don't know what caught my attention but here I am squatting among the exposed roots and the smooth, paler ivy roots. The hum of bees greets me and this wave of fear, curiousity and excitement. Immediately I recall my dream figure, Thangoz, the man living in the thorn tree with a little owl or hawk on his right arm. He is standing on a ground of mineral rose quartz. He is, I am sure, a male warrior guardian of the land.

The haw berries already brighten the scattered yellows and browns of ivy. Magpies rattle their stone bags and sheep graze below; a single willow stands in a pool at the head of the brook. Wasps patrol the branches above me but I do not look at them. This feeling of apprehension and excitement grows, bringing the word source, something I need to support or be a channel for. It is to do with the land and walking, trees and water sources. I eat some haw berries.

When I sit here, I am alone and yet I am connected. A daddy-longlegs scales a twig but it does not have the strength to go higher; only the breeze can carry it away... All morning my little exima man has been surfacing into my body, my limp left leg, the feeble grip in my left hand and arm, inexplicable pains in my right elbow and other muscular tensions. Sometimes I want to decorate my left leg and arms with beautiful ribbons, drag my left leg on the ground, bend my left hand rigid, twist my fingers into sticks and walk smiling in honour of this part of myself; original, there at the beginning, at the source. This profound begger is as common as a meadow brown butterfly. Is it in the land, too? I cry as I write this... There is something death-like about these thorns; they have their own protection. They are not to be played with. Nothing grows in their shade except ivy. A red admiral with white shoulders swings and meanders brightly by. A man with a child on his shoulders walks below me. I wave... I notice that the air is alive with moving lights, insects and the gliding swaying lines of gossamer. They are all going somewhere, a destination unknown, into a wall of frost. I will meet death there, too, one day. An old man, out for his Friday walk, stops to say hello. He tells me he wishes to see the coal-mining museum at Radstock. The daddy-longlegs, when airborne, sail by in stately fashion, none of this scrabbling on the ground. They appear serene.

When I stop everything appears, I notice things; the way the hoverfly lands on this page, crouching, shifting its weight slightly, the better to get the feel of it. I don't know who Thangoz is but he wants something... The man with the child on his shoulders steps out of the wood. The old man passes below and waves. Grand-father, father and infant. I collect some of last year's weathered seeds. My aches and pains have subsided though I am very conscious of my left side. I will not label this dis-ease. I will call it blessing, opening. (Priston, Autumn, 1994)

DIADEM CONNECTIONS

The day after the storm wracked the Moray Firth, we raced our gardener's wagon along the sandy backroads to Lossiemouth and Cummingston to collect the bladderwrack stacked onto the beaches. Redwings, the newly arrived winter migrants from the farther north, landed forlornly on the shoreline as we stuffed the seaweed into plastic fertiliser bags for compost making. A hard overnight frost made handling the seaweed unbearable, and for the first few minutes I cried with the pain of frozen fingers; yet miracles, a few minutes later the same fingers steamed with heat. An hour later those same bags of seaweed would be steaming and almost too hot to handle. We stacked them by the wooden compost bins and out teemed myriads of tiny kelp flies, miraculously incubated by the fermentation of the seaweed. They flew out of the bags into the webs of the diadem spiders shrouding every crevice of the garden shed. The diadems made a hundred curtain calls gorging themselves on this harvest – and they were the fattest ones I have ever seen. (Findhorn, 1975)

THE KING'S SIGNET RING

One glorious autumnal day I visited the lake above Rhayader in Wales. I sat on the shore, the dwarf oakwoods behind me, the mountains ringing the rest of the lake. The setting sun high-lighted the flaming reds in the bracken. The clouds glowed opal and seemed to be fused to the sky. In a flash I imagined that I was at the bottom of an opal ring, the King's signet ring. My skin tingled with an overwhelming fear that I might literally be carried away – but only for a second. Then I was back sitting on the shore watching the sun go down. Peter Bidmead recounts a similar moment: he had picnicked by another Welsh lake near Machynlleth. Rather than go home to sleep he climbed into his boat, lay on his back and gently pushed off from the shore. Is this safe? he asked himself. Yes. The darkness closed around him; the only lights were the pinpricks of stars. He idly gazed at them, relaxing to the gentle motion of the boat. He listened to nothing in particular. He dipped his fingers into the almost still waters. He said it felt like being in a womb, the lack of any spatial orientation. He can't recall how long he drifted neither asleep nor completely awake. The sound came gently as if a breeze had woken up. The boat rocked a little faster. Very clearly he heard the murmurs grow until they whooshed past his ears. His skin tingled. The boat appeared to be going faster and faster. 'I felt I was on a magic carpet and any moment I would take off.' Immediately he sat upright. There was no breeze. The water was absolutely still. He had no obvious explanation. (1995)

CAT AND MOUSE

I notice the big whiskers on the black cat skulking outside the dairy. A small family of five or six live in the rubbish to appear twice a day when the Jersey cows arrive for milking. The big whiskers are in fact a large mouse. Clever cat, I think, doing a good job. The mouse twitches its little pink legs. Poor thing, but still the cat has to live. The cat flops onto its side and drops the mouse. It shivers and runs towards the edge of the concrete hardstanding, three feet away and freedom. The cat easily clamps a paw on its tail and pulls it back, the mouse scrabbling its front paws hard. The cat lets go, the mouse runs and is caught again. This happen several times. Cruel cat, I think, but this is nature. A second black cat appears and lounges beside the first one, both with their backs to the edge of the hardstanding. They play with the mouse chewing it in turn and dropping it until it refuses to move. Wicked cats, I think now, but I do not interfere. I hope the mouse will escape. The cats lick each other making a furry bridge and through this the mouse scampers and *stops* when it finds the back of the first cat. They search for it, turning their heads, looking at everything – except their tails. They creep forward sniffing, the mouse scampers away behind them and drops over the edge. Perfect timing. I walk away pleased, questioning my neutrality and wondering whether I participated in this drama at some subtle level. (Dunsford Farm, November 18, 1993)

SAGE

I know someone who thinks a food chain is a string of super-markets. Once, I offered him some herbal sage leaves from my bush thriving in rubbly soil facing south. 'It's beeeootiful as tea or rub it dry to burn as incense.' He declined politely. 'I'd rather get it from Sainsburys... I know where it comes from then.' (West Ilsley, 1979)

SAY THAT AGAIN

Malcolm Weare, a horticultural therapist and a natural story-teller, taught me three basic rules of running courses: make people feel at home, build on what people are already doing well and give them something to take away. Once he was asked to start a gardening club at a home for elderly blind people. He took along lots of scented and aromatic plants, pots and compost. Two things shocked him on entering the purpose-built building: the big hall lined on four sides with residents sitting on chairs, and the silence between them, as if they were walled into their own worlds. He unfolded the table, heaped on the compost and placed plants around it. One by one the residents were helped over or pushed across in their wheelchairs. He guided their hands to the soil, touched their hands on the plants and pots, and encouraged them with his friendly banter. They stroked the plants and then forgot them. 'I feel sick,' one said. He put more plants in front of them. They touched them again. The hands slid back into the soil. 'What did the cook say, Doris?' 'I can't remember.' He put lovely smelly plants beside them. They knocked them over as they crumbled the soil. 'I can't stand that boiled cabbage...' And so on. The hour alloted for the session ticked away and not one plant had been potted up. His plans had ended in failure. He packed up morosely. 'When are you coming again?' asked an old lady as he was leaving. 'We did enjoy it,' said another. 'Enjoy what?' said Malcolm. 'You didn't do anything.' They smiled and said, almost in the same breath: 'But we had such a nice time talking.'

* * * *

He once taught a boy who would not climb the stairs. Each time he stood with his hand on the bannister he wobbled and collapsed into a carer's arms. He could only go up with someone's support. He had to live on the ground floor when he visited the special unit of the children's hospital in London. They taught him how to tie his shoes, stir sugar into his tea, cut paper with scissors and many other skills, but the stairs were always out of reach. Malcom mixed up the potting soils and planted bulbs with him. He wrote the boy's name on the label and they put the pot in a dark, cool place. Then they brought the pot into the warmth and light, and the boy could not believe that the shoots came out of *his* tulips, that they were growing. The problem was this; the water supply was upstairs and someone had to take the pot there. Of course, it was necessary to hold the pot in both hands. The boy did not trust anybody to carry his bulbs. He carried the pot and walked up the stairs for the first time in his life.

* * * *

A nursing worker told me this story. An experimental residential home had been set up for young adults with learning difficulties. The idea was that if they lived as a group, took responsibility for the household chores, the cotton padding of institutional life with nursing care and cooking staff would be eased away. Instead of having all the time to do nothing, they would have time to learn from experience. Six young men lived in one house and took turns to cook the food. Joe prepared the Saturday evening meal and invited two nursing staff to join them. The tables were laid immaculately, plates with side plates and a separate knife, and everyone sat around the table waiting for the meal. Joe brought in the main course, a mini pork pie lost in the middle of a plate. He cut it slowly into eight slices unaware of the silence around him. When the first of the tiny slices was served the suppressed laughter rocked the table. Joe laughed, too. He never made that mistake again. (Frome, 1986)

LITTLE OWL

These birds are masters of disguise, the way they turn into stone on rooves or make a gatepost longer. I notice one because part of the roof turns when I walk past and then stops when I stop. I associate stars with little owls because they appear together, and something of that strange immensity, nearness and farness, clings to this little pear-shaped bird. It is one of the very few successful introductions into Britain, originating from southern Europe. They are curious about humans. Twice I have seen them perched on the Beckington bypass fence tilting their heads at the busy traffic yards away – yet surrounded by miles of open farmland. This elusive bird, living between the worlds, is the totem of Athene, goddess of battle, wisdom and culture-making. She lives outside our ordinary senses, hearing distant things and brings them closer. I think one eavesdropped onto a conversation two days ago. A lady was describing to me the birds in her garden. 'Do you get little owls?' I asked. 'I don't think so,' she said. 'I've never heard one.' 'What's that?' I exclaimed on hearing the familiar short, yelping cry. I pinpointed it to the roof and a starling mimicking a little owl. (Norton St. Philip, November 3, 1994)

THE COW PAT

What do I say? I chose this moist cow pat sheltered in the Red Barn field and facing this cumulus sunlight. I want to sit beside it for an hour doing nothing. I gaze befuddled as an unknown beetle whirrs into the fold of a volcanic crater, folding back its wings to descend into a shaft. It's gone! A turdy, nondescript beetle emerges and spirals up into the sky. It's a very ordinary cow pat. A Devon steer investigates too freely and involuntarily I find my feet and immense height. That does the trick. This lava flow is regulated and shows all the marks of a descent, a short and sharp impact, a dark side of the moon on the grass. I am ringed by their makers all smoothing and tearing the grass. I peer closer. Minute iridescent wings scull the edges of fissures, the texture and colour of old leather; they are compressed into ranges of parallel mountains. This page is a cloud across them. A sleek spaghetti beetle surfaces but only for a micro glimpse. I notice everything that moves including my tilting shadow. The whizz of wings deafens me and I lean back as the picture-wing fly claims the highest ridge. It's enough. Gone! Smaller flies appear as drifting shadows which vanish when they land. Two more spaghetti beetles rove in tandem. One heifer blows its baby horns, setting off the others into a raucous chorus; half lie down. A beetle, dull and black with red-tipped antennae, violently grips the dung then flicks its blade-like wings. Gone! A tiny paddle-winged fly makes a lonely consort before the clean lines of a bluebottle; it walks sedately along a ridge seeing both sides. I have always wanted to do this, to be a visitor to this stage. The cattle are restless and follow their leader into the hummocks of the next field. When I am still the cow pat flickers with flies, all sizes, each kind with a style of walking; distinctive with busyness or plodding and patient... The dung flies are spring-loaded and made from the colours of grass and twigs; they launch themselves into the air. The black edges crease the cow pat when the moisture goes, first along the highest crest and then around the circular rim, a darkening landscape at odds with the jewelled greens of grass. I stay silent with this pen as three buzzards patrol the sky over my head.

I wonder what's beneath the cow pat, which rich seams do the beetles mine? Mostly I am with the surface of things. If I close my eyes I hear the metallic trajectories of flies as zip fasteners. The big picture-wing returns; white eyes, rusty wing corners; a daring precision. It walks two steps forwards, two steps to the side and nose down into the good life. I see insects I have never seen before; a walking grass blade with side legs. I blink. Gone! I haven't smelt this world yet. I resist. I dont want to scatter my insects. Head on, the picture-wing is invisible, its sleekness disintegrating into an illusion of bulges and rusty bits. By contrast, the dung fly decked in brown corduroys jumps out... I notice that the colour drains out of the older cow pats, the rain and dung-beetles recycling the craters until the grass grows through. Strangely, I forget all about cows. They are far away... I realise that the flies have funny walks because the turd is bumpy; they have to go up and down and sideways to cross gorges and craters. A single-minded weevil confounds this theory; it scales the foothills in a straight line. I have strayed an hour squatting here. I am still perplexed scratching this surface. I am no wiser. For myself, I am content to have undertaken this foolish journey. (Dunsford Farm, 1995)

LOST AND FOUND

One windy autumnal day, while living in Lower Weston, Bath, I walked around Victoria Park enjoying the leaves cartwheeling on the paths and drifting under the trees as gangs of waifs and strays. They clattered and grated the tarmac, roamed the kerbs and gutters, going the way the wind took them, this way and that way. 'It's here. No, it's there. Don't follow me. I'm lost, too.' I kicked my way through a mile of leaves. When I reached home, I found that I had lost my father's watch, an expensive Swiss 'Omega'. I returned to the park with the hopeless task of retracing my steps. Everywhere I saw leaves, and they were continually moving. I arrived at the beginning empty-handed. I stood by the stone lions at the park gates and looked one last time at the beech leaves, the way that they glowed, or appeared to, when the wind vibrated them... A sudden gust swept some aside and, for one moment, I saw the metal strap of my watch glitter. (Bath, 1984)

FUTURE SHOCK

These experiences are without obvious explanation, quite different from each other, yet I cluster them together as they provoked in me a similar response: wonder, panic and sadness. The first happened at Plumpton Agricultural College in Sussex where I had arrived to run a day course on therapeutic gardening. I parked the car, walked along a gravel path into a dell and along another path to a reception building. At the end of the day, exhausted yet happy, I retraced my steps back to the dell, along a gravel path...to a broad view of steep valleys with beech hangars and headlands of rolling downs. I stared. A surging fear panicked me. The car park had vanished. I looked quickly left and right. I spotted the corner of the car park. The relief flooded through me and I did not know why. The second time was desending steps to attend an evening class held in the basement of a convent. I went through the door at the bottom, crossed the landing with three doors, opening the far one into the hall. At the end of the session I opened the door, crossed the corridor, opened a door and went up the stairs. Halfway up I panicked. They were not the same stairs. I walked quickly down, staying calm. I opened another door on the landing and stepped into a small, dark room. My heart accelerated. I opened the third door on the landing. My familiar stairs! The relief hit me like an arrow. The third occasion was in Sardinia near Cala Luna, a beach beside a mountainous coastline. I had ventured out of the village along a hot gravel track bowed on both sides with olive trees, dark volcanic boulders and tantalising glimpses of emerald green lizards. I turned a corner with a picture postcard view of the sea and lots of people promenading along a track. I blinked. They wore strange hats with horns. Imagine that! People with horns. I played with it until it startled me. I looked again. They were goats. The sadness comes last, how tightly I grip the familiar, how frightened I am of dying to something new, something unknown. (November 19, 1993)

* * * *

Peter Bidmead, a traveller of sorts, recounted a similar incident. Once, while camping near Bury Hill, Coleford, in the Forest of Dean, he left the field just before dusk and strolled down a broad green track into the forest smitten by the high summer oxygen and gladness. He was wearing only shorts and a light shirt. He reached the stream at the bottom and calculated that he had plenty of time to walk the mile back up the wooded slopes to the site, one of the Rainbow Circle camps. The slope seemed unusually steep, he recalled, and only by clinging to tree roots and rocks did he scramble back up – in time see the the sun slipping below a densely wooded valley. But not the campsite. He scrambled back down the slope and reached a path but not the stream. It had vanished. He walked quickly along this path with the dusk fast obscuring the light. He saw no familiar landmarks. He was lost. He walked far along this track until he reached a small trail diverging from it. He stopped, unsure whether to follow it or continue along the main path. He chose the little path. A mile later he heard a steady, hard padding sound and a man stepped out of the dark in front of him. 'Excuse me,' said Peter, 'but I'm lost.' The man laughed uncontrollably. 'You're the first person I have ever seen on this path,' he said, 'and I've been walking it for fifteen years.' He walked through the forest once a fortnight to play chess with a friend. 'That man knew every stone, twist and tree of that wood,' said Peter. 'As it is, when I finally got out, I had to walk five miles along roads back to the site.' (January 9, 1994)

EPITAPH

I can choose any strands. It doesn't matter where I start. I have delayed this moment of saying goodbye. It is too final. The first thing is this; thank you for loving me. Thank you for your questions, your way of taking each moment seriously. You were the midwife to the artist in me. You showed me how to take myself seriously. Thank you for sharing the gift of parenthood. This doesn't die. They are inseparable. Thank you for sharing the mundane ground, facing the world together, just being there; making you tea in bed, waking up in each others' arms, listening, consoling, love-making. It's a sterile game now to apportion blame. Tigers by nature, both highly independent... Already I lose my way. I loved you, you know. This love did not save me from pain. Sometimes I think the happiness of the first part of our marriage – rented accommodation, managing on pennies and providence – was like an extended childhood. Two peas in a pod, your mother called us. Perhaps we are. You are a good mother. I see this in the boys. How hard it is to say what matters. I have fallen into the abyss. I am confused about relationships. I'm glad I am not perpetuating my male derelict side on the children. Sometimes I think that by leaving I have spared them this. It hurt being alone, the intense experience of feeling abandoned and struggling to find the parent in me, the father to organise support. I think the hardest thing is to be an

adult. I have suffered. I have lost my home and this security. I have discovered who my friends are. I have lived with the despair of being misunderstood, especially by my children. Our marriage floundered because we had to grow up emotionally. I thought for a long time that we would never separate as the children would suffer. I realised that this masked my own fear of suffering. I often wish that I could return, slip back to this comfort of family life. Then I remember our power struggles, the sexual stalemates. I gave my power away. I didn't know how to keep it. If I'm honest, the collapsed child in me wanted you to be stronger, to take care of me. Death, death of Eros! How hard to own my own power, to acknowledge my boundaries. Boundaries keep polarity, keep Eros alive. That damaged male side has a chance to be healed now it is separated, out in the open. I'm amazed our marriage lasted so long, really. I think it was a good marriage. I'm sorting things out by finding what endures. These are some of them: the wayside is a place of healing; parenthood is a continuing relationship; homelessness is a crime; a father needs a home; work is how I express myself in the world. I feel tremendously sad with all this loss and grief out here on this wayside. (1990)

FOREST GARDENER

I gave him three nuts I had collected from the Tortworth chestnut tree. Robert Hart held them in his bandaged hand, several of his fingers cold and blue, and only his eyes moved gleaming with interest. He nodded his head. He would plant them in his garden. I was both touched. and saddened by his acceptance of this little gift. His characteristic candour and willingness to serve the future came with us along every faltering step he made in his forest garden on Wenlock Edge. My worries surrendered to the peace I found there. Within an hour of walking those strawy paths I had been returned to my gardening self, brushed lightly by tranquillity. In appearance he is an English gentleman, recalling strangely the self-effacement of that other soil pioneer, Lady Eve Balfour. Yet the fragility is only on the surface; the decisive nose, focused eyes and prominent listening ears belong to a patient, enduring face and the plodding frame of a peasant. Over thirty years ago he decided to be a peasant, he said, when he moved to Rushbury with his aged mother and handicapped brother. It's only one and a half acres bordered on one side by what's left of a monastic fish pond and on the other by the hollow-way of a prehistoric packhorse trail. His forest garden is his contribution towards restoring the primeval forest of Long Mynd. In the growing season the dappled shade of his Peace Arboretum is the centre of his day; in the evening, in hot weather, he weaves his hosepipe among the trees. He walked at the speed of an infant and introduced, one by one, the members of his edible creation; I tasted the mushy acidity of Sorbus aucuparia 'Edulis', the most northerly of fruit trees; the curdy appleness of Chequers (Sorbus torminalis); the lushy bite of the Wisley crab, the salad leaves of an exotic mallow pleased me – and there are more and more.

His age is a trade secret, he says, but he must be in his eighties. He belongs to the world of the originals, those motley spirits seeking a renewal through a culture of the land. He calls his garden a peace arboretum and many of the trees jostling into a crowded canopy are dedicated to his mentors: the land historian H.J. Massingham; the Japanese farmer who brought a conservation ethic into production, and others. There are no views in his garden. The many small crab apples – 'Crittenden' is a favourite – and over forty varieties of cultivated apples, gooseberries and blackcurrants, tall lovage, exotic vegetables and roses temper the light and tease out surprises from the winding path. It is a very private garden yet, paradoxically, this enclosed horizon is linked to the forest gardens of Java, the permaculture gardens in the inner cities. Hunger is his life work, he says.

Robert Hart is both a writer and a gardener. His latest book Forest Gardening (Green Books) has achieved cult status, and I am amazed at the names in his visitor's book – the world arriving down this unmarked lane. They're his family, I think. For a moment *(and it keeps returning) I glimpse his profound solitariness and out of this, a fruit which is tasted worldwide, his contribution to resolving the conundrum: how to feed people* and *nurture the biosphere at the same time. This touches a nerve in me, the business of artistic withdrawal and public-cation; they need each other like lover's hands, yet to embrace this is to live an individual life, a creative life. 'I am intensely interested about healing,' he stammers out, characteristically passionate and earnest at the same time.*

On the walls in his spartan home are the posters of nature's warriors; Greenpeace, permaculture, the greening of deserts, of inner cities, the rights of natives, the Celtic British heart... Nature is already halfway into his home. He does not mind if people think he is eccentric; 'bien faire et laisser dire' could be his motto. I like to think that I will see Robert Hart again, that I will come back to take a photograph of him standing beside me. (Bridges, Long Mynd, October 12, 1995)

WINTER

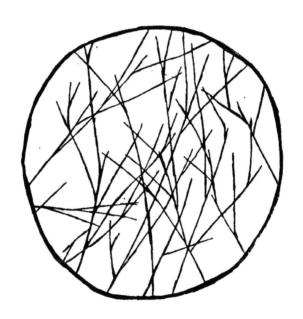

FROST ROBIN

A robin I called Perky lived on the sand dunes at Pineridge next to the Findhorn Bay caravan park. Its favourite perch was the fence beside my Sunseeker caravan door and it was there, hunched and feathery, one bitterly cold December morning when I stepped outside. I shook my head. Sorry chum, no bread today. The robin stared at me. I leaned over to shovel coal into my bucket when I felt several sharp prods in the small of my back. I turned expecting to see a mischievous child's face but there was no-one. Not a soul except for the flutter of the robin turning quickly on her perch. The truth dawned slowly. What a cheek! You're not getting bread from me – but it did, and I swear I saw the glint in her eyes as she gobbled the crumbs. (Findhorn, December 3, 1976)

* * * *

One spring, the hungry eyes of a robin watched me as I dug a small vegetable plot. I whistled to him. He cocked his head darting among the turned clods and sprung backwards into the air for a fly. I whistled again and once more he listened, scanning the steaming earth for squirming grubs. He flung himself under the fork and emerged with a fat chrysalis. The third time I whistled it flew to the fence post and peered at me steadily and carefully. It leaned forward, half crouching, and drew deep from its belly a long plaintive call, without irritation or hurry, a single note quivering with steady feeling. I received it as gratefulness. Then it flew to my feet and we started working again as if nothing had happened, me digging, the robin grubbing. I never heard him make this call again. (North Oxford, 1977)

GRANDPA'S CITY WALK IN REVERSE

Ronald Please, my father's younger brother, had taken the train from his ex-council house in Surrey and knocked at 55 Portland Place at midday precisely. I had bet Michael and Ben, my two sons, that he would arrive on time and he did. The two sides of my family sat across the kitchen table: Rene and Yoyo LeClezio, originally part of the landed Breton nobility, and Ron, part of the Please family and the back lanes of the City of London. I wanted the boys to go on grandpa's city walk, the one he took my father every Sunday morning from the Battersea tenement flats. I wanted

them to know part of their roots; Golden Lane, Roscoe Lane, Whitecross road, Banner Road where grandpa got knocked down by a hansom cab one hundred years ago. These back roads with teeming street markets, tailors' sweat shops, Peabody flats for the poor, were the workers' quarters for the City business world in Ludgate Circus, Fleet Street, The Strand... 'It was a village,' said Ron, pointing out the crumbling, black-brown brickwork dwarfed by city skyscrapers. Here grandpa had lived as a child. Down the road at 2, Old Street, his own parents – my great grandparents – had worked as booksellers. Grandpa's brother Bill was a professional boxer at Blackfriars. I kept asking Ben and Michael what they thought of the place. 'There's Uncle Bill in Ben,' says Ron winking, drawing me into the Please ancestral world. I smiled, but I am far removed from this place, but not the bedrock of survival upon which these people stand and trade. They are people on the ground. Ron talks a lot about money; he has umpteen insurance policies. He is a catholic convert and complains about the profiteering among today's poor. 'It is the poor robbing the poor.' He wants to get out of the suburbs as his estate is going downhill. He points out the cafe (the same one) near Ludgate Circus where grandma worked between 1922-1936; she earned 12s6p each week to keep grandad and Alfred, my father... Then up to St. James's Park, Downing Street, Regent Street, not forgetting our visit to Buckingham Palace and the Houses of Parliament. This walk must have felt like a walk around the world for the working class tribes of Golden Lane with hand-to-mouth poverty and comradeship. Ron started as a messenger boy with the Post Office and delivered the telegram to Downing Street on the death of King George VI. 'I was on television,' said Ron, beaming across his broad, muscular jaws. Both Ron and Rene's world of international trading are similar, bound by banking, timetables, ambition... They are circumscribed by convention; the real difference is a social one. I belong to neither of these worlds. This London world is grit and realism; I admire the independence of spirit of my French connections. Ben and Michael, I felt, saw Golden Lane for what it is, a tiny warren of streets far away from their lives. It's far away from mine, now. I no longer feel driven by these social opposites. Perhaps, for the first time for several generations, I have the opportunity to be me.
(February 13, 1993)

FRENCH CONNECTIONS

The names Giraud, LeClezio, Le Gras, Roussel belong to the southern French, Breton and Mauritian world of my mother. Up until the French Revolution most of her ancestors lived in the ports of Vannes, Quimper and Lorient, merchant people sailing and trading far overseas. I was brought up on their stories. With the Revolution and the indiscriminate slaughter that followed, they made a momentous and irrevocable decision. They left their land and houses and sailed away with their children to an almost uninhabited island in the Indian Ocean – Mauritius, the land of the dodo. Their descendants still live there, and, like the English on Barbados, are more French than the French, my grandes tantes still wearing Victorian and Edwardian outfits into the sixties.

The story I remember best concerns a certain great uncle who hankered for the fine old days. On his visits to Paris he searched the public records and unearthed his forbears, Les Jubins de Kerivilly, nobility before the 16th century. He tracked down two descendants, one at an illustrious Paris arrondissement, the other at a chateau in Brittany. The moment of reunion kindled his pre-Revolution imagination. He knocked at the great door of the baroque mansion in Paris. A servant answered; he presented his card. Madame Kerivilly? Oh, she is not available at present. Pourquoi? 'She's on duty cooking dinner.' He took a train to Kerivilly; the chateau at least was real. He presented his card. The owner eventually appeared. He looked my great uncle up and down. 'I'm sorry but I have no money to give you.' He shut the door.

TECHNO-PEASANT

I have always liked those teasers where someone has to get across a river with say a lion, a bunch of flowers, a butterfly and a rabbit – and she can only take one thing at a time on the boat. All must arrive safely on the other side. Force will not work and going slowly will be no help: thinking too much can be as dangerous as thinking too little. The solution is both highly practical and imaginative. Those extra, seemingly fruitless, journeys are necessary to accomplish the task. The teaser makes us see that we need a strategy to swim upstream. There are many hazards going against the flow. In 1977 I wanted to write and be

a gardener. 'The boy's a good egg but he's hopeless.' I teemed with questions. Thinking. Thinking. Thinking. Where am I going? I had no idea. I dreamed a wind blowing through my life, a great pearl coming out of the sky. I said goodbye to journalism and almost immediately resurfaced as a part-time meadow keeper with Merton College, Oxford. In the mornings I scythed the banks of the River Cherwell noticing extraordinary things; a worm in the act of casting, nodules of nitrogen-fixing bacteria on clover, a greedy jay dropping an acorn. I let nature touch me. I worked.

In the afternoons I wrote, wandered around Blackfriars or in the Parks, or sat in George's cafe as a spy on the world. I was happy. I no longer had to say: 'That's marvellous, thank you,' put down the phone and think, 'Idiot.' Techno-peasant (a phrase of Frank Herbert, author of 'Dune'), was my strategy to write, keep my hands dirty, pay the bills, have more fun! I wanted time and experience more than I wanted money. From the beginning I lived in the cracks of life, neither in nor out, alone as a journeyman gardener and sometimes lonely (a bad combination). It was not success I wanted but courage and fulfilment. I felt like the traveller in the fairy story who is told that he will fail five times before he finds his way – rustic dweller, herb grower, therapeutic gardener, community seeker, facilitator... But that was all to come, as well as the failure in other people's eyes, belonging neither to the professional or the artistic world. The bits didn't add up. Every time I panicked – trying to salvage myself as a professional – my plans blew up in my face. I burnt my fingers many times trying to be sensible. It wasn't fair! Yet I chose this way.

Twenty years later I still call myself a techno-peasant and it is still unknown, a traveller's way carrying me into the future. The menagerie has become my inner family. I like to think we are all going the same way now...into a planetary culture of communication and valuing what's at home, what supports us; food, people, the land, animals and flowers; a technology ethic: do the job in the simplest way possible; a native heart...half cultivated, co-operating with nature; a measure of wealth as listening spaces; of knowledge as also forgiveness. I was always looking for my voice – it's here!

DECEMBER CHANGES

What's left behind? The bones of trees, the ghosts of insects. By day the sun is a white hole in a tissue paper sky; solitude is the first door above ground – dewdrops on branches reflect bare trees – swirling greys and maroons in ploughed chalk fields – leafless trees at the beginning of month – song-birds congregate – swans are floating white lights in hoar frost – stones sing like high-tension wires across ice – fungus steams on tree trunk in snow – last yellow hazel leaf is a torch-light in the wood – flash rains bank leaves into cliffs and gullies down steep footpaths – straight lines: beaks of starlings, spores of hart's-tongue fern, side shoots of blackthorn – cat leaps on icy pond to catch fish swimming below – ivy flowers bright yellow on rusty black field maple leaves – river floods reveal burgeoning green tubers of ramsons and fisty shoots of butterbur – shrivelled damson fruits on bare branches, squidgy rosehips on bushes – bleached black bryony stems threaded with red berries – winter gnats, dung flies and bluebottles crowd last ivy flower – Medusa seed heads of old man's beard green with algae – dog's mercury collapses last of all – puddles in fields mirrored by puddles of seagulls in fields – plastic rubbish rears up from leafless hedgerows – silver lines appear on sides of trees when rain stops – skeletal wings of field maple seeds carry fresh rodent dung – rabbit burrows sparkle as frosty geodes – trees by street lamps are jewelled with raindrops – missel thrushes throng berrying hollies.

MORNING OF HOAR FROST

I have picked a yellow rose from my bare frozen bush at the back of my garden. It drips as the silver edges vanish. It is easier to start here in this sitting room listening to the wrackle and swoop of passing traffic than to enter the ornate world of hoar frost outside. I stood on the grass, soft with squashed frost but hard as iron underneath. And what I noticed were the bright silver outlines of the hedgerows against the frozen haze close to the skyline and above that the colours changed from watercolour violets, chalky blues to a light blue in the mid-heavens. Back to earth I could see my footsteps leading across the field to the ash tree with matted woollen keys; the two crows in the branches looked like lumps of coal, the starlings little black holes. I seemed to be the only thing moving except for a few leaves falling from the weight of frost. The grasses by the barbed wire fences, for once looking kind with their spangled lines of frost, resembled fallen wands thick as my finger with the frost growing on one side only. I felt lonely and peaceful walking by myself and I am still like this now. I am intensely aware how I identify with the bits and pieces of things outside me as if they are inside me, too. I find an inner peace when I consciously respect myself...this bits and pieces person, instead of projecting him outside onto the world. When I keep the centre within the world becomes whole, too. Along the wayside I noticed the red breast of robins, the bulldozer lilacs of sentry pigeons fluffed up to keep warm, the red flash of rosehips and silver blankets of old man's beard. The cow parsley stems looked like satellites and I could not resist thumbing the frost from the grooved stems. Crows in trees, spider's webs wrapped around pine bark emerged strongly against the hoar frost, along with solitude, a sky seen as blue mosaics under water and the sense, emerging steadily, that this winter solstice is a doorway to emerge above ground. On the walk by the factory chimneys, I realised that my dream of the sweet chestnut road, the healing pictures in the azure night sky, the shower of stars and streaming lights was also a sign from Zeus, the father god, that this way of the heart leads to fulfilment. (December 11, 1991)

THE TEDDY BEAR ROAD

Paul French is a traveller from Devon. In the winter he pulls up at the farm with Blossom and Samson, his two cart-horses, Rowan the whippet, Dolly his travelling goat, and stays until the grass starts growing again. He has just left the travelling Dongas in Dorset, indigenous road activists with hand carts, mobile benders, donkeys and spinners, opposing the Government's road building programme which threatens 800 ancient monuments. 'They have so much integrity those people,' he says, 'they didn't want to arrive at an action in a car.' He cuts no conventional stereotype; his wide-brimmed hat with a feather sets off his bright eyes and clean teeth; the quality Edwardian cotton coat is matched by courtesy, sharp intellect and lightness of touch. He still keeps accounts in case he ever wants to come back. 'I had a panic attack this spring when I met some of my peers and they all had good jobs. But I get homesick for this way of life.' He told me some of the lessons he had learned while walking up and down England, visiting the Priddy, Appleby and Stow fairs; be positive, want things but not too much, don't be scared of fear. The last one he saw in a dream back in the early 1980's about the time he bought a horse and was making his first excercise cart. 'It was an initiation ceremony before the God and I was sure that I was going to be sacrificed. The acolytes took me trembling to the curtain and pulled it back. The God was a giant knitted blue teddy bear.' He can talk horses until the cows come home: Samson's moods, the horse's nose for a dealer's hands, whether to leave his stallion entire or to cut, but the story which touches him most he repeats twice, at different times. It's about an old Frenchman he met in North Yorkshire, a muleteer in the Second World War. He was captured and sent to work on a German farm, escaped and joined the Resistance. He was caught again and exiled as an alternative to being shot. He was sent back to Britain after the war. Paul met him at his tiny smallholding near Thirsk. The old man had always wanted to go for a longer ride in a bowtop and Paul agreed to look after the smallholding in his absence. A week later the horse pulled up on a village green, and the old man was still sitting in the bowtop except he was dead from a heart attack. 'I was very sad,' said Paul, 'but what a way to go.' (Dunsford Farm, December 9, 1994)

GLASTONBURY MARKET

The day starts with a drama. The battered red Bedford van won't go. Mark Prior and I push to bump start and fail; we squirt damp start and it still won't go. We get the tractor out and that only starts with the jump leads. The mud, by now, has worked its way up the sides of the wellington boots (by friction) and is on the inside of my trousers. Halfway down the farm drive, with the tractor towing, the van starts and the day's first hurdle is cleared. For several months I have got up before dawn, banged Mark's Mercedes home-mobile, packed the egg boxes, the cold boxes with yoghurt and cream cheese, then driven to the west end of Dunsford Farm where we fill the van with grey trays of organic vegetables – Spanish black radishes, moolis, fat yellow turnips, Japanese winter greens, Queensland blue squashes, red kuris and more exotics – then negotiate the back roads over the Mendips for the Tuesday Glastonbury market. I know the road well now: Paulton, Chewton

Mendip, Green Ore, Wells and Glastonbury. Yesterday, a hare stepped into our headlights and bounded away into a sleeting solstice day. Above Wells, single lights crawl across the black plain of the Levels, miles of glittering necklace. The Christmas lights of Wells, empty streets except for the dustmen, affect me with a peculiar nostalgia, a consciousness of this unique local journey. It's always colder on the levels and the hoar frost bites the back of our throats.

It takes an hour to set up, off-load the trays, screw the legs onto the tables, balance the boards, the scales, and arrange the vegetables in the circular woven trays. Breakfast is always roasted cashew nuts and coffee. The first customers arrive just before nine, mothers coming back from taking children to school. It is a privilege being behind the stall, the culture of Glastonbury comes to us: the travellers from the droves, the long, short and river droves near Butleigh; the Frenchman Sylvone, a stub of a man with a pear-shaped face, and a metal wolf in one of his dreadlocks. He is gentle, humorous and a hermit when he is not busking. He reminds me of the early Irish saints living in their wattle huts like others of his ilk from King's Field, Dragon Hill, Tinker's Bubble. They live on pennies and providence. The locals from the Levels, dressed against cold and damp, appear barricaded against the world, the older men in dungeness green raincoats, caps and pitted necks. They stand by the stall looking without speaking, weighing up an important decision and then they cart off pickling onions (22p/lb); beetroot (36p/lb) or broad beans (5lbs/£1). They love broad beans the best. Yesterday, a man called Sweetman bought potatoes and carrots in part exchange for a bough of mistletoe; with his fresh cheeks, guileless eyes, clean white teeth and trimmed beard I easily pictured him in a black frock coat, a white ruff shirt...

The women, exotic visitors to Avalon, are beautiful and belong to many divinities; TM, pagan, rebirthing, starchild, dongas, land rights, bender goddesses, new age, gothic... Mark has cute come-on eyes and I a sexy listening ear. We laugh wickedly at one of our jokes; two things are endless in this world, ignorance and a long line of sorrowing women looking for our predecessor. Each week I have my little fantasies and always someone else comes along. Our oldest player is Marjorie Seedling ('as in plums') who always asks for Mark. She is ninety two. 'You heart breaker,' I tell him. Once the market stopped trading, the voices dropped and people stared at *the glitter storm of hoar frost brightening the air around us. At other moments, with a cold westerly wind driving into us, I wonder what I'm doing selling vegetables to the new age. Is Glastonbury really the place of great beginnings? The only Christian church not to be ransacked by the Saxons? They had converted by the time they reached here.*

The stuff of Avalon is carried in the quirky hearts of the individuals. Glastonbury gives people permission to be unique, to be dignified when they are poor and own nothing, to trust in their process of renewal, wholeness even when they cannot recognise it. Glastonbury is a sacred dustbin... The familiar latecomers appear; the big-whiskered tom cat skulking by the pet-food stall, the trader regularly throwing things at it. Anna, the flame-haired Donga, drags £34 of vegetables away with a helper. I give a pumpkin to Zeb on Dragon Hill. He overwhelms me with gratitude. Children with rubbish bags appear in the twilight feeding the grinding, municipal van. The drovers and colourful goddesses scavenge the remaining refuse dumps. And I am left with this: I arrive bedraggled and stressed and after eight hours standing in the elements I return invigorated, a stronger sense of me as unique, as theatre, vulnerable, trashy and deeply lovable. (December 22, 1993)

SILICA 30

I showed the homoeopath the thorn in my finger and she recommended one dose of silica 30. 'It works,' she said knowingly. Even her mother believed her now. 'She had a splinter in her finger. She tried to get it out with a needle and couldn't. I tried and I couldn't. So I gave her silica 30. Nothing happened for a day or two...except the spot she always had on her nose where her glasses rubbed got bigger and bigger and bigger until it was a girt big boil – and then it burst! A day later her splinter popped out. (Glastonbury, 1994)

BINNED

Glastonbury Joel, with little Gaia high on his shoulders, has an ear for tragi-comedy. He met this geezer sleeping in a bin-liner with his worldly possessions transformed into a pillow. He saw him again sleeping like that. So the next time he gave him a present: a silage bag. This man spread it out, got inside, stretched out his arms and legs. He smiled at Joel: 'Now! I'll be able to start a family. ' (Glastonbury, 1994)

SOME FINDHORN STORIES

I knew Peter Caddy, the co-founder of Findhorn, as a tall, restless figure often seen walking at speed along the warren of pathways in the caravan park. I usually avoided him. I never knew what to say. One day, he stopped in front of me as I was cutting the edge of a lawn and carefully avoiding a daisy head. He shook his head sadly. 'This is sentimental. A lawn is a lawn and the daisies on it are weeds. It's no use taking the others out and leaving one or two in. They should all be taken out.' This is an attitude that has spoilt many gardens, he said. He knew a woman in Inverness who lived many previous lives as a deva and was now experiencing life as a human. 'She hates to cut anything growing in her garden. The beech hedge is 80ft high. Can you imagine that? The roses have never been pruned. They look spindly and miserable. The carrots are no bigger than her little finger. She can't bear to thin them.' In the end Roc, the intermediary with Pan, had to clarify the situation. Then Peter strode off. Two weeks later I was collecting the feathers of another small bird hijacked at the pond by a cat when the gravel crunched to a standstill. Peter stood before me. 'There are too many cats in this community,' he said straightaway. 'We put out so much love all the strays come here from as far as Forres.' He said that he was prepared to tolerate three cats but no more. How were they going to be reduced? 'There has been some work on the inner but action is also needed on the form level.' His blue eyes searched mine. Summoning my courage I said that I would catch the strays and take them away in a car. He digested that and strode away to another core meeting. A week later, while scarifying the lawn, the grass squeaked and Peter appeared. He spoke cheerfully: 'This cat deva knows his business. As soon as he heard of your plan the cats vanished.' Then he spoke softly: 'In our two conversations I have observed a curious thing. On one hand the extreme of taking a lawn mower around a daisy and yet you talk of murdering cats.' He shook his head sadly. He strode away, and I don't think I ever spoke to him again.

* * * *

'Everyone here may be cool on the surface but underneₐₜ
is a cry for help.' These words were oxygen when I heard them in
1975 at a men's meeting. Someone said that there's a light at the
end of the tunnel. I didn't even know about the tunnel. Shyness,
judging as bad our low places, were common threads as well as
an acknowledgement of the basics 'I'm confused, I'm lonely and
I'm horny.' Dick Maxwell, the veteran among us, had a soft voice
which filtered out through his white beard; with his mass of
white hair, he appeared a patriarch burdened by unknown
things. I never knew him well but this story made us laugh.
Once he had been working in the Nevada desert for a few
months on an alternative architectural project. He returned to
San Francisco with a huge beard, bigger than normal, and while
walking down his home street some secretaries giggled as he
passed. This bothered him. The next time he came back from
the desert he shaved off his beard before arriving in San Franciso.
He walked down his home street and saw the secretaries. Again,
they giggled as he passed. (1976)

* * * *

An investigative reporter (and there were some who flocked to
Findhorn in the early days in search of orgies and fairies) interviewed a frail, elderly lady in her caravan. He noticed the bottles
of coloured water on the shelf, the rainbow woven textile on the
wall, the small-framed affirmative sayings: 'Trouvez votre
plaisir'; 'S'écouter'; 'Life Is Only Real Then, When I AM'.
Tentatively, he asked: 'Don't you think you might be a
little...cracked?' 'Cracked?' she answered straight away. 'Of
course, I am. It lets in the brightness.' (1976)

* * * *

Bart, an American from Idaho, said he played this game in his
youth on the family farm. At harvest, they left a large block of
ripe corn in the centre of the field. Then a group of his teenager
friends would go there with a box of beer, a tractor and a
harvester. They'd drink the beer and all the kids except one
would hide in the wheat. He climbed onto the tractor's seat,
blindfolded himself, and then tore through the wheat – hence
the name, 'run and kill'. A twist to this game was that those
hiding in the wheat could jump onto the tractor and box the
driver's ears. So it was in his interests to steer as erratically as
possible. (1976)

DRIZZLE BLANKET DAY

The hind leaped out of the thicket of elm suckers, flashed the silver brown rump across the field and stopped, glancing back for the waiting fawn to appear. It walked out slowly and then the pair melted into the drip drizzle shrouding the field and tree outlines, and the upright silhouettes moved farther and farther away, side-stepping among the corn stubble fields beside the River Frome. These are natives, I thought, running against the grain of distant car lights cutting straight lines between the hedgerows. This ambivalent feeling of hunter and being hunted stalked me through-out this walk, the futility of one person wandering among these ghostly byways in search of grandparent trees. Sometimes I'd stop and let the earth take my cares and concerns, let the ground do its work without me knowing how or where or why.

The winter sky merges with the land, the drizzle clouds combing the tree tops, spreading the colours of sleeping, squeezed-out browns, smudged greys, making the land smaller, shortening the view by taking the perspective away so I seemed to be walking into a fish bowl. These things stood out: silver lichens, single yellow ivy leaves, the crack of a gun, the yaffling laughter of a green wood-pecker... I squelched up field edges taking this feeling that something has died in me, that I am incomplete. The blurred outlines mirror this numbness, soothing and sedative, masking the dead and the sleeping land. I hear gunshot below ancient nut-brown trunks of sycamore skirting Orchardleigh and I go the way the deer go, dropping down through the winter rye, stopping to listen then side-stepping to the field margin. I notice things: great beetle stumps by Brookover Farm, an oak tree cleaved in two and perfectly hollow, the straight beaks of starlings, the pentagram at the crown of every hawthorn berry. I get tired of noticing things and again this aloness crowds in and I wonder what I am doing. Perhaps I am suffering from a terminal disease. My new walking boots collect gallons of mud and I heave and swivel my hips to move one in front of the other...

This walking about business is my work. I choose this limitation and boundary. It has a weight; sometimes it is a coffin lid, some-times it is a perch from which I sing. Today I feel the weight of the earth, I feel my weight... I root into my ground, ordinary, maker of fine old messes, traveller at home. I am a techno-peasant. I choose not poverty. I choose creativity, connection. I do not receive *these thoughts outside by the beetle chapels in old stumps or the flaking bark of sycamores... Here, on this stone floor in my den, the bigger picture arrives, speeding this pen across white paper. I know all parts of this walk now. I know myself better. I returned the way I started, along the banks of the Frome river, green except at the white water of the weir which thundered persistently. On such a day little things become signposts to bigger things: silver lichen show brooding grey walls; fresh emerald circles of nipplewort opens a door into rocky crevices; single yellow ivy leaves reveal rusty black woodland floors. This feeling of death, this immovability as limitation, is the stage scenery in place for next year's show.* (Frome, December 15, 1992)

WANGAL NARBO

This twenty two-year-old Tibetan refugee was carried by his mother who walked from Lhasa to Kathmandu fleeing the Chinese invaders. He lived in a convent until his family restored their fortunes and then came to England to the Ockendon Venture where I met him. Life in Nepal, at best, was often precarious with little food and a hard bed, but it wasn't until he came to England that he discovered the word 'insecure'. He had no idea what it meant. In Nepal he had heard many stories about Christianity and assumed Europe to be very religious. He marvelled at the churches in each English village and the lack of religious feeling in most people. He noticed our tolerance, humour and stiff upper lip. 'A boy was knocked down on the street and people said how sorry they were to hear about his death but no-one expressed their feelings. When I came to England I had to learn to hold back my feelings'. In exquisite Tibetan script he recorded some Tibetan sayings: 'A little spice in an elephant's mouth'; 'A beard won't stop someone from eating'; 'There is hope 'til there is breath'; 'At these twenty two stone taps the water flowing is very sweet and pure.' These are stories his mother told him as a child:

* * * *

Once there were two flies, both husband and wife. Now it happened that the fly wife became pregnant and her husband went off in search of some butter, a luxury in those times. He found himself on the rim of a large pot and looked down upon the butter; but no matter how far he stretched he could not reach the tempting butter. He used a long stick as a spoon and scooped up a large piece, but it was so heavy that as he lifted it, he lost his balance and fell in and died. His wife became anxious at his disappearance and cried and cried and cried. At last she gave birth and when the little fly had grown up a bit she asked him to go and look for his father. This the dutiful fly did and by and by arrived at the butter container. He was so young and energetic he was able to lift the body of his now frail father, and with him on his back, set out along the river bank. As he went along a fish popped out of the water and pleaded with the fly for a bite of his dead father as he was very hungry. The son said that he did not want his father to be broken up on the mountain or given to the birds, nor did he want to give a piece to the fish for the same reason. No, he wanted to bury him in the ground and plant a fragrant tree on the spot, so that every time he passed, and the same for his grandchildren, the sweet fragrance would bring back the memory of his old father.

* * * *

Once there were two farmers, a husband and wife, and they had a large granary to store their grains. Now it happened that the wife became pregnant and in due course became very hungry. Each evening she would silently go into the grain house, shut the door and start eating the grains. After awhile the husband noted that the grains were going down and so he decided to watch the granary. One evening he saw his wife go in, and after she shut the door he crept up and looked through the peephole. He saw his wife eating the grains and suddenly there was a loud noise and the husband was blown from the door. The grain scattered in all directions and the wife became very embarrassed for she saw her husband had seen her farting. She ran out and wept and wanted to commit suicide.

She ran to a monastery where the monks beat the large drums and spun the prayer wheels. A monk asked her what was the matter. At length she told him and he said that was no reason to end it all. Was it as loud as this, he said tapping one end of the drum lightly. 'Oh no! Much louder.' 'Like this,' he said beating the stick against the drum. 'No, still louder.' Summoning all his strength he whacked the drum sending a roar down the valley. 'I think it was louder still,' said the distressed farmer's wife. 'You must be a liar,' cried the monk, 'I have never heard of such a thing. I won't believe it until my ears hear it.' The woman consented to his request. She farted and the monk's hat and robes went flying into the wind, along with the large prayer wheels stacked by his feet. The woman ran away even more frightened and embarrassed and lived off the wild grain. The baby was near birth and one day she heard the baby inside her say it was very hungry. This is very strange,' she said to herself, 'it must be some kind of monster.' So saying she took off her clothes and put them on a pillar. She gave birth to the child and hid behind a tree. She saw the baby indeed was a monster and it went up to the fake mother and ate her up and then went up eating the villages and corn in the fields...' This story goes on and on,' said Wangal showing me his white teeth, 'and I never found out the ending.' (Oxford, 1980)

THE DONKEY AND THE BIRD OF PARADISE

There should be a story about these two but I have never found it; the beautiful bird finding a home on the back of the plodding donkey, flying away and always returning. When she leaves the flies settle on the donkey's back and he sinks into earth and the dusty road, the nuts and bolts of routines. She returns with far away stories and whispers them into his ear; he dreams a little. She needs the shelter, warmth and contact of the earth, a grounded energy, earth and sky working together. There is harmony when they go in the same direction. I made a picture of them once. They are looking at me now.

JURASSIC STONE (II)

falling falling   falling falling almost like snow falling falling
falling falling falling falling down through the millennia
falling falling   falling falling falling falling falling horse-shoe
crab falling falling falling falling falling falling millennia falling
falling falling falling falling belemnite falling falling falling
falling falling falling falling falling microscopic snow falling
falling falling falling falling falling falling plesiosaurus falling
falling falling ammonites falling falling falling snow falling
falling crinoids falling falling sea lilies falling falling falling
falling falling falling falling falling falling coating grains falling
falling falling rings calcium carbonate falling falling falling
falling falling snow falling falling falling falling falling

microscopic snow falling falling falling falling falling falling
coating shell falling falling coral fragments falling falling falling
falling falling falling falling falling falling falling falling falling
falling falling oolitic spheres rolling rolling rolling crinoids
rolling rolling rolling grains at heart rolling rolling rolling
rolling buried half an inch a century rolling rolling oolitic snow
rolling rolling bivalves rolling ammonites rolling rolling rolling
rolling rolling coated with lime rolling rolling ammonites rolling
rolling rolling rolling rolling rolling rolling down through the
millennia rolling rolling...

The Jurassic seas retreated and expanded, the coastline changing
as the ocean bed tilted and faulted, raising and lowering the sea
levels. The Bath oolite vanished beneath coarse and shelly
limestones, coral deposits with starfish and sea urchins, the
stems and arms of sea lilies (crinoidal limestone), and thick
deposits of blue, yellow and brown clays from muddy prehistoric
seas. The weight of millions and millions of years pressed the
oolite into golden stone seams between three and ten metres
thick. The seas ebbed and flowed. Microscopic foraminifera,
sea-floating organisms, built the future cliffs of Dover over sixty
million years ago with their minute cathedral skeletons; alluvial
clay deposits established the site of London forty five million
years ago. Britain continued to drift northwards into more
temperate latitudes, helped twenty five million years ago when
Africa, during one of its shunting movements, bumped into
Europe. This created the Alps and the shock waves tilted the
oolitic beds into a gentle, south-eastward slope. The visible rim
of that collision is the limestone outcrop running from Portland
on the south coast of England, up through Bath, the Cotswolds,
to the North Yorkshire moors.

The giant Irish elk (*Megaceros giganteus*) knelt against the frozen
earth. Its breath steamed instantly. It shovelled away the snow
crust with slow, ponderous movements of its three-metre antlers
to reach the tips of shaggy moss. The wind scuffed the artic
wastes and veered northwards across the thirty-metre ice wall.
The clouds merged with the ground into one horizon, sky and

earth frozen, a never-ending view of snow fields scarred with black scree. By night the elk sheltered in caves, the mossy side of boulders or sought the protection of bison herds. By day it followed the melt-water cutting the snow into ribbons, steering clear of rock terraces concealing long-toothed predators. Tiny blue flowers starred the snow. The elk skated across the mushy skin of permafrost until the uplands encircled an extensive iced lake in the hollow of the hills. Here the wind dropped and scrub woods of alder contoured the slopes above the vast beds of bulrushes. The elk saw the narrow river winding to the west but not the reeds sinking annually, layer upon layer, building first a spongy mat, enough to support a snail, then a frog, a rat, then a deer. The elk saw the gorge slicing the ring of hills but not the small islands appearing slowly and growing heath, willow and enveloped in steam gushing from the earth: the beginning of the place called Aquae Sulis, later Bath.

Sean Borodale, the printmaker, remembers finding a fossil in the shaly cliffs at East Quantoxhead when he was four years old. That memory brought him back, when he was sixteen, to look for more. He scaled down the cliff breaking off a rock with his hand – on the other side he found a perfect fossilised fish.

TURKEYS

A few feet to my left, up several steps of hay-bales, are the many craning eyes of turkeys. They stare at the eight pigs slopping up dregs from the sheep trays below them. The birds are hunched into their backs of bronze obsidian feathers and emerge like vultures with skinned faces no bigger than a walnut. They are mobile with intelligence, tilting now to question me. I am fascinated by their strangeness, their ugliness. In some lights, the folds of skin hanging below their beaks glow a translucent red, and in cold weather the pink delta of blood veins shed a ghastly glaucous colour. Most weird. And to add to this, the neck skin hangs in folds of fat, strung as beads in the males. One fact is clear: in fifteen days these prodigious fowl, nestled and muttering melodiously in the hay (the rats have cut the binder-twine), will meet a spectacular death. They will screech futilely as their legs are caught, their flapping bodies upturned and then plunged head first into a funnelled, metal container. *A blue flash, an aura of vibrating light from the electric Stunner, will render them immobile. Their thoats will be cut and the blood will drain into a bucket. Their legs will be bound by a noose and the feathers plucked while they are still warm. It is an outlandish death, almost a ritual death.*

These birds originate from the Americas and were once the royal birds of the Incas. Absurdly, the image of the teeming sacrificial victims of that culture appears, the one the Spanish looters loved to publicise, the young victims cut open while still breathing. I cannot get rid of this association of ritual death. There is something royal about these birds as if they were once free, more individual. They could be an exotic buzzard but the caustic-dip head spoils the effect. They barely fly, limping a few feet before crash-landing. They continue pecking the grass, waddling, switching their big white-edged tail primaries; others do nothing except stare. Their eyes are soft alternating browns. They are waiting for something but it might as well be Godot... I whistle gently and I am listened to, the shuttering of their eyes flickering on and off. They laugh together, it explodes in their throats as some dirty hilarity then vanishes. The piglets return below, heaving the soft earth in the orchard with sighs. The farm track to the house is a broken, muddy mirror with slop and sludge and bare winter branches. It's hard to move this pen. I am none the wiser about turkeys. Once again, I perceive the turkeys are not interested, one way or the other.
(Dunsford Farm, December 5, 1993)

LAST ORDERS

Frome had many small grocers handed down from father to son, sometimes with the grandfather serving, too. They lingered into the nineties, relying on street corner trade and supplying boxes to regulars, but they died of old age – and everyone else went to the markets. We won't see those names anymore – Parry and Son, Sparey and Son, Reynolds and Son... Nor touch that web of gossip and local ties. The shop near Selwood Road closed down in stages shrinking to a few boxes of veggies, cheap tins and biscuits. One morning the sign on the door said, 'CLOSED FOR GOOD.' But the pigeons couldn't read it, and every morning for weeks afterwards, two or three queued patiently outside the shop-door between 6.45 and 7am – the time the owner used to feed them when he opened up. (1991)

BARN OWLS

Chris Drury is a man easy to romanticise but that would be to miss out the uncertainty, the self-discipline, the whole-heartedness of his walking about landscape work. He often walks in the wild places – in Caledonia, the Rockies, across Ceylon, on Irish boglands – making womb-like shelters, building cairns on ridges of mountains, lighting beacon fires, touching one hundred oaks or taking fly agaric spore prints and giving them away as presents. An artist, a weaver, he is a big bear of man yet, strangely, he lives in a smaller frame, stocky and with broad shoulders. His brightly blue-flecked eyes glint mischievously from his smooth, compact face. His grey-black hair is cuffed around his forehead and, with his fleshed-out hands and the way they emphasise his words and bubbles of laughter, he gives the impression of purpose and contentment, an Irish sprite with more than a leaning for the religion of the present moment. This encounter with a barn owl is typical of that natural magic which weaves its way through his work. One evening in the flat fenlands, as the watercolour oranges lit up the sky, Chris cycled home on a long, straight road listening to his wheels squeaking. Suddenly a pale luminous shape appeared a few yards behind him, skimming the verge at bicycle height. The white, embroidered wings beat silently in the dusk. Chris pedalled, the bicycle wheels squeaked, the barn owl scanned the verge. They travelled like this for several minutes along that straight road, the barn owl hoping the squeaking wheels would disturb the voles. Or perhaps it thought they were voles? (Frome, 1992)

* * * *

Some incidents happen quickly but the meaning unfolds slowly: Tim Baines is a landscape gardener in Bath who escaped from an administrative career with the Milk Marketing Board. He is a gentle person, the godfather of the local organic gardening network. He told us this story quietly, hesitantly at the Earthkids Conference in Swindon. One Sunday he walked with his wife and son along the Avon lanes when, from behind the hedge, came a dreadful screeching noise followed by hollow, beating sounds. They stopped, the noise stopped, then it started again even louder. They crawled through the hedge and astounded an adult barn owl caught fast on the barbed wire fence. It screeched fearsomely as they approached. His son held the owl's head, his wife the talons, while he freed the wings from the wire. They held the bird for a minute and then released it. That minute was the longest minute for, in a way he could not explain, the owl and its plight and the freeing of the bird released some long-standing tension between themselves. He could not explain it but he was was aware of this bonding feeling for weeks afterwards. (November 1992)

* * * *

This tiny incident keeps reappearing in my memory, a side-drama in the more serious business of watching barn owls by night. This particular nest in the Cam Valley, Avon, belonged to a pair of the lucky birds reared in their nearby stronghold on the Somerset levels. In the wild they may live three or four years; in captivity, over twenty years. (There are more barn owls in captivity than in the wild.) Their favourite food is short-tailed field voles, and they will quarter the rough grasslands in search of this prey, and, in harder times, they do this by day. Andre Fournier, an amateur naturalist with the Cam Valley Wildlife Group, was sitting quietly with a friend, their backs to a hedge and watching the nesting box in the fork of a tree by the old Somerset Coal Canal. A vole chose that moment to twitter past – just as the heart-shaped luminous face appeared at the nest-box entrance. The vole stopped and side-stepped backwards until it crouched between the two men. For half a minute none of them dared rustle a blade of grass. The two men and the vole watched the owl wondering where to go next that starlit night. (Paulton, January 26, 1994)

DUMFRIES

I can see that lonely person trudging the back roads in the rain, up the buttress of Criffell or along the Nith estuary with the swans lighting up the dusk. I walked with my *Oxford Book of Wild Flowers*, identifying for the first time toothwort, eyebright, sea pink, lesser celandine, and each one of these flowers light-ened a darkness in me. I dreamed of longer walks, great journeys following the Euphrates from its source in Turkey to the Persian Gulf, tramping the pampas in South America and astounding people with my repertoire of sad Irish songs. I even wrote to the

National Geographical Society for advice on expeditions. I was full of longing. For what? I dreamed myself away from those rambling Dickensian offices, up the heavy elm staircase, past cubby-holes and back stairways with dark rooms, reporter rooms, boxes for the regional editor, past the door going down into the oily steam of the hot press and the broad Lowland talk of compositers, proof-readers and lino-type operators. I followed the sign, *The Sub-Editor* – a painted finger pointing to my door. I worked on a huge table of coffee-stained wood with ancient copies of the History of Dumfries peering out of glass-fronted bookcases, the shelves and ledges covered with dust-weary hand-outs, old clippings. They were put there for a reason; no-one remembered why. The nave-like ceiling opened up to the sky-light, possibly for inspiration but it made the room impossible to heat. I listened to the pigeons in the attic. The smell of accumulated droppings overpowered me on hot days: tiny mites occasionally landed on the copy I edited. I thought I had lice. I looked up at Tom Phin, the editor, tall and wiry and always working, his waterfall of wrinkles above his canny hawk of a nose and his greying toothbrush eyebrows. He epitomised indu-striousness. I heard stories of notable failures, a reporter who had never initiated a story in ten years, one who always preten-ded, if someone rang for him, that he was someone else – until someone caught him out red-handed. I was an outsider in this insider world of Scottish journalism.

Books took the place of parents, grandparents and advisors. I filled my journal with wise sayings from Wabasha (the Sioux Indian), Mother Teresa, Kropotkin, Sufi masters, Pierre de Chardin, George Borrow, Ghandi – anyone who could pull me out of this turmoil and ballooning sense that I needed to change, step into the unknown. But where? Of course, the signposts were there all the time, in the gaps; while cycling to Kirkcudbright or the old military road to Castle Douglas; in lover's walks on the coast near Kirkbean; in every alkanet and sea pink; while noticing the solder-and-sailor beetles mating, the tiny penis visible against the sunglow. These details were the signposts. They were too small to see. This gently growing love of nature slowly opened my eyes, gave me the spaciousness I needed to imagine, the time to notice the white moustache of a reed bunting in a flock of winter finches, the feints of the snipe, or the heron's glistening eyes staring down its beak.

I tortured myself with yearning and indecision. Nemesis came in disguise outmanoeuvring my inertia. One weekend in the Moffat Hills, I panicked crossing a ledge over a stream. 'And you want to go down the Euphrates?' I asked myself incredulously. Everybody I met wanted to own a house. Why not me? Under Scottish law I made an offer on a cottage in a nature reserve and waited for a week. They refused, then changed their minds on the eighth day when it was no longer legally binding. I changed mine. I was not going to marry Dumfries after all! I had had enough of journalism. I resigned and was amazed by the kindness of my superiors, and set off with my rucksack to the North of Scotland. Not long afterwards I dreamed that I was standing on a back road in front of the cottage I had wanted to buy. I examined it carefully. I decided against it and carried on until the road joined the main road. The traveller going down that was dressed in red and yellow, the colours of joy. (1975)

ALAN PEACOCK

Alan Peacock was the first writer I ever met. His family befriended me at a lonely crossroad in Scotland; I was their lodger for a few weeks. They had long ago sold up in southern England and rented the house at Thorniethwaite Farm near Lochmaben. He lived a domestic life, writing and tending his chickens and vegetables, his wife carding and spinning wool. I suspect they lived on peanuts and happily. He died suddenly from a heart attack a few months later. I remember him fondly for he kindled the hope of writing in me. Quintessentially English, the son of a British family born into the Raj, he belonged to the theatre. 'I love the rompotomp drums. Don't you?' 'Never heard of them.' 'There are no rompotomp drums.' His puckish eyes gleamed. I had passed the test. The British war machine he mimed magnificently; the absolute precision of bugling, the pacing forward; the first volleys, marching forward, bugling again and firing... He twice remembers seeing Ghandi, once as a child in Amritsar where his father was the colonial administrator. He said the Indians respected his father because he was fair and stood up with no nonsense. One day Ghandi's car sputtered to a halt in the dusty plain outside the town and no-one knew what to do. His father latched a rope to the car and shouted PULL! Ghandi delivered his political speech. He saw him again near Delhi. As a special parachutist he had landed in a forest clearing after reports of suspicious movements of Indians. On the ground they heard the villagers shrieking, 'BAPU BAPU!' and staring at a skinny figure up to his knees in the local shitpits. It was Ghandi haranguing the crowd about building their cesspits around the village. Didn't they know that their health was in danger? They agreed, setting fire to the old buildings. Ghandi led them to a new site. (1974)

TRAVELLER – SEX

When I was 38 I dreamed I came spinning out of primal swirling stuff and that I had a tiny cock. I saw it, real titchy. I had the clear impression that it was there before the beginning. But from where? A second dream: I find a sculpture in a wall, a curious ivory phallus on two legs, with little rose-red hearts engraved into it. As I hold it it grows into a cross, and upon it is Jesus Christ with an enormous erection and a blissful smile. I bow down before Him as if He is blessing my sexuality.

I did not want to make a special subject out of sex for that is what I was brought up to believe, that sex is in a special box and you can take it out and put it back and all you need is the key. But I can't get away from it, sex for me is a special subject, an uncompromising teacher at every turn of the road, a blessing in every disguise. I would have liked sex to emerge naturally, not just the delicious act of coupling but the fateful attraction of gravity for all the things that move or fly; the honey bees smudged with May pollen, the smell of fresh cut grass and rolling in it, the hands in the earth, clouds over a tree, games of hide and seek, the touch of a woman; these myriad intangible connections are erotic and beautifully unknowable. But the nitty-gritty is where I stumbled and I must go back there. I don't know where I got my ideas about sex from. Not from schools (they gave me silence) or my parents (they gave me a leaflet on the dangers of masturbation when I was sixteen). I suppose off shithouse walls, the big dripping cocks and vaginas like barn-house doors, names of queers and slags and girls that shagged; the bragging of elders (they were begging for it); the wrath of God at Sunday mass (the polluting body, the retribution of venereal diseases, the syphilitic cripple; love everybody except yourself); the cynical advertiser's dream of cut-out muscle men and cute, surrendering women.

I never had a chance. I walked onto this world stage an unexceptional boy, shy and not-knowing it. I didn't know what hit me. I copied my peers staying silent about myself. I kept *me* private. I didn't know about the hole growing inside which I would fall into one day. I closed the door on that. Of course, I coped. I masturbated in silence, with friends; a bonding secret among boys. I revelled in my hidden erections on trains; sex and silence, this secret world a secret in public places. It was a way of affirming my sexuality though I never graduated into flashing...but I had the potential. I loved passionately, shyly from a distance, hopeless love for my friend's mothers, elder sisters, or distant faces in congregations. I drew the line at nuns. I had no boundaries. I was a sexual amorphic, dreaming myself into every bed, into every shape and size. The rub passed me by: the bigger I saw myself, the smaller I felt myself to be. And by this vicious logic I needed somebody else to be that small man, to be that whipping boy. It was survival, remember.

The cultural homophobia, the taboo on intimacy between men, stopped us learning about ourselves, our needs. I resented men in groups. They had let me down. I was frightened of them. A lot of the time I felt like an orphan and on the run. I was lonely and mother bound. The hippy era allowed me a softer side but the hashish at eighteen opened the door to the first descent. The experience of nausea was my awakening, the first knock at *that* door. I could not escape it. That small man with tiny cock rose to the surface and no matter how much I bashed him back down he kept popping up, opening up the sewage gates: vivid pictures of me being tied to a tree and ravished by girls, crawling through minefields, waking up in bed with my mother. I lost my self-confidence and felt different from my friends. They were normal, *me* was rubbish. Bit by bit, I believed myself to be impotent, or a homosexual at least. How could I be potent with such a figure inside me? Such a changing, rubbishy figure no earthly good for any woman. I didn't know that he was on my side, that he had an enormous heart. I found some solace in the wayside of my childhood, walking down the back lanes going nowhere in particular, mooning with nature. I started to walk with that sad person. Sex, unwittingly, had become my teacher. I longed for sexual love, normal love and lots of it, yet the old pattern of coming on big and feeling small did not work. I usually lost my erection. I either blamed the women, too demanding or insensitive to my needs, or collapsed in self pity. 'I'm no good.' Or I talked and let some of my sadness out. Bless those women who listened to me. They helped me carry on with my life. But this bogeyman had other plans. He was like a magic thorn; the more I tried to pull it out, the deeper it wriggled in. I was 23. I could not banish this sadness in me. I looked elsewhere for an answer.

I travelled. My catholic world came with me, my yearning for transformation, my lascivious imagination. I was always on the rack between God and the devil. Above the Sea of Galilee, I walked through a cornfield with a devout Jewish girl and when we lay down I kept thinking: perhaps Jesus walked here, broke bread and fishes for the multitude... I could not defile this place with sex. In the hot springs at Tiberias other men's cocks always appeared bigger. The vicious logic ground on; big men equals bigger cocks equals big sex, impregnable steel phalluses, with push button control; one after the other, always on time. Better than soft little dwarf ones. And so on. I had a hole where my cock should be. Oh, this little man! The self-torture. Truly, I was a wolf in sheep's clothing. I knew all the sad Irish songs, the long-distance lonely walks; I was outspoken for the downtrodden; a friend of lame-ducks; I behaved lecherously when the booze got out of the bottle, then collapsed into purity. There seemed no way out of this mess. It had long eclipsed my modestly successful career. I felt full of piety yet eaten by desire.

At 25 I was driving a car submerged in water and I had no idea how this had happened; at Findhorn, provoked by happiness, I cried as many tears. I melted a little. The process of self-rejection encountered a serious obstacle – tenderness. In bed, I surrendered a little. I still have a postcard sent by Ling, a Canadian Chinese woman; two butterflies dancing in the light. And though I schemed and bungled and tried too hard, I discovered the obvious, that sex can be a dance, a passionate conversation.

ADAM THE GARDENER

Adam came to the Findhorn Foundation back in the early 1970's, one of the Blackpool bikers and would-be rock stars who found a home working in that famous garden. He always

85

represented for me the essential gardener, steady, unflappable, with a knack of combining gentleness with authority. He worked as a rock climber instructor on Skye, managed a caravan park for years then resurfaced with his first love, trees and plants. 'For two years I had been saying shall I get back into gardening or shan't I. Then I said yes and here I am.' He grinned and his very blue eyes animated his oval face, furrowing his laughter lines. We sat on the wooden seat in the herb garden sharing a roll-up, listening to the babble of voices on the other side of the fence. No-one came along this little path. I said that I was standing in front of an empty place in my life, my practical endeavours having failed. He grinned even more showing the full extant of the gaps in his teeth and told me this story. Once on LSD (a long time ago) he looked up and saw the sky open and then he was up there, too, and the stars came out one by one. Up, up he went and it seemed to him that he was at the centre of a galaxy, that the curtains opened on heaven, and the stars gleamed and glinted all the way to eternity. He looked at me and stretched out his arms. 'I came to the end of the stars and there was a wall up ahead. I put my hands on the top and very slowly peered over the other side. I stared into the greatest emptiness, a void of space, unending. For a moment I couldn't believe it or move, then very, very slowly I got back down, and I have never been back there again.' (1992)

RICHARD ST. BARBE BAKER

There is a kind of logic that I should glimpse this gentleman visionary in that other place of visions, Findhorn. That a recluse living in a tumbledown keeper's cottage in a wood knew this man as a bit of a father, a bit of a brother, a bit of a friend, and above all as a teacher. In the seventies, I searched the catacombs of Hay-on-Wye for cheap copies of St. Barbe Baker's Books – *I Planted Trees*; *The Brotherhood of The Trees*; *The Redwoods* and others. Always I glimpsed the paradox of this strange man, quintessentially English yet looking at the world not as an Englishman, someone thinking about trees for the sake of the planet. A private person yet a consummate showman if it could put another tree into the ground; a friend of aristocrats (often notable foresters) yet someone who dreamed of living in a caravan community in a wood; the forester with degrees from

Cambridge University and a blood brother with African chiefs. I could not pigeonhole this man; even his closest friends did not know he was a member of the Bahai faith. While contemporaries embarked on doomed peanut schemes in Tanzania, he urged people to plant trees to halt the spread of the Sahara. He liked to be called 'Sahara' Baker. A man, definitely, before his time.

I was on familiar ground in the insect garden of Bruce Burdass, off a lane and down a track near the Wiltshire village of Compton Bassett. An unlikely place for this urbane pilot who once owned 500 acres in Kent. I never sought for an explanation or got one. He had been a friend of Richard St. Barbe Baker for thirty years, at 40, the youngest council member for The Men of the Trees, the organisation founded by his mentor with the Kikuyu tribes in Kenya in 1922. That helped to change the traditional attitude of planting trees as God's work, to the work of warriors, comradeship against the desert. Bruce recalled for me the tall, meticulous man in dress and manners (but never showy) he first met at Penshurst when St. Barbe Baker had politely announced that he was vegetarian, refusing the leg of lamb. 'He had walked twice around the Sahara when I met him. And later I walked a thousand miles with him in ten African countries bringing seeds and knowledge to the tribal peoples. In 1974, as a birthday treat, I flew St. Barbe Baker over the plantations which he had personally planted by Mt. Kenya.'

He was a man who considered he had a purpose, said Bruce, yet at 70 felt his plea for reafforestation, particularly, in the Sahel, were not not being listened to. His treatment of the African as equals in the 1930's, his lack of interest in bureaucracy and the codebook of rules against new ideas did not endear him to the colonial administration. 'There was no tittle tattle in him, or any falseness, just factual. He could see through people. A lot tried but you couldn't fool him, yet with a genuine audience he could talk about trees for hours... Some people found him intense.' St. Barbe Baker often used his London home as a bolt-hole, arriving on his doorstep with rucksack or suitcase and sleeping bag. He travelled all over the world with his tree message, largely at his own expense, Bruce emphasises. His training as an ex-army officer extended into his civilian life. (Once he had been a cavalry officer and in his youth retraced Cobbet's ride in Hampshire). Up at 5.30. writing for three hours before breakfast of nuts and berries. 'He was very hard-working and deeply conscious that if he could only get his views across he could save millions of lives.'

He thought about trees in big numbers. Bruce remembers sitting on a verandah at Tree-Tops, a reserve near Nairobi, listening to the bush at 3am. They watched a beetle the size of a plate crawl to the waterhole, then two torchlights appeared and a jungle owl swooped down and grabbed it. Crunch! 'It's larger than life,' I said. 'That's what I wanted you to see,' said St Barbe Baker. 'It's the scale that matters.' *He pictured the world as a new tennis ball and the fluffy bits are trees. When they wear out the ball spins faster and the earth's natural equilibrium is endangered.* 'He didn't see the world as an Englishman. He didn't consider himself to be any particular nationality. He was a citizen of the world. He was a loner though he never considered himself to be out on the edge. He felt he was the one in step. I think time has proved him right.'

I'm proud that I met him once even though I never spoke to him. In 1976 I saw his face in a candle-lit meditation, alive, alert and serene. He was 87-years-old. He told a visitor at breakfast that he was always intoxicated by the love at Findhorn. He is buried under a tree in Canada.

TREE MAN

Ken Day was felling a 400-year-old oak with his chainsaw. He was intensely aware of this great continuity being felled by his own hands. He closed his eyes and tried to commune with the tree, expecting that he would encounter sure signals of distress. Instead a sudden feeling of peace enveloped him. He continued his work with a light heart. (Bath, January 4, 1984)

* * * *

I always notice the tree where the lower branches have been cut back; despite this loss the tree still grows, the wounds transformed into swelling bosses of healing tissue. It's a picture of hope.

JANUARY CHANGES

The rain keeps coming: the yawning squelches, the soft, wet isolation of drizzle blanket days, soggy soggle boggle days, mud-gasper days, the saturnine low pressures. Everything is pared to the bone waiting for signs of spring – purple haze skies, smudged trees below masked with glinting cats's eyes – a saddle of whirling white flashes on a long black back: a magpie – primrose flowers in sheltered hedgerow near Bath – seed husks of the spindle (*Euonymus europaeus*) are pale brown – dog's mercury opens claws under woodland leaves – robin sings sweetly his courting song during hail-storm at Frome – first felty arrow shaft of burdock (*Arctium minus*) – starlings fluff their feathers on steaming roof slates with frost tideline – tadpoles of moving water slide beneath ice sheets on Egford Hill, Frome – cobwebs everywhere with hoar frost – soggy pigeon feathers on bare branches – when the sun shines, the hoar frost tinkles – piles of chewed berries grow under holly tree – purple alders with russet flames of weeping willow – rhubarb shoots emerge as rubies – meadow grass, half dead, half green, glows after storm – hazel catkins land on ground – under the boulder ants herd white aphids along tunnel – after the storm, rafts of russet alder seeds float on River Frome – fat pigeons gobble black ivy berries – the red-bursting buds of hawthorn, the dun clusters of blackthorn – oak-posts creak and submit to the wind.

TRAVELLER – IDHP

I know it saved my life. On the day I decided to do this practical facilitator's course I dreamed myself onto this perfect seashore with the stone of the world carved there. I pushed off from the sand and became an eagle and every time I thought it, I flew higher watching the land shrink into little squares. I returned safely to earth. Then I saw this shabby, stuck together house, a sort of Okie's home, make-shift and full of adolescent paraphernalia. A surreal hawk-headed woman in silver stood outside with her sharp profile to me. I needed her discernment. I glimpsed my power to destroy and recreate, the work of reconstruction required; for that house represented my patched together emotional body, the fact that I had never got through my adolescence. I didn't know that it would cost me my marriage, that the next ten years would be a descent, a

disintegration and a profound social reappraisal in my life. I had
no idea of the world of sorrow in me, belonging not just to me
but somehow passed down generations, the clothes that did not
fit. In a dream I clung to the edge of an abyss. I surrendered and
free-fell into the darkness and up struggled butterflies into the
tender rain. By facing my grief, I believe I have spared my sons
this grief. Sometimes I think that's the bravest thing I ever did.
For two years I discovered an intimacy and support beyond
anything I had experienced. We became mirrors to each other. I
discovered boundaries. We broke each other's hearts in a hundred places. We put some of the pieces together and afterwards I
accepted that some did not fit. Perhaps it is only necessary to
put enough together to journey across that chasm. Strangely,
with hardly an exception, those courageous people have slipped
out of my life. I remember the remark that this generation has
stopped to heal itself. It's the work of our times; it belongs to
everybody. I'm amazed when I thumb my journals, the angst,
the heart-searching, the never-ending soap opera. Was I really so
intense? So self-obsessed? Yes. The task of giving faces to that

grieving silent world, giving voices to ghosts, burying others, leaping into living still continues. I'm definitely not all good. I'm often well nutty, and I'm all right. (1984-1986/1995)

BOUNDARIES

Boundaries are the edges of things, they point to what's inside. The shape of a bird's beak and its delight in insects, the touch of lovers when boundaries yield with pleasure, the way a chair fits a table, or glasses cover the eyes. They fit because they are different. The boundaries help maintain polarity, the myriad patterns of energy in the world.

Boundaries tell the truth, the outer line shows what's inside. I embody what I feel. This is a dream for myself. I have always had a problem with emotional boundaries. It has taken most of my life to distinguish myself from my family. I lie on a hotel bed and I am flooded with impressions from previous sleepers. What is mine, theirs? I visit a friend and I am overwhelmed by his sombre mood. It goes when he goes. I cycle in Scotland and I am assailed with collective garbage about the Scots. It goes when I meet a native. I am amazed by this confusion.

My little girl is BIG
And sits eternally on her mother's knees.
She watches, with her big eyes she sees.
You are a big man, she says.
There is no escaping the truth;
Each little moment, it unfolds.
She is there always, all ways:
Daring me.
She terrifies me.
I love her.

THE UNSUNG HEROES

Paul Darby admits he is becoming more eccentric: the spider ladder in the bath, wall-to-wall natural history books in his living room (now his office), the burgeoning piles of conservation correspondence on the carpet, the lawn surrendering to the wild flowers – these are signs. Conservation is Paul's life; the only other distractions are his taste for obscure real ales and singing in *The Dubious Brothers*. He has a fine bluesy voice. Paul is tall and slender and slightly bowed like a Masai warrior leaning on a stick, except he has no stick. He's outgrown his woollen hats decorated with badges – 'Save the Whales' or 'Badger Patrol'. Most of his free time he busked in city arcades for Greenpeace. You could easily pass him by unless he is singing – something like The Last Leviathan – then the passion from this secretive man pours out and will hold you spellbound. Very English, really. He is part of an extensive network of ordinary people believing in the future, the unsung heroes of these times. In the dimpsey hour we leaned on the bridge at Dauntsey. The moon made a valley of light on the water. 'Perfect,' whispered Paul.' They'll be out soon.' Something *big* ruffled the surface below us. 'The pike.' A heron retreated over our heads scaring us The wing-beats trailed oil on the water. They arrived on time: the pipistrelles darted by our heads, the water bats skimmed the surface. 'With the bat detector you can hear them tracking a mosquito...zip zip zip ZAP!' The puckish folds of his cheeks matched the contentment in his voice. A perfectly understated picture. (Dauntsey, 1995)

THE GIRL FROM IPANEMA

John Green comes to life when he picks up his guitar. He leaves his troubles and cares of scratching a living as a performer in the nineties and loses himself in a gypsy jazz style all his own. Most Saturdays he busks to shoppers in Bath, and on one particular day he was singing, 'The Girl From Ipanema,' when a tall, elegant, dark-skinned lady stepped out of the crowd. She waited for him to finish. 'Did you say Ipanema?' she asked. 'That's the title of the song,' said John, 'but don't ask me where it is.' 'It's a beach near Rio de Janeiro,' she answered. 'But I've never heard of that song before, and I'm a girl from Ipanema.' (December 2, 1994)

FRED BARTON

He was a father to me, the first person to call me 'gardener'. In appearance he was the grand gnome, stoutly built and cladded with duffle coats in winter; a tapering white beard completed the effect. I'd have to guess the colour of your eyes but it was your buoyant sanity, listening ear and perennial puckish humour that I remember best. I start getting sentimental when I think about you. I suppose I never knew the real Fred who could be stubborn, didactic, somewhat old-fashioned, only Fred the Gardener. Our ideals came up against the rock of you. On the subject of curses, Fred listed perfection quite highly. It doesn't exist he maintained. 'A garden is never finished. You dig the earth and get it looking good but the weed seeds are laughing: 'Ha ha little does he know we are all here. The beauty is that a garden is never finished. What do you do when you're perfect anyway?' The last time I saw him he did not remember me, not that he was senile for he had happily remarried a woman half his age. I was disappointed but then life can be like that. I recorded this conversation on New Year's Eve, 1977. He died some years ago.

* * * *

I arrived while Fred was watching the Bruce Forsyth show and Rowena (his first wife) was busy in the kitchen baking mince pies. The white scottie dog immediately dived for my socks; Fred looked sternly at it and the dog curled over and went to sleep. 'Well, how about something to drink,' he said. He poured cider for me, sherry for himself. The smell of mince pies floated into the room which closely resembled a badger's den; comfort was the key note, a splendid place to relax. The conversation was soon on gardening. 'My working days are. over. I'm an old man now,' said Fred. His silvery hair and beard had recently been trimmed showing a determined, chewing profile. He leaned forward and rubbed his knee joints as if they were in pain; a prolonged damp spell put him to bed with lumbago; the hazards of a gardening life. To his mind, the community was no place to linger if one was young. 'There's a whole world out there; it's mixing and working with every kind of character that develops character and individuality. An old man like myself can give of his experience here; the young people should pick up as much as they can for the first twelve months and then go back into the world.' Fred's voice grew stronger with feeling.

The community jargon concerned Fred; he thought it could confuse people's sense of identity. 'Who am I? What am I?' he suddenly said, leaning forward and touching the floor with his hands. 'Put your hands in the soil. It's always the same. It never changes – but don't leave them there too long at this time of year.' Fred was no believer in groups, only in individuals. 'When I first came here Peter Caddy asked me to focalise the garden – the last thing I wanted – I gathered the gardeners together one day and said that if we take on our areas of responsibility, we will have a group without trying. They visibly cringed.' He turned his face into a cringing gardener. It was on a Saturday morning that Roc came to his caravan and suggested a walk around the garden. 'I hear you have been having a bit of trouble,' said Roc. He told Fred the youngsters were still unsure of themselves, groping in the dark. They were apprehensive of Fred's authority. 'You are both going to the same place but coming from different directions. What you have to offer is the breadth of practicality and experience.' He recounted this story with relish.

Our task is to live life. 'If you're working with the earth and nature you can never forget your spirituality. It's always there. You don't have to make an issue of it. You can never lose sight of it if there is that contact.' He leaned forwards. 'You know, I have plenty of time here and I watch people. I notice them, I see their mannerisms. There are some people here who have nowhere else to go. They are running away from life.' As usual Fred would never name names. A good frost was a godsend, he said, peering out the door. It produced a fine tilth, neutralised fungi spores, any harmful pests, encouraged the birds to really get down to all the cracks. It also broke down the ordinary sugar in parsnips and turned this into sucrose. 'Nature gives so freely... Abundance is giving away our energy.' (Findhorn, 1976)

OLDFIELD NURSERIES

I worked here not much more than a year, a superior old-fashioned nursery, family run with its retainers – one of the last of that tradition. We propagated most of our plants and they were hardy for that part of Somerset. Customers selected the larger field trees in summer and we dug and root-balled them in winter. We gave the customers personal attention as well as our expertise. Everybody seemed to know everybody else. We had our jokes: 'Excuse me,' says naive customer. 'Could I have something to climb up a 16ft wall and flower this summer but not get any bigger.' 'I'm sorry madam, we've run out of plastic.' We humbled the know-alls. A gentleman comments on sly chive flower inserted among yew foliage. 'Ah yes...the rare chinese yew. What's it's name? Taxus er...' 'Dontknowensis,' volunteers the assistant. The nursery closed down some years ago – here are some snapshots from my journals:

* * * *

Potting shed: It's tea-time. A clock ticks relentlessly. The plain wooden boards creak wearily under pressure. B comes in humming 'When the blue of the night meets the gold of the day.' A newspaper turns and Olly wheezes a little on his roll-up. The old phosphorescent wickerwork chair creaks when B flops into it; somewhere in the loft the young starlings ascend the upper octaves when mother arrives. The dog, Honey, scratches the floor, her thick fur raised in hackles at the slightest sound. M strokes her. 'Rough as a badger's back,' she exclaims. Her face flushes when she is the centre of attention. No-one comments; we drink our tea in silence. On the wall behind her are postcards pinned in three rows and six deep; on the table is a half-eaten packet of digestives, a Queen Elizabeth coronation cup, a yellow parrot container with a bunch of flowering daphne. The cream coloured fridge is dining table for the resident cat; this morning the rear legs of a rabbit are discovered behind a chair. A dusty room, still and quiet and ordinary. By the door are the ancient file boxes, clip-boards, a little brown suitcase, a framed 1961 horticultural diploma above B's desk. A pre-war paraffin heater does the same job. The place still works, is still afloat, just.

* * * *

Olly: He's like me, on his own and on the sidelines. He's the handyman. I like his ability to name things. ('Ship's timber was traditionally soaked for seven years in baulks and then stored on land for seven years. It removed the resin which the beetles were after.') He sits on a tea-chest next to the wet boots and Katy-cat in the apple box. 'Living a life of luxury,' he says enviously. He always eats four ham rolls for lunch. His hands are knuckled and large as dinner plates, all mounds and valleys, a great wedge of a thumb and deep lines from constant use. He holds the Sun open at page three. He looks steadily with his eyes when he talks. No messing. He says he was working on the gutter at Crowe Hall in Bath when he sees The Lady looking under bushes, under tree stumps, shouting, 'Mr Brown. Mr. Brown. It's the pet jackdaw.' He laughs, showing rows of smile-creases but frowns when staring out of the window. His hair is brilliantined and falls across his head in two cow licks. 'I'm going to tell you,' he says, a favourite expression when a revelation is due. He can take any thread of conversation and sometimes his eyes wax behind his spectacles as he searches for the words. 'I readily can't remember what I did yesterday.' When he exhales he blows hard and watches the smoke drive across the room.

* * * *

M walks in as if she is riding a motorbike, arms bent and stuck out. 'What did you have for dinner last night?' 'Lamb chops, potatoes, carrots and gravy, and cream and apples for pudding. Lovely!' She says that she always tests doubtful food by giving a piece to the cat first; it never eats anything that's off. X has the habit of speaking as if she is in pigtails. More than once she says about her husband, 'I can talk him into anything,' or says that she will trade him in for a new model. I am amazed at the amount of back-biting that goes on. Rarely to the face. The males are one side, the females on the other. Olly squats in the middle rolling a cigarette from his 2oz tin. He's wearing a parka and blue cords; somehow the top of his fly is always undone. The cold northerly wind brings a togetherness of sorts. 'Did you see Combo last night?' At least four different television shows are discussed. Other conversation subjects are meter thefts and a police stabbing in Bath. B talks about an oil platform disaster. He yearns, I think, for something heroic in his life to upset these daily routines. He often mentions the comradeship in the war. He was the only one to walk through the blizzard of the last winter. His words glow with the struggle... C is always defensive. Every innocent question is treated with suspicion. 'Did you see...' 'I've already seen him.' 'Are you going to...' A long blank stare. 'I already do it.' Everything is matter of fact. 'It's raining outside because I can see the rain.' 'It always snows in January but if it doesn't there's no snow.' B suddenly gets steamed up by accumulating work. He flies at the dust on the table and flings his leggings across the floor. 'Those ruddy boys never put anything away.' Two minutes later he is purring over his cat, his lady.

* * * *

The shrub foreman's hat: It's a tartan based on black and dark brown and fawn stripes, speckled with peacock red and sky-blue threads. It has a rakish, sloping brim, a foxy flavour. It's rarely cleaned; there are tar stains and greasy grime along the brim. Two tired feathers are stuck to one side, pheasant and nondescript pigeon. The gloom of a bramble patch coming into leaf; the colours of concealment. A gentleman's hat, yet I don't think of sheep or sportsmen or the dyes. I think of a limpet, a tenacious quality like an elder tree in a crack which won't give up. The colours are earthy, maroony red on black; a corner of a ploughed field in winter.

JUST A STORY

Susan Seymour, mother of Aelfrieda, wrinkles her mouth in consternation. 'I can't think of a story but there must be one...it's just a story,' she says shyly. Some years ago she worked at a centre for adolescents. One of the visitors there was Bernard, a youth diagnosed as autistic. He kept his face expressionless, hardly made a noise and avoided any eye contact. She took him on an outing one weekend and they stopped at a post office to draw some money. Bernard handed his book to the postmistress. She handed back the money and vigorously date stamped his book twice. 'Temper temper,' exclaimed Bernard. (December 9, 1994)

THE CUPBOARD

I won't say his real name for I fear I will embarrass him with this story. His terraced house in a better part of Bath attracts no attention from the outside – but inside it is different; a tideline of clothes, books, plates, toys clutter up the ground floor and hallway, threatening to climb the stairs or trip me up. I'm amazed that anyone can accept such chaos as normal; the peeling wallpaper, the doors not shutting properly, the rotten woodwork by the windows. On leaving, he stopped beside the stair-well and took out a key. It fitted perfectly the well-oiled lock. He turned the polished brass handle on the door...inside were rows of tools on the walls – hammers, screwdrivers, fret saws, draw-knifes, old cross-cut saws and much more – all immaculate, polished and oiled. He picked out a chisel, fingered the box handle and touched the white-sharp, cutting edge then put it back. He closed and locked the door. I have never seen that cupboard again but I've always remembered it. (1991)

FEBRUARY CHANGES

The black month, everything hangs in the balance. The gaps are big enough to step into. Thoughts are elusive; they accompany the winnowing winds. I think of butterflies in August: the sun opens sallow flowers, the doorway for the insect world – first leaves of elder are purple-tinged and folded into zip-pencil pouches – young trees in bright sunlight show algae tidelines – fresh greens of arums peep above rotting leaves – first grass shoots overpower sodden leaves by wayside – fat yellow pollen sacs on male yew (*Taxus baccata*) ready to burst – sheaves of daffodils but no flowers – drowsy drone fly on sunny dandelion flower – wolf spiders emerge warily looking for sunny perches – blackthorn with nutty bud clusters casts purple shade – beacons of silver lichens, silver leaves and silver undersides of brambles – every bud of hawthorn is flushed pink – flowers of cornelian cherry (*Cornus mas*) are paper bags with yellow bon-bons – hazel catkins dangle firmly above tufted red crowns – a February bloom; hairy bittercress (*Cardamine hirsuta*) – lesser celandine flowers on sunny bank, leaves are shining thumb prints – flies and dust roam the back lanes – *Lumbricus terrestris* tie lovers' knots by stones on mild, damp nights – hazel catkins fade as hornbeam catkins open – goosegrass already one third way up hedgerows – old and new hemlock seen together – berries of guelder rose (*Viburnum opulus*) still hang on trees.

EDGE OF HAZEL COPSE

The sun is a welcome stranger, a warm hand on my cheeks, cool outlines on my nose and eyes. I smile showing my teeth. I gaze around me, squatting on my haunches at the field edge of over-grown hazel copse. I have forgotten this world sound: throaty

pigeon raspings, sudden peal of laughter from the green woodpecker, the instant softer reply, the small twitterings and clickings, pipings, the tap against old wood, and hardly one bird can I see or name. I am calmed by this warmth and the raucous trumpetings of the rooks. Hazel catkins dangle to earth, not straight but bendy, opening firm and pink-flushed in twos or threes. The tiny male parts are often a node below, a tufted red crown on a scaly head. I have never looked closely at them before. A long-tailed tit, a form of streaked unknown, purr-titters and is gone. I nod my head. Out come more words: the oldest tassles – some are three inches long – are stacks of eyelids sheltering the yellow baubles and the emerging dark flecks. The shade side of each tassle is yellow. The old hazel leaves retain their rich brown colour, curling both sides to the centre rib, miniature boats or coracles... Depending on the sun the light dapples each burgeoning thicket with veils of flecked yellows. Glossy ivy pillars, tracings of old man's beard, and red or underside silvers of brambles catch my eye. The earth remains. My memories of this place are as fleeting as the marble white butterflies seen here last July. These brambles with their vicious downhill lancers are the first colonisers of this field, stealthily cartwheeling and creeping under the tree shadow intent on plunder. Old thistle heads, the standing soldiers of another season, are scattered face down or are caught by the brambles. The wind has blown them down, their hooks are anchors in the earth; the plumed seeds are still inside.
(South Stoke, February 28, 1991)

TOAD AND RAIN

Intermittent thunder and a sudden downpour once forced me to abandon scything the docks and figwort from the banks of the River Cherwell and take shelter under a red horse chestnut tree. As the rain dripped down my neck I crouched lower and lower covering my head with my hands. I stared at the ferny shoots of new cow parsley. A long dry spell had cracked the earth but that morning it steamed with a lovely sweetness. The rain dripped from my chin onto the ground, a coat of autumnal leaves all twisting, grey-wracked and curling. Then the earth directly between my feet heaved itself from side to side. A stony back, dull in tone and marked as the worm-chewed earth, rose up on four legs; instead of grass roots there were bumps and craters of the common toad (*Bufo bufo*), nearly round in shape, lying low on its marbled belly. We eyed each other in silence and I couldn't

99

help smiling. I was crouched like a toad and both of us were doing our best to keep out of the rain.

* * * *

Another connected picture is walking across the Abingdon Road at Folly Bridge and noticing three mallard ducks sitting on the parapet, facing the road and watching the day go by. I stopped and leaned against the bridge, a bit farther down. I watched people walk past and each time I turned my head to look at them so did the ducks, and when I turned back they did the same. (Oxford, 1977)

DIRECTION

When something comes out of nothing it is always like a gift. An Australian told me that and this story. When he first visited the Findhorn Foundation he could not make up his mind whether to stay in the community or not. So he wandered among the sand dunes next to the Moray Firth. They stretched for miles in both directions. He walked up and down the sand hills wrestling with his question and did not notice the sea mist sinking into the hollows, spilling over the gorse and lapping the crests of the dunes. Too late, he realised he was lost in thick fog. He retraced his steps but they vanished into stony stream beds. He walked in straight lines but they bent and meandered with the dips of dunes, and the panic hit him like an arrow when he crossed his own tracks. The fog was thicker than ever. He was dressed in a tee-shirt, wet through, and he started to disappear into a suspicion that he was being followed. He heard it faintly at first. He thought it must be some strange stick creature with narrow legs and big saucer eyes. He wanted to run but didn't. The sound faintly boomed then receded. It wasn't in his ears. He listened harder. It was the sea! He walked towards it, stopping when he lost it to listen, then walked again. He hugged the coast to get back to the village and in that distance he made up his mind. He decided to stay. (1976)

HOMESPUN

Gary from Oregon taught me how to hammer a nail: 'See that nail? Hit it square. Hold the bottom of the hammer and let it do the work'; how to saw – 'Cut your niche first, hold it steady and level and don't push, just let it glide'. He trained with the

Swedish carpenters in Oregon and recalled their favourite remarks: when Gary was trying to be too precise: 'Well boy, we ain't trying to build a piano.' If a side was out of square: 'I reckon that side's heading out to Jones's.' Working out in the winter snows, he would be told: 'Well boy, if you hadn't spent all your money in summer you wouldn't be here freezing your nuts off.' (1977)

TRAVELLER – FRIENDSHIP

There are no words to bring back the voices of my friends, or fathom the bonds of a lifetime, or ordinary moments watching the box together. Some friendships lie dormant for years and suddenly reappear as desert flowers. Some are mayflies and bring sadness when I hold onto them. They puzzle me. They mark the hours in my life as accurately as a clock. Some appear unexpectedly at times of openness, crisis or change and then vanish – yet they are here still in some special time zone. With some, hardly a word is spoken, yet by time alone a bond is forged. Some are inherited with families, landscapes or friends of friends. A very few have become brothers and sisters. The majority simply drop out of my life. Sometimes I blame others or myself for the way friendships change. Or perhaps we change, more likely. They have their own lives. Friendships always seem to be gifts. There are more faces than names, and these are some of the names, starting from childhood: Alfred Please – Marie-Thérèse Please – Miriam Giraud – Carlo Barrow – Linda Orpin – Ronald Please – Anne Please – Anne Arnette – Bobby Porterman – Peter Callister – John Ham – Pino – Rene LeClezio – Yoyo LeClezio – Sister Gatzien – John Please – David Starnes – Keith Gartzien – Russell Needham – Julian Clinkard – Howard Moore – Tony Hannaford – Milly – Stephanie Harrison – Carol Berry – John Cook – Tim Spalding – Paul Fox – Giulio Masetti – Dominique Bares – Clive Postlethwaite – Sandy Tait – Paul Darby – Hugh Shewring – Alistair Warren – Brian Rafferty – Alyne Jones – Ramesh Lele – Jane Crosen – Michael Buck – Sprague Cheshire – Tom Wilson – Pam O'Neil – Claire Underhill – Ling – Mel Kaushensky – Judith Handlesman – Fred Barton – Tom Welch – Lynette Navez – Vance Martin – John Ballot – Giles Christian – Marianna Lines – Tim Rees – Simbana Please – Phil Ahearne – Dennis Hills – Simon Fletcher – Julie Fletcher – Dan Lupton – Caroline Waterlow – Marko Michell – Tim Baines – Robert

Taylor – Benedict Please – Keith Spencer – Alice Taylor – Bridgit Green – Freddie Smith and Layla – Paul Cheshire – Susan Bland – Ken Day – Richard Seccombe – Russell South – Michael Please – Rob Ackroyd – Linda Perry – Alan Peacock – Robert Palmer – Peter Barnes – Rosie White – Helen Felton – Nigel Felton – Conrad Martin – Laurence Yeoman – Lucie – Annie Spencer – Sooze Douglas – Peter Bidmead – Neil McDonald – Chris Drury – Keith Paddock – Charlie Dunfield – Jill Westcott – Bill Harvey – Andrew Bartkiw – Darren McClane – Susan Seymour – Medard Atiopou – Toots – Rob Burns – James Waters – Jamie – Jess Taylor – Mark Prior – Maggie Jeffrey – Jill Maggs – John Huckett – Paul French – Queen – Aelfrieda Seymour-Please.

BILLY

Dear Billy, This is not a letter I shall send you. I imagine you slumped in your chair at the farm, Peter Bidmead, Susan Seymour and Phil Sumption talking to you and getting no answer. You didn't move and they touched you, and you still didn't move and this frightened us. I am not sure what I want to say. This white space frightens me. You always talked about being frightened about the future, and you would stare out of your thick-rimmed glasses and say something like, 'It's all in God's hands,' or 'You have to trust.' And I would say, looking around at whatever was closest, 'This is paradise.' You would add: 'Everything is a gift, that's what I think.' It's hard to know your age. Sometimes I hear your grandparents in you, talking of all the wise things that come with a lifetime above ground, and this wisdom is also sad because you are only twenty. They speak through you. Your own blood parents are dead, and then there is your diabetes and sudden attacks of cliff-edge immobility. I notice the softness of your skin, your pale face, thick fingers and that wonderful way of listening with your eyes looking big behind the glasses, and the smile tucked into the corner of your mouth. I can see you were teased mercilessly as a teenager, your gentleness mistaken for timidity. The sheepdogs love you and understand you best. Queen, the old one with the hair falling out, follows you around hoping you will throw the ball, and she heads it back every time. They trust you and you trust them. I suspect that you have passed your young life in the care of older people playing the part of parents, you playing the role of worker and hoping that one day you will have a job. I know that you stay at home playing with your canaries, talking on the CB radio, helping your mother with her chores, or work at the farm.

In small ways I have played the role of provoker, helping you sing louder, swear more easily, express some of the poison in you; that love and anger are not enemies, and that it's all right to be uncertain about the future. I listen to you repeating all the things that people say you need to do: to be clean, work on time, not to swear, how they have taught you to be a good person. I am a bit like you, unsure of myself and fearing rejection. I like your spontaneous way of speaking, telling things as they happen, the way the cockatoo you call 'Warrior' (after the Gladiators) turns his head to listen to you. You lighten the atmosphere with your anecdotes from home. It's when you try to please us that you speed, talk too much, lose your way. I feel free in your company. I'm not sure why. I feel free to be silly, to sing tender songs, to make mistakes... I feel safe with you as Queen does. I do not censor my feelings but I'm careful what I say, sometimes choosing songs to say something, me Buddy Holly, you Depeche Mode. The music is a lifeline. Words are not the best way; you have heard too many...

Dear Billy, see, I am getting through this page, this unknown space. It terrifies me this uncertainty; it can appear as a dagger aimed at me or it becomes the point of this pen. I enjoy the ease I find with you, your lack of judgement, willingness to listen. I return these qualities to you and this is why we appreciate each other, I think. When I let my younger self I call retarded reveal its head, I open up, I play in the uncertainty, gaps and silences. I discover tenderness lurking in the cracks; absurdity and laughter at the pomposity of know-alls. I discover tears and sadness that I can't say the things I wish I could say, and miracles! I can say them. How this happens is a mystery. When I'm with you I'm connected to myself, reminded of someone close to home... God bless you Billy. Tell them Queen has teeth, and so do you. (1993)

DOGGY STORIES

A Brighton youth worker described this incident which incensed him. One Sunday he went to a local park for a walk when he saw a silver BMW pull over to the side of the road. An immaculately dressed man appeared and opened the back near-side passenger door. He helped an alsatian out onto the grass, where the dog did his business. The man returned the alsatian to the car, carefully wiping each of the dog's paws before letting him in. (Earth-Kids Conference, 1991)

* * * *

Eric Preisler, an American naturalised in Britain, was once in Leningrad when he saw an old man taking his dog for a walk. The dog looked as old as its master as they both hobbled on the pavement. At a street corner the dog stopped and carefully shifted its weight, so that it could do its business without falling over. Its legs wobbled, and so the old man bent down and widened its legs, adding his own support. He wrapped the turd inside some paper. He put this back into his pocket and they continued on their way. (Findhorn, 1976)

* * * *

At Barnard Castle, I passed this dog coming towards me walking along the pavement. 'Good morning Mr. Rottweiler,' I said. He lunged for my near-side leg. I flipped it over the cross-bar to the off-side of my bicycle. I managed to carry on pedalling. Try as I might, I could not get my leg back again. There's the power of fright! (Barnard Castle, May 17, 1995)

* * * *

Becky says she was drunk at the time. She had just started scaling the security fence at Glastonbury when the guard and his alsatian appeared. 'COME BACK OR I'LL SET THE DOG LOOSE.' 'Go on then.' He set the dog loose. It bounded towards her growling. Becky got on her hands and knees and waved the dog to her. 'Come here beaut.' The alsatian stopped and licked her face. The guard called back the dog and marched off sulkily. Becky scaled the fence and cut her hand badly in the process. (Glastonbury, 1995)

GHOSTS

When I was married I often stayed in an old farmhouse in Haddenham, Buckinghamshire. On the wall, opposite the bed, was a gilt-framed picture of a stern woman dressed in a low-neck gown from the 18th century. She stared across the room with such cold eyes that each time I slept there I hoisted the picture down and turned it face to the wall. One night, unable to sleep after a late meal, I stared at the ceiling with my eyes half closed.

I was not asleep nor was I perfectly awake. I heard a faint tapping sound as if the radiator had suddenly come on. It hadn't. I opened my eyes a little wider. I listened. I stared blankly around the room. I settled on the dust-lined space where the picture had hung. The more I looked at it the louder became the tapping until it changed, bit by bit, into a faint drumming sound. My heart beat louder. Then something moved in the dust-lined outline on the wall. It bulged with the drumming beats, ballooning out. I watched it, unable to move or make the slightest sound. A tiny fist came through the wall and disappeared. It came back again with another fist. They disappeared and came back with an elbow; a baby's hands and arms. I sat up sharply, wide awake. The hand disappeared. I stayed awake the rest of that night and I never slept in that room again. (Haddenham, 1985)

* * * *

It should have been paradise, the walled garden in the depths of relic woodland swimming with orchids each summer. Beside it were the veterans of a Victorian arboretum and a lawn bigger than a football pitch where the ancient manor house had once stood. Perhaps the ghosts were there. They were somewhere. My friend Tim Baines told me this story, and somehow it captures that macabre quality which could well out of cracks in the day, the tired part of the afternoon or when the rain buffeted the gaping glasshouses. At the back of the house was the swimming pool, and Tim remembers visiting it early one summer's day. He saw the young roe deer floating in the water; the next day, a fox, and later that week, a bloated rat. The combination of brightness and the floating dead animals, the innocence of the deer and greed of the fox and rat prompted him to leave. Afterwards, he learnt that someone in that household had died during that period.

FISHY

On a winter's day in the Parade Gardens in Bath, you can see something quite remarkable. If you walk along the garden side of the river Avon you will find a shadowy circulation of steam arising miraculously out of the cold waters. If you stop and stare long enough into it the fish start to appear, the smallest strung into a crescent and all facing the bank; behind them are larger

udd and roach – and they, too, are arranged as beads on a
:e and facing the bank. I fancied I glimpsed even larger
fish in the murkier waters behind them. But why? That very
spot is the outlet for the steamy waters of the springs of Aquae
Sulis. It must be the oldest intact view in Bath.

WINTER ROAD – THE RIDGEWAY

*I wanted to walk the Ridgeway, that part of the old winter road
from Streatley to Avebury. I wanted to go back to the young man,
twenty years ago, who ventured into these larkhall downs following
this wayside road. I can picture him: bearded, smiling yet sad, a
reporter on the Berkshire Mercury, living in a dizzy daze of bars
and business, digging up stories from municipal burrows, yet
unaware of his own story. I see him as inarticulate about his needs,
gentle, shy; a solitary, though surrounded by people all day. It's
impossible to hold the many strands of this walk. I am lost before
these Downland landscapes, the ploughed earth and chiselled winter
fields, the Ridgeway snaking behind and before me, a gashed path
of muddy, green-top strips. On the early commuter train to Reading
that morning I heard the words, 'Your eyes that see the world...'
They opened the tear-locks and I sheltered behind my hands with
the image of a blue-eyed boy, who is exquisitely sensitive. With
darkness I searched out adolescent memories at Reading; the
College of Technology (unchanged) where I idled two years away, a
hibernaculum; looking for 1933 pennies at Cemetery Junction;
bearded Howard Moore reading Ferlinghetti in Hamilton Road;
hashish nausea in Denmark Street... This time traveller did not
stay long. Reading had become a London suburb, a stepping stone
for another generation of strangers. I could hardly remember who I
was here nor could I find the Honeybear Cafe or The Star Inn in
Broad Street, or hear the voice of the beatnik Hamlet or the canal
boat gypsies, George and Albert, with caps and rings and swathes
of hair down to their waist in 1966. Reading Gaol with the ghost
of Oscar Wilde reminded me of the old Reading and so did the
black-timbered pubs (The Saracen's Head) and herringbone flint
churches; the former Reading Chronicle offices in Valpy Street were
now a wine bar... I stood outside them remembering my editor, Big
'G' Garner, David Bowyer, Tim Spalding, the Dickensian clutter,
the oily burning fumes of press day. Gone, all gone now. I left
Reading glad to escape the plethora of boarded properties.*

The shining thumbprints of celandine delighted against the moody greens of ivy and spindle; the unfurling arum leaves parted grand-mother's winter cloak; snowdrops splashed white over it, blackthorn and hawthorn ripped the seams with bulging buds, dun-coloured and scarlet pointed. The smudged hedgerows became shorelines encircling the land, interrupted only by clumps of beeches. I saw nobody. I sat in a grove of thorns, wind-rocked and virtually uprooted, and blew tobacco smoke at them and my best wishes. I am contented when I stand with my back to a tree, just touching it. Nothing happens yet that unique moment is enamelled some-where... I pause for breath. I hear the plush-ploughing wind on the sharp thorns, the thin, hard whistling of wires. I clap my hands, and piles of flints far away in a field, lapwings, flash white as they bob and flutter as so many butterflies. Partridges explode and throttle into the wind before resigning themselves to a greater power, and swing in a huge arc to land back at the hedgerow...

At White Horse Hill, beside the tattered pennants of mugwort, I smoked a cigarette to the memory of my father, the best memory of all, for we had walked from Upper Lambourn to that hill twenty years before. The burden of the ramparts stepping lightly off the hill, the timeless blue sky, by these associations I saw my father's face, that moment with the red kites flying. I cried out: 'It's so short.' I did not shelter behind my hands this time. The tears cooled my face and I relapsed into silence. Then I imagined my first-born son on my shoulders. He never met my father. They meet only in me.

I turned my back on these old pastures, thousands of years old, and enjoyed the thorn-edged Ridgeway snaking to that megalithic spirit temple, Wayland Smithy. I played with a sliding movement, turning up and down my hands and hips. I liked it. The tidal clouds overshadowed the lonely barns, the hillsides dotted with scalloped pig-iron shelters. The turf and white oozing mud lulled my swelling blisters but not the erotic thoughts, the rocking earth had its own rhythm, and other rocking intimate moments intruded as naturally as the shining rosehips garlanding the thorns. I treated them just as gently, allowing them full rein before kissing them goodbye. I collected crab apples with good seeds and planted them in hedgerow gaps...

It's the last part of the walk I see now, Barbary Castle to Avebury with the clouds brushed into vast feathers... At this dimpsey hour

107

the darkness creeps out of the ground inking trees until, by some magic, I only noticed the pencilled edges of everything, the least silhouette of bent grass against the horizon, their brittle golds submerged by water purples and an ocean of yellow haze. The wind subsided, and that lonely trackway became a winter road. I looked for the old man sitting in the fork of a tree, the darling first-born son of the mother, and her protector. I looked for the yellow glinting eyes of the little owl perched on his shoulder. I looked knowing that he is not out there. I laugh at this childishness, the stuff of story books. Great sarsen stones, boulder erratics from the Ice Age, appear beside Fyfield Down; painted on one, were the words, 'Trust your God.' Avebury is a circle of orange lights three miles below. It is now dark, Orion is above, and I am very, very tired after walking thirty miles this day. I am disappointed not to see the old man, as my son never saw his grandfather. I picture this sculpture of a man holding his child, not just in age, but whatever is youngest, most original in us, whatever needs our protection. (January 29, 1994)

SPRING

FLOWER STORIES

Dutchman, Jan, worked in one of the large bulb glasshouses in Holland. Most of his day he cared for the nursery beds, crouching for hours in the constant draughts – the cause of the lumbago in the small of his back. One afternoon he weeded a bed of tulips and discovered that he could not stand because of the pain. He was stuck staring at the earth. Then something cool and satiny stroked his skin and the pain disappeared. He turned and saw that one of the tulips had touched the small of his back and that he was able to stand again. (Findhorn, 1976)

* * * *

When Heather Goacher told this story, her shoulders shuddered with the memory, as if it had happened yesterday, rather than fifty years before as a child in Kent. It happened twice, when she was eight and ten, and while out exploring the bluebell woods near her grandmother's home. Her apprehension vanished as she recalled the scent of the flowers wafted in the evening down the lanes. She had gone to pick bluebells (*Hyacinthoides non-scriptus*) growing abundantly in the coppiced woodland. She spotted a single white flower in a sea of bluebells and tiptoed to pick it. She touched the flower and the smooth, angled body of an adder coiled around the root. Two years later, in a different wood, she saw another white flower in a blue ocean. She touched it and recoiled when she saw an adder staring back! (Frome, 1992)

* * * *

An American bonsai gardener went regularly on long business trips abroad. While away he gave his collection to a friend with explicit instructions how to care for the crooked miniatures. He returned two months later and they were in a terrible state though his friend had carried out the instructions to the letter. The next time he went abroad he gave them to his friend again but this time he took a photograph of the plants with him. Every night on that trip he said 'Goodnight, bonsai!' On returning he found them alive and well. (Findhorn, 1976)

* * * *

Judith came from New York. She intrigued us with her stories of cooperation with nature among the city skyscrapers. In May of that year her marriage had broken up when she felt that she could not bear the child that she had conceived. She asked for a dream to help her and she saw a vision of petunias growing in a field, and a voice said, 'Take note Judith, this is the dream you wanted.' A few weeks later while working on the balcony flower beds at Harper and Row she saw petunias growing where none had been planted, the exact sequence of colours from her dream, the last petunia with a violet star pattern. (1976)

TRAVELLER – TRAINS

I am still in love with trains. I have no idea why. When I am cycling I often imagine that I am the driver of a lone Trans-Caucasian express, and the canal towpath ahead of me becomes a vast expanse of night I'm disappearing into, crossing mile upon mile of uncharted forest, chugging down snowy mount-ains, over canyons and across red-land deserts... And I am the pilot. I hum to myself monotonous two-tone notes, a deep, steady rumbling balanced by a lighter, rising note, a rhythm which strangely soothes me. I stop at Moscow, the last stop before the wastes of Sinkiang, or hurtle through ghosted stations in the middle of a foreign city, and always I am alone in the night in a strange country. I can take this back to when I was eight years old and I used to run around the centre island of our housing estate for hours on end, the same fantasy of making a journey. Trains are always about journeys. I can see the photo-graph of a railway shed with a steam engine emerging out of the mist. After school I often sat on the main station at Farnbor-ough staring up a long, straight track. The early hum of an approaching express would magnetise my attention long before it hovered on the horizon, a mobile blur growing stronger as I watched it, the dim speck blackening into a dot until the hum rattled and I stepped back as the great thing rushed through the station. I glimpsed the number, the cream and brown pullman coaches, the businessmen and newspapers, and then the startled pigeons and platform litter would swirl with hot steam, soot and sparks and come to rest with the ricocheting rails, and the feeling that I had witnessed something *real*.

Well-meaning yet ignorant people would smile at my train-spotting trips to Eastleigh, Reading, Barry or Swindon, always with the unspoken statement that it was a shame I could find nothing better to do. Yet I was only ten or eleven-years-old and these journeys were pure adventure. I planned each campaign carefully for I visited the railway sheds without permission. I knew the weakness of the most impregnable, Stratford in East London, how to coincide my visit with the tea break so I could crawl beneath the window of the sentry office. Then down the tunnel I'd run and cab as many locomotives as possible before I was inevitably caught and thrown out – but by then I was happy. At the Great Western Railway shed at Swindon I waited hours by the main entrance to melt into the rear of an an organised party. At Barry scrapyards I wandered sadly among the rusting giants of the Manor, Castle and Kings' classes searching for screws and bolts to take back with me. I still have black and white photographs I took of those trains: County of Glamorgan is one. I underlined each number carefully in my book, or wrote 'Cabbed' or 'TB' (travelled behind) against them. Now, thirty years later, I recall the excitement of travelling to a new place, alone. The numbers then, as now, are irrelevant.

In my early teens I dismissed train-spotting as childish and was careful to distance myself from the popular stereotype of spotty youth and zero-rated intelligence. Shortly after puberty (sublimely unaware of its implications apart from the hair between my legs and a cock which had the habit of staying erect) instead of longing to visit railway sheds such as Crewe or LMS Willesdon, I diverted my attention to girls, another kind of hunt conducted by both sexes, mainly in packs. The solitary trainspotter, traveller, became a mod and dressed like everybody else with flared trousers and parkas, and I dreamed of owning a 200cc Vespa sprayed copper and without learner plates. The traveller in me went underground. The horizon at fifteen extended to working in a petrol station, filching fags and sweets to buy protection from my elders. I loved having spots and scratches on my face so I would appear hard and worldly. 'He's a bit green,' I remember one of my heroes saying, a squaddie type with podgy face, square-set legs and hands always in his pocket (no doubt for checking his balls were still there), razor-cut hair and a reputation for screwing everything in sight. The motto at that time was find them, follow them, feel them, fuck them, forget them. I was frightened of my male counterparts and that's why I copied them. If I were like them then they could not see me.

MIDNIGHT BUFFOONS

In March, 1973, I wanted a break after my apprenticeship in journalism. I boarded the Orient Express at Victoria Station, London and hurtled across Europe in seventy two hours, each one longer than the one before. The train stopped at Trieste on the Yugoslavian border before midnight and it was freezing. On the platform were several plump people loaded down with packages, western luxuries from across the Italian border. Two men struggled into my compartment, men in their fifties, with stony faces and each clutching about a dozen parcels. They were so fat they barely got through the door. They concealed parcels under the seats, tucked them next to my rucksack and scattered them as far from themselves as possible.

At midnight two cold-war custom generals, with the obligatory rifles, pulled open our compartment door. They wore stonier faces. They were not interested in me. They squinted at their fellow Yugoslavians. They knew exactly what to do. They prised the parcels from under the seats and the four corners of the luggage racks and dumped them on the floor. They ripped them apart and noted what they found: towels, soap, socks, wine, salami and other trifles. The Yugoslavian consumers grimly paid the excess duty in cash. Eventually the train skidded out into the icy night. Two minutes later the grim faces melted and my companions smiled, then they warbled with laughter and flung their arms around each other and me. They undid their coats. Underneath was another identical one, then a jacket with a string tied around it with a clutch of ties and stockings neatly folded over. They cut this free, took off the jackets, the jumpers, pairs of shirts until they got down to the frilly negligees, bras and braces folded over a string tied around their waist. Then the plum brandy appeared and, for the rest of the journey to Ljubljana, they laughed, smiled a lot and patted my back just because they were happy. (Trieste, 1973)

MARCH CHANGES

The sun lowers winter's draw-bridge and stirs up the wind. Clouds race across the sky, the wind chasing dark and light shadows across fields, drying the earth, germinating seeds. Everything is coming and going; the old twisted, drying and curling, the new soft and pointed. I walk around feeling hundreds of years old – rooks in pairs are black flapping leaves meandering into the wind – a solitary leaf clatters along the tarmac path – beech hedges sigh – a blackbird carries nesting material early in the month – jet-black jackdaws laugh like jangling keys – whenever a cloud appears, no matter how small, a breeze blows up – sequence of colours in ivy berries: apple green, arsenic green, washes of mauves and reds, purple black – oak leaf speared by shoot tip of ramson (*Allium ursinum*) – miner bees appear smudged with pollen – wych elm flowers on bare twigs – dozens of honey bees swarm on yellow and violet crocus flowers – crocus bulbs which fail to flower have neatly chewed mouse holes – spider seen re-arranging web – brimstone and tortoiseshell butterflies in pairs at Wadbury gorge – solitary bee ecstatic in dandelion flower – horse-tail cones release pollen when tapped – wolf spider (*Pisaura mirabilis*) dangling by a thread above floodwaters of River Frome – spiral stars of hemlock in water meadow at Lullington – tractors spreading nitrogen fertiliser balls in fields – ash flowers emerge like insect eggs, turn dark purple against fading hazel catkins – first leaves: tiny stag antlers of elder (*Sambucus nigra*); viking helmets of wayfaring tree (*Viburnum lantana*); blackthorn a candle flame inside a shell; fat chrysalises of new beech leaves – white poplar catkins drop as exotic caterpillars studded with salmon red bobbles – paper cocoons of burnet moth still visible on bent grass – hedgerows noisy with small birds – tiny picture-winged flies (*Sepsis fulgens*) paddle wings on crocus flower – queen wasps visit *Euphorbia robbiae*, queen bumblebees goat willow – hazel catkins make small rafts on River Frome – snail impaled on daffodil stem at Mells – four buzzards soaring on thermals.

HOLINE (II)

I start with the coltsfoot deity, finger buds bursting little suns on the wayside. The scaly stems without leaves and some still flowering had been dumped on this trodden ground. I mention this word holine and it evokes a picture of all things having their place, even the ones which don't fit – and just by being there they make the picture complete. I picked up a clump and gave it to the friend who showed me this walk along the Wadbury Valley. Old lover she is, lifesaver, sometimes sister and sensitive woman, and I get so confused about her. Already I am losing my way and it doesn't

115

matter. These parts belong somewhere... She shows me how to love sexually, to allow sexual energy to move me, to allow spirit to touch our bodies, to return us to our senses. She loves the Fussell's labyrinth, the 18th century ironworks where the waters cascade into gushing weirs. I can stay in the past with you, easily transferring your voice to my own sister and wanting her to never leave me. Brimstones dallied in the sunlight and hurtled over glossy hart's-tongue ferns; small tortoiseshells sunned themselves on collapsed umbellifer stems by the Mells Stream. She leaned on me as the sun warmed our faces. 'Come to Australia,' she whispers. 'I can't,' I say. 'I'm a traveller in little things.' 'You can't just have a bit of me,' she says. I know that. At Mells there is a field belonging to moles and their straight love tracks criss-cross it from all directions. She lay beside me and I could feel the energy move up my body. 'This is just the starting point,' she says, her blue eyes glinting, daring me. She is right: I can't just take a bit. I need a whole bite. I love the idea of love being a 'vast, uncentred energy' across our bodies. This holine business — the word came in a dream — gets to me. When I collapse and nurture myself, curling up, being needy, asking for help, going swimming or making myself a hot drink, notice new leaves, hold my son close to me, reach out, I let the world come back into me, I feel whole again... I am calmer now, not so panicky when I wailed that I would never see you again. I can choose how to express my energy. I feel my power when I am vulnerable and reveal my needs, especially with men.
(March 8, 1992)

WOLF SPIDERS

I notice them as I walk slowly across the bark mulch; it's the movement I see, the one per cent of the mulch. Each footstep scatters two or three ahead of me. I blink at the flick of peacock butterfly wings. The spiders scatter farther into the mulch. They love these sun traps. I cruelly forced one out into the lawn and prevented it from returning to safety. It attacked me and clung onto the side of my boot. I stamped my foot to release it. I did it once more forcing it back into the great unknown. It fairly flew over the grass, stopping twice to take bearings, or so it appeared to me. A brimstone butterfly just rustled against my neck. Instinctively, I brushed it away. I'm disappointed how I react. I brush away the unknown, the crack in this day. What am I frightened of? One other hunting lesson: when I move the wolfies move, when I stop, they stop...

I stopped in the sharp-edged sunlight, taking care to throw my bending shadow far from the line of the low retaining wall. The tiny etched shadows I recognised as *Pardosa amentata*, the common wolf spider. I counted a dozen in a two-metre section, stopping and starting, jerking sharply as they approached each other. These were the small spiders I saw clinging to their mother's back the previous summer. This was a game of bluff. Despite having the entire wall to pass each other, they invariably chose a collision course. It ended in the same way: the spiders facing each other, until the nerves of one snapped and it jumped into the void, free falling until it touched the ground and scurried away, apparently unharmed. I happily watched one brute's progress dislodging several spiders, before fleeing in its turn a particularly large one. (March 29/21, 1990/91)

SUNNY BORDER INSECT

I am enthralled watching an insect I have never seen before; brown and furry, shrew-shaped with a probiscus longer than its body. I can only call it a humming-bird bee (actually, a bee-fly). The legs trail as it manoeuvres for position over the cartwheel vinca blooms. I creep stealthily, a sleuth, upwind of shadows. What is it? I never knew it existed before. It rests on a leaf, invisible if you didn't know it was there. I am a clumsy predator, a fool squatting here. A queen bumblebee roars up the drive, pokes its head into my business and directs itself away. The housekeeper is in the yard. I don't move. I don't care. I creep closer and see the black blotches on the wingspans, a shrew with wings and sunbathing; out stretch the legs as it withdraws its probiscus, arching back its body. The black beady eyes search the aubrietia carefully for drops of nectar; the needle drones constantly, only changing as it darts sideways or is annoyed by this moving pen. It hovers like a kite flicking its legs backwards and forwards staying focused on the flowers. So precisely still and full of movement. It relaxes on an ivy leaf pulling back its wings; these silver oars reflect the light. That's it! The wings are switchblades and create the illusion of stillness; the two legs are held back, strangely human, like someone skydiving. Once again the only intruder is a dive-bombing miner bee with the distinctive pollen smudge. 'Here I am. Watch out!' A bully but not dangerous. What

117

fascinates me is how insects and spring flowers appear so significant – yet for thirty years I have never thought about them. (Upton Cheney, March 29, 1990)

SALIX

Frantic burrowings of insects make me stop by this strange weeping salix. The hefty baseline of a queen bumblebee says that the nectar is flowing. The bumblebees are almost as big as catkins and have the backsides of baby elephants. I see old familiars, the yellow swarming fly, not in vast numbers but in ones and twos, sandy in the sun and hoppers on land. The jet-black fuselage, shiny and big against the yellow pollen fields, must be the picture-winged fly, (Sepsis fulgens); they walk like ants paddling their wings. Still shiny green-bottles, washed-out house flies, dreary dung flies, a tiny ichneumon, a striking solitary bee all slink or hobble into view. Hoverflies, broad-headed, fat wafer bodies with horse-riding legs, work methodically at each catkin; the honey bees frantically fill their honey bags. I notice the solitary bee again, more rufous, quick flying in a straight line. An independent character. This is the opening of the insect year when salix is in flower, as ivy is the door which closes it in winter. A two-spot ladybird closely resembles the nutty sheaves of the catkins. The dung fly is nut brown, brackish green as a country gentleman with soft brown corduroys. I, alone, still feel tight in my winter's shell, in a torpor. I often wonder how seasonal or self-induced this is. I find it hard to loosen this pen, let down this winter's drawbridge. I am still frozen with little to give or feel. I am hundreds of years old at the moment. I don't know what's happening in my life. The insects are only interested in the flowers, none venture into the woody interior of Salix caprea, 'Pendula'. When the clouds come, only the yellow swarming flies remain. (Upton Cheney, March 21, 1991)

ABRAHAM

'All that you know is a handful of sand, but what you don't know covers the whole earth.' Abraham, the Indian priest, wrote this is in exquisite calligraphic Tamil in my journal. In his open shirt, flannel trousers and chubby boyish face with a prominent nose and curious eyes which watch you without judgement, he looks a typical tourist. Except for one detail: his skin is the colour of soot polished in oil and he walks in the bleached white landscape of central Turkey. This catholic priest from Madras is following the footsteps of the apostle St Paul who made three journeys here using Konya as his base. At each relevant place – Antioch, Tarsus, Konya, Antalya, Miletus – Abraham read the appropriate epistles. 'I was very ecstatic,' he says smiling.

I met him on the road to Goreme, a surreal landscape of tufa volanic cones and cliffs with doors and windows carved by the anchorite monks in early Byzantine times. The absence of Christians grieved him. He was the first Indian to visit the catholic church at Konya. The Turks could not believe their eyes. 'Arabian, Arabian?' Another made his hands into horns and asked if he believed in cows. We shared a pension at Urgup ('Your stay will be a soccess of care and comfort'). His energy never dried up. In America he travelled by night, sight-seeing by day. Before dawn Abraham had showered and meditated on a passage from St. Luke, and had read the relevant bit in the Guide Bleu for Cappadocia. He fell in with my plans to walk and hitch and the day went as smoothly as if it had been planned, a taxi driver giving us a cut-price rate. Abraham said that he did not push his plans as he believed in providence. 'Everything has worked out better than I could have planned and it has happened without me doing anything.'

We visited the underground city of Kaymakli: endless stone steps down down down into darkness, ice-cold air, huge circular stones by doorways ready to be rolled and seal off intruders. At the fourth descent Abraham met a friend from Antakya and shook hands carefully. Several hundred people once lived on these eight subterranean floors. He walked in a trance inside the volanic tufa cliffs, touching the brilliant yellows, reds and blues of the frescoes telling the story of Christ; the Nativity, the gifts of the Magi, Mt Tabor and the Resurrection – all miraculously preserved by dry air and lack of sunlight. The double portrait of the Emperor Constantine and Helena dated them to Christian Byzantium. Abraham said that all the churches in Greece are designed on the cave churches of Goreme: a narthex (entrance), main hall with the domed roof resting on four pillars, and an apse embracing an altar. Down a cobbled lane in Urgup a schoolboy pulled us into his stone house. In the front room with a double bed, hand-carved cupboards painted green and a post box boiler, his mother and grandmother worked the loom, swiftly choosing colours and cutting them to fit with a knife. It would take three weeks to finish this Anatolian carpet stoutly made in blue and red floral design. The grandmother smiled at the pleasure she had given us. Abraham said that during his five years in Europe he had rarely seen the angelic smile familiar in India. The weight of materialism and unhappy home life was to blame. The example of his own Christian mother and father had led him into the priesthood. He consulted them before making any personal decision, however minor. When his younger brother wanted to become a priest his parents got down on their hands and knees and begged him to reconsider, as he was their last son.

Abraham believed, without a trace of conceit, that he would have been an outstanding success in civilian life. However, his progress spiritually, or lack of it, sometimes made him miserable. For every step forward he took two steps back. To console himself he quoted St. Paul that the evil of the day is enough. I last saw him when the lights of Urgup had fused to a pale luminescence (this was during the Cyprus troubles). He said that in 1964 the Pope visited Bombay and like every other Christian he wanted to shake hands with him. The night before the Pope left the country he prayed that his wish would come true. The next day crowds of priests jostled outside the entrance to the government building along with Hindu fanatics pressed against cordons of policeman. Abraham waited by the Pope's car parked at the back for a quick getaway. One of the very very few to shake the Pope's hand that day was Abraham. Years later at the Vatican, Abraham personally presented to the Pope a copy of the Bible in Tamil translation. The Pope told him to give his love to the people of India, a country rich in spirituality. I can still see Abraham's white smiling teeth as he told me this. (Goreme, Turkey 1974)

HORNETS, BELOVED HORNETS

I have always been frightened of wasps and hornets, the menacing bands of blacks and yellows sent the pins and needles skating down my back, pumped the blood a little faster and generally got me ready to spring, wave frantically with both arms as if my life were in danger. No doubt because of this fear I have had close encounters with hornets. Once I stayed at a Cevanol farmhouse in southern France with a real cave in the cellar and a huge white room with fireplaces lodged in the walls to warm the silk-moth caterpillars. The munching of thousands of silk worms on mulberry leaves (*Morus nigra*) thundered day and night, I am told. I stayed in an outhouse with my wife, Caroline Waterlow, the painter, and our small son, Ben. It's important to picture this room accurately, the square ground floor, a staircase leading up to a sleeping platform and the sloping roof without a window. All three of us slept there. One night, and somewhere in the middle of it, I listened carefully to a hornet revving and changing gears each time it hit the ceiling below us, our floor. I prayed it would find the door. It found the hatch instead, motoring up the stairs ominously. The hornet arrived in our sleeping space, head-butting the sloping roof, dropping angrily, rising and hitting the ceiling again. It was definitely on target for me. I picked up my book, *The Wheel of Compassion* (I was in a Buddhist phase at the time). Fear and anger sharpened my senses. I couldn't see in the dark. It revved closer and closer I hit it first time and batted it against the ceiling above my face. My wife and son slept through it all. (La Font du Rouvre, 1981)

* * * *

Some years later at Wood Cottage, Tellisford in Somerset, I made peace with hornets on one of those balmy, cow parsley days in rural English paradise. A helicopter woke me from my sleep but it was in the room next door. I saw the hornet scrabbling on the inside of the window. I stood nailed to the door unable to pass it or walk out of this picture. Instantly I saw the great jacaranda tree overhanging the track leading to the waterfall at Nahal Arugot by the Dead Sea. The only way to reach this paradise was along this winding goat trail, hard between mountain cliffs and a ravine below. The sound appalled me from half-a-mile away: hundreds of hornets swarming over the red trumpet flowers. Each day I walked there and walked no farther. I was terrified. I walked to the window and trapped the hornet with a jar and postcard. I held it trembling in front of my eyes. Her sharp, penetrating voice radiated menace. I stared intot her liquid chocolate face, the abdomen with bands of sherbet yellows; she looked made up from different parts, as if it were a toy. I sat with this hornet for over an hour and then I let her go. I have liked them ever since. (Nahal Aragot, Israel, 1973/Tellisford 1986)

* * * *

In 1991 I bought a semi-derelict house in Frome and, in the attic, I discovered a huge wasp nest glued to the rafters with wing-like legs. I examined it carefully. The first paper-makers had constructed a brownish dome three times the size of my head. They made it from crescents of chewed wood, streaky browns, reds and whites, a maze of closed doorways with narrow, horizontal spaces for ventilation shafts. The attic eerily magnified sounds from the road below, a dog barking, cars passing, and I easily imagined the hum thrum and thrust of this waspy world. I touched the paper breaking it. My hand trembled. I was frightened to shine the torch too long in case it awakened a sleeping queen. (I knew they abandoned their nests each autumn but it made no difference.) Pictures appeared: wasps cutting holes to steal nectar from comfrey, waiting on flowers to ambush flies, searching dustbins for sweet wrappers, bits of cake and other discarded things. At a sun-dance camp we danced for three days and nights to remember our children. I sat in front of a black rubbish bag swarming with wasps. The night before I dreamed of a beautiful woman who lived in this rubbish bin. I decorated it with coloured streamers. The wasps liked this place. I cried when I said, 'my rubbish she is beautiful'. Up in the attic I thought of things that I throw away or belittle: my uncertainty, nuttiness, gentleness, shyness, vulnerability, embarrassing silences, nice sexual fantasies, evil humour, resentment, ecstatic thoughts. That's enough about wasps. (Frome, April 24, 1992)

* * * *

How similar are leaves and wasps in death – they curl up slowly as the life goes, becoming lighter and lighter, unbending without a mortal break. They turn brittle and dusty to touch – how strange that in death one must handle even more carefully. (September 23, 1987, Pilton)

STONE

This is my hunting stone, a tender to my heart stone. This journal is my journey through the seasons, the little things in nature's wayside and the sideways walk with my heart... I wanted something solid in stone to stand for the fleeting, ever-changing and not-changing world of my hopes and dreams... This place, at the foot of an ancient field maple, beside the dragon wreck of a fallen oak, the hoop of a branch; in a clearing colonised by dog's mercury, I choose to make a sort of stand... It faces west by choice, where all things come to their rest, the journey's end. This stone phallus, about three feet high, I carved from an old lintel from Trowbridge Railway Station. I made it in the woodshed at Wood Cottage, Tellisford. I made it with songs, ceremonial puffs of tobacco. I knew I was mad but I enjoyed it. I saw it first in a dream; Jesus Christ on the cross and with an enormous erection. This changes until it becomes a sculpture made from ivory or smooth white stone, and along one side are tiny red hearts, exquisitely carved. I made it first in clay, then as a small stone sculpture I placed in the garden of a signal box near Pylle. It is a fertility stone, the image of the sperm chasing the egg. This winter has taken its toll, wrung me out with flu deliriums, of frenzied planning, stoked my fears of homelessness. I don't think I have been more unsettled in all my life, facing an emptiness and depth of negativity I never knew was there. I would like in my fortieth year to learn to love myself. If I can love myself I have a chance of loving others. (Dragon Hill, Launcherley, March 16, 1990)

123

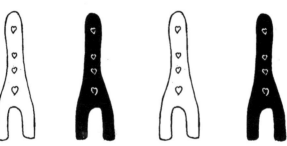

BIRTHDAY BOY, DRAGON HILL

I breathe out deeply. I don't know where to start. A small bird trills from the woods cutting through the splits and splats of rain dripping onto the bender tarpaulin. The wooded horseshoe combe reverberates with the huffled puffled omens of contentment from pigeons greeting this drizzly day. I drank real coffee by the fire at 6.05am this morning. This germinating rain I love – but why, oh why on my birthday – and I long to feel the soft, rounded thighs and look into the cheerful eyes of a woman, and I'm not too particular at this moment. I see pictures of the dazzling precision of bee-flies investigating the yellow tape on my handle-bars; the excited fluttering of four amorous tortoiseshells, the spiral majestic glide of two buzzards ringing the sun-laden air above the hill. Yesterday I looked for a stand of flowering goat willow, and several times I gazed into the fuzzy catkins above my head and the bumbling bodies of bees smudged with pollen. I wanted to write about the opening of the insect year, and always it wasn't quite right...

I had cycled the Bronze Age track over the eastern edge of the Mendips, now a minor metalled road between Egford, Whatley, Chantry, Beacon Hill and so onto Wells and the hummocky burtle hills of the Levels. I loved that view and the wonderful alchemical associations of a techno-bronze age culture, which appeared in my mind, out of the land, a technological culture conscious of its well-being, a culture valuing wealth to create variety, stability, one definition of beauty. The Bronze Age still speaks in this landscape. Of what? My knowledge I could balance on a pin and it makes no difference. I am a dreamer. I always have been. Why else am I sitting on this rocking chair, draped in my red blanket in a wattle bender with windows for badgers to peer through. This bender is made by a woman and is luxuriously appointed with two-tier pallet stagings, carpets, insulation, a Rainbow Orchard stove, gas cooker, shelves for cups and black pots, an entrance hall where the wood is stacked... Outside a bundle of hazel sticks leans against the shell of a derelict bender. It all looks so impossible. The one permanent resident here is slightly mad. As soon as I say hello he launches into the intricacies of the Gregorian calender and how it straight-jackets our perception of the hidden realms. I like him, all the same. He maybe right for all I know, but it is disconnected from this moment, as the benders tucked into the woodland are from the farms at Barrow, or Quaish at the bottom of the track.

I am sad thinking of those properties I passed yesterday, with sentry gates and guard dogs; the people enclosed in their cars on a beautiful spring day. I am sad that families have shrunk to this nuclear pair bond, feel that they have to fight the world. I shivered with cold in the bender, so cold without a stove burning in the morning. I return to this fire and the tintinnabulation of the stream (a world first for me that word) and what a good word stringing liquid sounds together as syllables. A wooden pig still stares at the holly oak planted five years ago at the sun-dance camp here. I will let that madness and beauty in equal measures rest. The intensity no longer appeals. Time for another coffee, I think, or to throw a stone into that empty bucket on the far bank of the stream. (Launcherley, March 16)

FORTY FOUR AND THE BIG SKY

This delicious moment keeps reappearing... It is this: a few weeks ago I wove a durable wattle fence on the farm beside the caravan of Maggie and Jill who share the duties of feeding and mucking out the pigs in return for rent. Together we had cut and carted the hazel weavers, rammed a palisade of posts into the bank, then constructed the fence by interweaving the hazels between the posts. Maggie and Jill served the tea and biscuits, and then this moment arrived, the one where I said goodbye and turned to look up the long Goose Meadow. The sky grew bigger. I felt smaller suddenly and this familiar meadow changed, now another country with unknown frontiers. I walked into it with the halo of a job well done behind me, Maggie and Jill waving goodbye. I was alone, free at the beginning of something new... Immediately another picture came, an association with the western film, 'The Big Sky', which I had seen as an eight-year-old, a panorama of wind-carved rocks, trails through awesome desert landscapes, wild and beautiful, and the back of a lone rider, Alan Ladd I think, disappearing into it. The two images connected as if I had clapped my hands. That feeling of completion I liked, then and now. This fugitive emotion mirrors something bigger, a yearning in my heart ever since I can remember, a conscious love of exploration. The fact that I turned my back on the women is significant. Part of the deliciousness was being alone with nature, away from women. Had I not always felt most myself, out of my mother's house, looking for snakes and animals? Is this escapism, classic macho into the sunset stuff, or is *it a trail of sanity? The fact is, I loved that moment of completion for it allowed something to end, and by drawing a line marked a boundary over which I could now step and experience something new. That something, not known, I wanted to follow, to trust, perhaps a dream.*

I am forty four. I am in an extraordinary state, a prisoner in some sense at this farm. I have time but no money. I have no distractions. I am surrounded by people and I have never felt so alone. I am the father of a beautiful daughter, partner of a woman. I have given up any ideas of a professional writer or landscape gardener. I appear naive to myself, only the doing makes sense, the step by step of the donkey. At forty four I have stopped rushing away from myself. I am disappointed. I like myself more. I like my tenacity. Even if I were to die now, in my eyes I am honourable. It warms me this dream, standing beside me all these years, a dream of making a garden of earth matters, making visible by whatever means the myriad invisible connections with the life of the soil. This is my big sky... When I remember my dream, I remember me, my strange brush with reality. Sometimes I see this man in a sort of rough woven Islamic overall; there is light and doves appearing from his heart where his hand is pointing; around him is a landscape of pines with diamond patterns. I am connected to this future man, British with an eternity heart.

I am back again at the Goose Meadow and knowing that I would have to walk there alone. Aelfrieda struggled to be born, Her mother couldn't see her being born. Birth is a terribly beautiful thing to witness. Already I sense a profound parting, an ending. I dreamed this is the time of the Madjuragora (a biblical cure for sterility), from midnight to dawn, a hard winnowing time when the ground will be rewoven. The trees will still stand but not the dead wood. Walk carefully. I am more contained, peaceful for writing this. I wonder if anyone will ever read it? (Dunsford Farm, March 28, 1994)

WILD GARLIC

Rosie White is a woman with a genius for noticing the details of flowers, the miniature worlds of perfection on the wayside. She told me this story about her father when he was a sergeant-major in the 8th Army during the Second World War. He was posted to an oasis encampment somewhere in the Libyan desert.

Her father, acting on impulse, decided that if he walked behind a certain rock be would find wild garlic growing there. He did. He pulled up the garlic and beneath it found a crusader's coin, hundreds of years old. He carried it around with him as a good luck charm throughout the war and still had it when he returned to Barry in Wales, his home town. On his way to see his mother at Claude Road West he inadvertently spent it as a tram fare.

A CURE FOR SWOLLEN GLANDS

During Rosie's stay in Mlalo, a village in north-east Tanzania, her toes became infested with the eggs of a nasty little flea-like creature which the locals called funzas. The English call them jiggers. Her diet was short on protein and consequently wounds didn't heal easily. The only way to remove these eggs was with a sterilised needle which left a hole in the quick of the toenail leaving it prone to infection. One time she had many funza cavities in her toes and the glands at the top of her legs became swollen and made walking painful. She went to the witch doctor, the father of a beautiful woman called Naida. He gave her a magical cure. He collected the barks of two different small trees. One was the wild pigeon pea. One of the barks had its outer papery layer peeled away, the other didn't. He put three knots into one of the strips of bark and four in the other, and tied them both together. They were long enough to tie below the knee of her infected leg. First he wiped the braided bark along the swollen upper leg, then he tied it beneath the knee. He said that the swelling should go within two days and, if it didn't, she should throw the bark away. But it did and her leg was healed.

* * * *

Once Rosie walked near Cellan, mid-Wales, with a friend. She climbed up a hill identifying bog plants on the way, the little pink bog pimpernel and flea sedge. A craggy tor dominated the bog and they settled in a crevice to shelter from the wind. A raven soared and plummeted above them, and higher still a buzzard circled. She scrambled down some rocks and, among them, out of the wind, she found scattered pink rose petals, sweetly scented. There was no rose bush on that mountain or anywhere nearby. (1992)

FOREVER AMBER

Linda Perry, mother of Demelza and Orion, migrates between her medieval terrace house and an Andulacian former olive mill near Velez Malaga. Unfailingly friendly with eyes shrewd with understanding, her long boned face sometimes shows the grandmother in her. She tells me a story about a piece of orange amber reminding me of my secretive childhood and how I once buried a pound note I had found on the street. Every evening I went back there and turned the stone just to make sure it was real. She found the amber lying on the seaward side of the sand dunes separating the Benacre Broads in Suffolk from the ocean. It was Easter day, and she was only a girl and her family had painted eggs to roll down the dunes on their picnic. She walked on ahead with a frying pan and bag when she spotted *it*. Her two hands trembled as they held this rock-size lump of amber, the ancient fossilised pine resin, see-through orange, light and smooth and precious. She couldn't carry everything at the same time. She hid it down a rabbit hole and concealed the entrance with marram grass. She ran back minutes later and looked into a rabbit hole and another and another... Thirty years on, her face flushes with the memory. 'And I could never bloody find it.' (1991)

SHE THINKS I'M REAL

I have not met many famous people but my collision with Dr E.F. Schumacher comes closest. I was brushing the lawn at Findhorn when I literally encountered a pair of shoes and standing in them was this distinguished man in a stetson. He asked for directions to the University Hall. This proves I have had my brushes with the famous. Dr Schumacher had razor thoughts: If you go to an African state and tell them what to do your stay will be either permanently prolonged or drastically shortened. This story is typical of his poignant observation. He was sitting in an airport restaurant with a couple and their six-year-old daughter. The waitress wrote down the orders. 'I'll have kipper, toast and some salad,' said the woman. 'I'll take poached egg, baked beans and French fries,' said the man. Then the waitress looked at the daughter. She stammered: 'I want beans and chips.' The waitress wrote it down, disappeared and the girl whispered to her mother: 'She thinks I'm real.' (Findhorn Foundation, 1976)

AELFRIEDA MARIE SEYMOUR-PLEASE

2.30am... Where do I start? Six years ago when Giles Christian and I trudged up Dragon Hill and set the stone phallus with little hearts next to the old field maple. Or eight years ago at the sundance camp on this hill when I danced my hopes for the world with David Urie and twenty other people...? About nine months ago Susan Seymour and I walked across the Mendips. We stopped at this wooded hillside on her birthday. In the middle of her infertile period, during a night of torrential rain and thunder, she conceived this child. (Twelve hours later I paused to smoke a ceremonial cigarette in a gorge beside Cheddar; a back-packing couple with a tiny baby passed us. That is the moment I believe Aelfrieda started life.)

Last night, at 11.55pm – on my birthday – and on a starlit night with lambs calling for their mothers, little Elfie was born, ten days late. It's now three the following morning and I can't sleep with this buzzing gratitude. I can hardly believe this has happened. I see the vagina opening up its secret doorways, the inner labia pink, clean and fleshy, opening up like an arrowhead; the appearance of that mobile, slightly hairy head cradled in the birth canal, moving slowly with a cap of viscous red blood. And Sue's face staring, oh! how she worked, long steady drawn pain, her face rock steady, crimson, puffing, pushing, the midwife Julia speaking gently, coolly: 'Don't be frightened of the pain. Go through it.' At 11pm the head had still not emerged, then the miracle – just before midnight the head appears then whoosh! on a flood of red waters out pops the baby. Creation is full of tears, blood, sweat and screams, then relief.

The baby appeared from another planet, strange, perfect, like an astronaut with an umbilical cord venturing into another world. We looked on dumbfounded with surging excitement. I don't know what to say. I had lots of pictures of grandmothers while sitting the long hours of the early contractions, old women with enigmatic smiles, standing there with us, inscrutable, fleeting impressions. Where did they come from? Then the afterbirth appeared, a big liver offal at the end of the twined cord. Strangely I was not repulsed, in fact I was amazed how clean blood could look. I shielded Elfie's eyes from the white inspection lights and hummed to her the tune I hummed to my son Ben at his birth... It was a dream that took me to Dragon's Hill, a dream which made me

carve the Thangoz stone, a fertility stone, a stone of longing...
Elfie is a child of dreams, a child of the nature spirits, hence
Aelfrieda. I, alone, have the satisfaction of predicting the time of
her birth. In truth I wanted this convergence... I am all a dither
with myself, my head resting in my free hand. Aelfrieda is the
feminine version of Alfred, my father's name. My grandmother
died giving birth to her third child on March 16th; I, my mother's
third child, was born on March 16; and Aelfrieda, my third child,
was born on March 16th. Elfie did not smile but only blinked at
this new world, unaware of these associations.

Dear Aelfrieda, what kind of world have you come into? A world
jettisoning much of its population and fertile lands; a hazardous
world of change... I am honoured to be your father, for though I
did not look for it I can see that I have set myself up, setting that
stone on Dragon hill, a stone of the heart's ways, and who knows
the ways of the heart? Because of this stone, did you appear? I
shall be careful next time I go a-courting there. We are both parts
of a story but I do not know the ending, or the next chapter. That
cannot be predicted; they belong to the realm of hazard. What do I
wish for you? That you will grow up with parents, know and trust
what you think and feel, share the sensitivity of a whiskered
mouse, the night eyes of an owl, the wrath of a badger, the songs of
the dolphin. That you will grow into your name, a counsellor of
the elves, of the earth. You came into this life because your mother
overcame her fear of pain; you came with eyes that wanted to see,
you came with a rush and literally perfect timing. A dramatic little
lady. What more can I say. I always wanted a daughter and now
you are here. The wind is still gusting and I am the only person
up at the farm; even the dogs Queen and Megan sleep. My tired
head sinks into my upright hand. My eyelids droop. I bid you
goodnight and smoke a cigarette, wishing you fulfilment in your
life. (Dunsford Farm, March 17, 1994)

BIRTHING WALK

The day started badly. I arrived at the bus station well before Sam
to be told by the conductor, 'You must be joking.' I had made no
reservation. I went to the railway station: £65 return to Padding-
ton before 9am, £34 after that. Outrageous! I had set my heart
going to London and walking to the place of my birth, St. James's
Maternity Hospital, Balham, then onto Streatham Common

where I lived the first five years in a prefab backing onto Streatham High Street; then onto 176 Muncton Road where my father, Alfred Please, lived next to the Old Kent Road, and finally to Golden Lane where my grandfather was born in the City of London. My childhood memories of my grandfather are hazy; a strong chin, a brass-buckled leather belt, a generous hand slipping half-a-crown into my pocket; a kind and quiet old man. My father came out of that city world of sweatshops, warehouses and street traders. This mix of street glamour and unglamorous poverty I associated with the Please family. And then there was Sparrow, the youngest brother of my grandfather, who reputedly died in Newgate Prison for stealing a loaf of bread.

I planned to walk twelve miles, in fact I walked twenty. From the start I felt shabbily dressed, and this was as true in Tulse Hill and Brixton, as in Regent Street. I did not belong anywhere. The only place I felt at home was with the Canada geese on the Serpentine and the overgrown holly trees, the tourists feeding the sparrows. The parks became stepping stones, tiny oases between the anonymous streets – Hyde Park, Battersea Park, Clapham Common, Tooting Bec, Streatham Common. After Clapham I felt I was walking into a black and white picture, or a woven cloth with unravelling threads. Treeless Balham depressed me; black spivs in fast red cars, old ladies struggling with shopping trolleys, though I liked the businesses sprawling out onto the street. I felt I was in Turkey... An African girl sitting on a wall had never heard of St. James's Hospital. She wore a silk blue dress, open brown eyes, and her hair was sleeked flat with oily ash. Around her were little red-bricked houses. An old man remembered it, and pointed to the houses. Only one ward remained, ringed by a barbed wire security fence, and a sign: Day Centre for the Handicapped. *I imagined my mother, from the tropical seas of Mauritius, nursing me under this chestnut tree those forty four years ago. This is where I appeared in the world. I felt nothing. I watched some people laughing on the roof. The carved inscription on the building said* Hawthorn, *under a knight's coat of arms and the motto:* We Serve. *I liked that.*

Smoke had coloured dark grey the grandparent oaks of Tooting Bec common, and everywhere I noticed suckers at the base of trees as if they wanted to start again. I wandered amazed down Streatham High Street with the teeming genes of Africans, Indians, Euras-

ians... I stopped by the adventure playground, pond and willows. Nothing remained of the original prefabs here nor their gardens. I felt a ghost, invisible to others; the old white willow where I must have played under as a child was real enough. I took three cuttings. The picture of the happy boy in the blue cap followed me by the old boating pond, now fenced and empty. Monstrous tower blocks with gardens smaller than a mini-car dominated Muncton Road next to the Elephant and Castle. A community garden marked the spot of the demolished yellow brick houses where my father had lived as a child. He escaped this poverty trap through education: a scholarship to King's College, London. Through his marriage to my mother, he joined the middle classes, and it must have been love for they returned to a prefab at Streatham far from the colonial mansions. I breathed gladly the cosmopolitan airs of London Bridge in the city rush hour, a desperate avalanche of purposeful humanity, midgets beneath sheets of iridescent glass... I stepped out of this by the Barbican Centre into the back-lane world of the Peabody Estate, underneath it the birthplace of my grandfather. I drank a toast to my grandparents in the Drum and Monkey and remembered their hard times, their laughter. The black poor have taken the place of the white poor. Sometimes I imagine that I'm living the dream of my grandparents, the life that was farthest from them, the dirty city, the cigarette factory... Like the mural I saw in Latchmere Road – a verdant world in balance with animals and people. I understood why the Please family are great walkers; it's free! My father loved books about roads, old roads, new roads. This road does not go back, it goes forward. I walk alone now but this road of fulfilment has strange beginnings, a long history.
(March 31, 1994)

APRIL CHANGES

Above ground now, spring-giving, a time of announcements, outings. The smell of earth is musty and sweet, everything shooting green – three miner bees escort queen bumble bee foraging a red deadnettle – when blackthorn comes into flower, hawthorn comes into leaf; when blackthorn petals spot the ground, hawthorn flowers appear – wild madder (*Rubia peregrina*) mauve-red beside white stars of blackthorn – spiral snails on the move along with spiral bosses of hart's-tongue fern – standard trees in woodland still bare, the shrubby coppiced layer in leaf – after the storm, the midges swarm, the bumblebees prowl – holly blue butterfly (*Celastrina argiolus*) sucking lime mortar – when ash leaves appear, beech leaves get erections – first house martin, first cuckoo – oak in flower – robber fly clutching victim on celandine, the yellow petals already fading white – honey bees visit hawthorn blossom – early spotted orchid in bloom with St. George's mushroom – cow parsley flowers with first hazel leaves – hungry bees investigate primroses and cowslips – fields with sweet vernal grass smell faintly of vanilla – dandelions everywhere when the sun shines – ash blossom on car bonnets by the end of month.

EASTER BACKYARD

I had to drag myself outside here, my thoughts telling me that there is nothing interesting to write about. I am leaning on a concrete wall looking at a forest of mammoth dandelions, great purplish-red cylinders collapsed across deeply-toothed leaves, with tiger-striped yellows in knots at their tips. A cold north-easterly is pushing grey-lined, blue-holed clouds across my horizon. I crouch to protect myself. I look around this flower border and up into the eyes of a sudden appearing fluffy, whiskery ginger cat. He rolls like a rhino on the paving stones and peers at me through the pierced stonework. He stretches to scratch the buddleia. I am pleased, comforted by his arrival. He sits on the red tiles uninterested in my Easter treat of a saucer of milk. He lets me stroke him and wanders off noticing a basking fly but without stopping. Apple leaf shadows flutter on this page. I like the way that something comes out of nothing, a miniature lion prowling alongside these – I nearly said – my dandelions. I am in this now. I have put myself here.

I suppose I, too, am out hunting with this pen, or is it wooing something out of nothing? Nature dislikes voids and, even if I hoe all the plants from this plot, it means the dandelions only grow bigger to fill the space. A miner bee, distinctive with its busy-ness, gives the dandelions a quick once over. An unknown fly of the hover kind is nose deep in the florets. How hard it is not just to write a list of things to fill up this white space. Perhaps we live our lives this way; the unknown day is already filled in. I look around attracted by the way the outer row of dandelions, collapsed by the weight of growth, still manage to keep the flowers facing the sun. Herb Robert, light greens cut with fine red outlines, likes this undisturbed ground with its thick thatch of plant stems, dry and bleached, a little forest floor. The blue spaces of sunlight are loved by hairy flies and slim waspies; they soak it up.

To return to the dandelions. I speculate that without competition they will grow enormous; wild flowers in cultivation are often two or three times larger. One dandelion plant is nearly two feet across; the flowering stem eighteen inches long. The drops of rain force me inside. This writing is sort of backyard writing. It's so ordinary! The demon boredom, a blank white cylinder, with needle black eyes and many narrow jointed legs, dares me, stands in my way. When I pass myself by I cannot pass him; he looks as if he can eat my best intentions. When I am here things appear, emerge is a good word: a ladybird huddles on a leaf; a phosphorescent green leaf hopper jumps and sails away, and does it again. Little things always appear to me to be asexual. I'm sure I do them an injustice. I come out with the sun, I come out with the lion, the dandelion, the ginger cat. They appear when I put myself on the spot. I am not afraid when I am content. (Wells Road, Bath, April 15, 1990)

SNAKE'S HEAD FRITILLARY

The North American Indians had a word for it, the art of seeing one to see the many. Stonechats were unknown to me until I walked the rocky headlands of County Clare in Ireland. The first day I needed three hours to hear one, the rest of the week I heard only their distinctive marble-strike calls. Watch out for leaf reversion said a radio expert one evening and sure enough the first thing I saw in the garden were the green leaves on the golden variegated *Eleagnus maculatum*. But the first time is the one I remember best. Once I scythed the banks of the River Cherwell for Merton College. Often I idled along the walk skirting the lush Addison's Meadow, a scrap of original Thames Valley flora. (This was saved from becoming productive grazing by Professor Tansley, I think, one of the fathers of British ecology. In 1911 he instructed the grass to be cut only in July to ensure the continuity of meadow flowers). The tall, waving grasses were almost blue from the flood waters. I went past this meadow twice a day until I spotted a single white fleck far away in the grass. I stopped and noticed other white flecks in the meadow. The shadows around each one appeared darker, almost mauve. Then, to my surprise, they changed shape or took shape, becoming round, lots of round mauve bells. They emerged from the grass shadows like dark stars, one by one. They were everywhere, thousands of exquisite, nodding blooms of snake's head fritillary (*Fritillaria meleagris*). (Oxford, May 1977)

CHERRY TREE

My mother, Marie-Thérèse Please, inspired in me a love of the unusual in life, such as dreams, aimable hopeless people, their stories and a catholic sense that it takes all sorts to make a world. Her marriage to my father, Alfred, is a real love story, he a reserved, calm and cultured man from the London working class and she from an aristocratic French family living on Mauritius in the Indian Ocean. He met and married her there during the Second World War and came back to live in a London prefab on Streatham Common. They stayed together all their lives. Little incidents often reveal so much. Once she stopped by a flowering kanzan cherry tree and looked at the hundreds of pink petals scattered on the lawn. In the half-light they were edged with pale blue. The background of spring lemon grass made them appear as jewels woven into some fabulous carpet. 'There are two kinds of people,' my mother said. 'The first one will stop and admire this picture of cherry petals on the lawn, the second will sweep them away as a nuisance.' (1982)

WAYSIDE

I stop, attracted by what? There is something uneven, mixed in height in texture and flower about this scene. Different greens, white deadnettles held singly and proud and patrolled by miner bees; seeding dandelions, all stages around the clock, their blooms opening yellow mopheads, bald heads to parachute factories with the doors wide open. Something draws me...the luxuriance of things happening: metallic flashes of flies; leaning, castaway stems of old dock, stems stitched with browns and greys, side by side with the soft rumpled leaves of new dock, the seed heads new-born. I see more details, the serpent-headed cleavers, the silvery cut-leaf of mugwort emerging straight drawn. This is opportunist ground. I notice the bits of cracking redbrick, the nettles and brambles fighting it out by the edges, the glossy eyes of black sheet plastic. I look

from one thing to another. I like the strip yellows of dandelions, the snow-capped peaks of fertilised flowerheads; already the dark leaves, freshly oiled at top, are rusty at the base, old age and youth in the blink of an eye. This is the wayside, thatched with last year's straw at ground level, pierced by sharp points of couch grass, dominated by basal leaves of plantain, the dark flowerheads sharp against dandelion yellows. There is no stopping these bramble benders shooting crinkled leaves from every sun-facing shoot. A concrete gas sign pokes through its tentacles. This is unmanaged ground of factory compressor sounds, moving metal buckets, traffic drones drowning bumblebees. I like this wasteland and I can think of no good reason why. I have seen more bees in this 10 by 20 foot patch than in a large ornamental garden. Ouch! The stinging nettles are everywhere... Two queen buff-tailed bumblebees are buried in the hooded lips of white deadnettles, crawling from bloom to bloom, wings folded, occasionally wiping their smudged heads, the only break they take from working. Old dandelion heads I see first as dull cream satellites attached to giraffe necks; they buckle over with age swallowed up by couch. Twenty minutes later I see the tiny orange-flash beetles climbing grass stems... I have nothing to say. I panic for an instant. I think: bees visit dandelions and in due course the wind. I peer at a tiny beetle; it unfolds its wings and flies into my face. I have only touched this world, its outer edge. The wayside, from this point of view, is literally unknown.
(River Avon, Bath, April 9, 1990)

* * * *

Tombstone for a mouse: Cedric Mouse – 'And when the earth shall claim your limbs, then shall you truly dance.' (Roboan House, Dauntsey, May 8, 1995)

SHOOTING STONES

I want to write about something ordinary, ordinary moments with Ben, my eldest son, and Peter Beatty, my sister's youngest son. I am remembering the stony, crackling seaweed lining the creek, and the high-banks with oaks spread-eagled along the top, many of the branches touching our heads. The oak flowers were soft and fragile to touch, and appeared with the leaves. Up the creek I could see the white stand of masts below the conifers, and above that the red brick of Dartmouth Naval College... Ben peared first coming with his funny Charlie Chaplin walk and flicking his blond hair from his eyes. He sat down beside me. I wanted to say, 'this is a good place,' but I didn't. Strangely, I felt no need to speak. We watched the wave-wash from the ferry tugboat rolling the small stones, the beached wood and plastic debris. I like creeks, knowing the sea is nearby and that I am still surrounded by land. Peter climbs down to us, smiling, changing the sometimes pinched look in his face. I wonder if he is happy. I tap out a beat on the oak and a rock; Ben taps his feet and then it changes. Peter throws a rock at the sewage pipe. 'This is it,' he says and wings it high and to the left. We all throw stones and they all miss, and every one is it! This is for the white buoy,' I say and unfurl a whizzer. It falls short. I cant remember much conversation: little bits like 'nearly,' or that's close,' or short exclamations of dismay. We never hit it. Then Ben placed little pebbles on a rock and, going in turns, we lobbed pebbles across a few feet to knock them off. Ben kept a tally but I didn't bother. Sometimes a ferry chugged by and we let this picture wash over us, not wanting to change it. Ben and Peter found skimmers, small flat stones, and bounced them over the water counting each time they landed. We never said anything to each other or talked about the weather or school or about ourselves. It just didn't matter. It wouldn't have changed this feeling of acceptance, allowing the picture to be itself, and allowing ourselves to be in it. There are no cracks in this picture. Shooting stones is something boys do and never tire of doing. This taking aim business, focussing, marshalling attention physically is in our blood. At a glance I could find the right stone for winging, straight and steady aim, and I made small and decisive allowances for the weight of the stones. When our arms ached we stopped. I found a bit of an oar and whacked stones from Peter into the creek. Ben walked behind me jumping each time I hit one. I feel better making the effort to record this mundane time... I stood in the garden at Maypool and looked at the estuary. I felt silly crying for the beauty, serenity of water and depth of vision. (Maypool YHA, April 12, 1992)

PLACE OF WILLOWS

I wanted to come back to this place of willows, big old giants tumbling sideways into a pool of brackish water. I went down to the water's edge by the square blocks of limestone which once faced this terminus end of the Somerset Coal Canal, known locally as the Paulton Basin, the turning place for the narrow barges. They took the coal from here to Dundas Wharf on the River Avon, and so to Bristol, Bath and London. In some ways this is a beginning place. This bygone industrial centre is now a rural scene; sheep and lambs nose the folded shorelines of field blending into the jutting rubble headlands, once the loading piers. The sharp-pointed flag iris encircles the open water, home to the three willows. Details catch my eye: the breeze rippling twig and leaf shadows; a dandelion flowering in the notched willow bark; young thorns at home with their feet in water; fertile arum leaves flushed twice their normal size; racing pairs of spring lambs; the angled face of stone peeping from the water. I smell the sombre, decaying leaves. There is something poignant about the stone blocks; their purposefulness, precision, man-madeness...in this forgotten place. Two moorhens crank and scuttle from the iris startling me. I haven't sat still like this all winter. I soak in the pebble chorus of small song-birds, unable to follow them or see them, and not wanting to... I remember the dream: the green boughs of willow at the turning into the main road, my main road. I stared at it until the tree vanished, changing into a glass beehive with a chair inside. I knew that it was a colour healing temple.

This cradle of still water I like, at perfect ease with the ruins. These trees are the inheritors of this canal, so well made that it still holds water. I keep looking back at the stone peering from the water; on sunny days it will steam I'm sure, and the water will reflect the sailing sun. This turning basin is a place for reflections, flooding up... What do I see? A man rubbing off the white mime paint from his face, no longer staying silent about himself. I see someone looking at the ruins of past attainments, wondering where he is: the artist in the garret, the terraced house at Frome. I am very unknown to myself. I want to work. What does that mean? To emerge from myself, to claim what was there at the beginning... I don't know why I give myself such a hard time. This is the cradle in my life, listening to my ancestors, burying some skeletons, clothing and feeding others. This sense I have of coming to the end of the line can be turned around and become a beginning place, a waterway going back out into the world. It is a place of peace, as this place is.

I have come to the part of this writing where my energy flags...it is the place in my life where the work is still to be accomplished, the garden still to be built. I am foolish before these dreams. I am alone. I want to trust this timing in my life, let go on a daily basis the fretwork of worries about tomorrow, security, loneliness...
(Paulton Basin, April 23, 1994)

JURASSIC STONE (III)

The steam rose above the strange, encrusted pools which stained the earth red. They were warm when all else was frozen and, around the sides, in the soft oozing mud, were fresh prints of crane, ox and wild boar. The Avon river filtered through a wide and shallow valley, between beds of cotton-grass and bulrush, meandering around gravel banks mottled with blue and brown clays and encircling the two low-lying islands of dense scrub cover. The ground mist clung to the surrounding marshlands, blue in the cool distance, orange in the sunlight. Beechen Cliff, the highest gorge, cast a violet shadow reaching the steaming pool. Here a man stood feeling the hot mud between his toes and watching the bubbles rise one after the other in the spring water. He dropped a silver weight into the pool. He crouched at the sudden harsh notes, echoed by others, and the reedy wing-beats of departing cranes. He ran stooping along the pathways of compacted sedge and climbed the bird tower, a look-out nest built from fallen branches. The trails were clear north and west, winding by willow and alder to vanish into the dense tree cover. Geese appeared flying low, startled from the south; an approaching pack of sky hounds. A column of men picked their way slowly down the boulders of the cliff. Cooking pots clanked against axes and picks; the short, metal aprons and iron sandals studs tinkled in rhythm. In front, almost by the river's edge, stood a strange man with an iron helmet and bronze cheek guards. He carried the ensign high for all to see – the Emperor's fluttering, purple banner.

They made the city in stone, a sea stone sawn by hand and dragged by oxen from the bed of the submerged super-continent Pangea. It was there beneath the Roman feet, under the turf of the surrounding flat hilltops. The seams of creams and golds and all the greys were exposed when the Avon river cut its way to the

140

Severn estuary. The great oolite lay squeezed between coarse and shelly limestones in bands up to ten metres thick. It looked like compressed cod's roe, with a grain varying with the prehistoric currents, tides and eddies. Fresh from the ground it was yellow, sappy and soft, but upon exposure it became white and hard. The legionaries – soldiers, farmers and exiles from bluer skies – built the scaffolding and the mobile cranes to lift the rock, free-stone to be sawn in any direction. The masons butted them together with iron straps and enclosed the hot springs, building on the earlier Celtic foundations. They laid the steps to lead visitors to the four fluted columns supporting the temple ped-iment, towering and gleaming over the marshland. It depicted a giant with the power of flight, and the torc around its neck were older links with the Underworld and fertility. And in the corners were mythological sea creatures, the Titans and the little owl, the bird of the night, the bringer of the dream. The old gods had new faces. The Romans dedicated the waters to the goddess Sulis-Minerva; to healing, wisdom and learning, the guardians of human culture.

Long before the Saxons breached the Roman walls in 577AD the rising water levels flooded the hot spring baths. The layers of black mud submerged the stone pavements and filled the scented alcoves. No longer were the cries of the hair plucker heard or the names of Lar invoked as the spirit of the home, or Vesta of the hearth. The floods washed the mortar from the joints, the frost flaked the stone and ice bulged the temple walls. The carved gods collapsed into the mud. Bulrushes, alder and willow returned and terns nested in the marshlands; the opal glints of dragonflies buzzed around the projecting deities. The Saxons recycled the statuary, friezes, pavements and battlements. Small hospitals for the poor and leprous were founded in the reigns of Athelston, Edgar and Ethelred. St. Augustine walked through the city in 597AD on his way to meet the bishops of the Welsh British church. He stayed at Caer Badon, modern Larkhall, travelling up the routes of Walcot Street, Guinea Lane and Julian Road on his way to Bristol. Bath, or Acenanescaster (Sick man's city) was now a border between the kingdoms of Mercia and Wessex. It had its greatest day on May 11, 974AD when Edgar was crowned the first king of All-England, and, at the end of the Te Deum, the Archbishop Dunstan dictated and Edgar swore three oaths: that the church of God and all Christian people should enjoy true peace forever; that he would forbid all wrongs and robbery and that he would command justice and mercy in all judgements. 'Let the King live forever,' the people shouted. After the feast he left for a long sea voyage around the island. He died two years later.

Out of the medieval streets full of dunghills, carrion for pigs and open sewers, grew the classical Bath. The architect, John Wood the Elder, his mind steeped with Greek mythology and druidical lore, dreamed his dream of a masonic utopia. He identified places around Bath with ancient rites: the Circus became a temple to the sun, the Royal Crescent one to the moon. He claimed he discovered a perfect model of the Pythagorean system of the planetary world, and Ralph Allen, the streetwise son of a Cornish innkeeper, translated it into stone. Beau Nash, the snobbish, kindly, eccentric gambler was the uncrowned king of the new spa. He took the dogs and cats out of the baths, outlawed swords from the city, forbade private gatherings, licensed the sedan chairs and ruled: The gentlemen of fashion never appearing in the morning before the ladies in gowns and caps show breeding and respect... That the younger ladies take note of how many eyes observe them.

In 1864, 100,000 tons of hand-cut stone were dispatched from Corsham railway station. It was the heyday of the chopper, the dayman, the ganger and the roadman. They had their own language: brigs, brogging hammers, chogs, cockles, ginny ring, gobs, razzer, squats, whim and windy drill. The mechanical samson coal cutters later replaced the sawyer with his frigbob and razzer, the picker with his jadding iron. During the Second World War most of the stone mines were converted into bomb-proof ammunition dumps, new temples of Mars on a colossal scale. Under total secrecy arc lamps were erected in the old cutting, illuminating the continuous stream of weapons arriving by train to be stored in the labyrinth of tunnels. Today diesel generators power the arc lamps shining on the dormitories, kitchens and control rooms hewn from the stone. Somewhere, in the empty mines, is said to be a great hall with tiers of stone seats, the same number as in the Houses of Parliament.

REALLY!

Six-year-old Rowan Harvey loves talking, telling everybody everything he sees and hears. His parents thought that snorkling in the clear waters off Zanzibar would silence him. The snorkel bobbed up and down then disappeared. The bubbles came up and out burst words: 'Gosh! Zebra! Look! Pincushion! See!' (Bradwell Mill, May 6, 1995)

BLACK MOUNTAINS

Two nights before this walk I lay in bed with little Aelfrieda beside me, listening to her slightly nasal in and outbreath. She felt tiny in my arms. This lulled me to sleep and much later, I don't know when, I heard her breathing but this time I knew that I was dreaming; her breathing now was big and steady as the sea, and it was I who felt small beside her. I listened intently to this breathing until it seemed that I was being breathed in time with it, and I did not know who was which; and the thought appeared this is how I should live in my life, one breath at a time. I remembered it while listening to the South African election day on the radio. 'Freedom walk,' I told my gentle companion Rob; he came to the farm as a volunteer after his marriage break-up pulled the world from under his feet. He says that he could not do this walk on his own. I think the same thing but don't tell him that. He talks about the night ahead, lighting the fire above Capel-y-ffin, sleeping in the silage bag, and the dull lights in his eyes vanish. His long-boned face is transformed; the gravity ebbs. For a moment he remembers the man who travelled across several continents in his twenties. It's that self he is looking to find again. He doesn't know where he's gone.

Every time I leave the path I find a trail, and this one led below the crags of Darren, a chaos of jumbled-faced rock encircled by grassy hillocks and single thorn trees. A peregrine falcon hurtled past, siren mewing, finding a still point with her wings before folding them back to drop onto the rocks. A raven appeared at the edge peering down two hundred feet. On the ground I stepped over giant black slugs every foot of the way, 'the reincarnated souls of sheep buggerers', a persistent joke. The trail wandered halfway up the mountains; away from the valleys of neat, improved pasture-lands with white dots for sheep, and along the older farming boundaries now surrendered to moorland and Offa's Dyke; a

143

poignant atmosphere of ruined hafods, derelict orchards, bulging drystone walls, tidelines of bracken... I imagined this grandparents' hand-made world: the donkeys and traps, chapels and routines, the back-breaking work without machinery, the tracks between the farms like badger trails. In the sixties and seventies I wanted that homespun life but I did not want the work. Rob still dreams of building a wooden chalet house in a warmer climate but with someone. I point out a hafod ruin, a gem of drystone still standing with walls three feet thick. 'Dream house,' I say, nightmare I think. This isn't it.

The horse-shoe valley is smooth above the boned ridges, dark and patchy with heather, red with bracken below to the springlines and woods. The eyes stretch along broad pastille sweeps, the sky shrinking the worlds below. 'Mama mia,' says Rob, clicking his tongue and whistling a fragment of song. He talks a lot in fragments as if he is confused. He says he is. Most of his time he holds together a home for his son and visiting daughter. 'I was another person,' says Rob talking about his marriage. 'I used to drive from Bristol to Swindon every day for contract electrical work. I'd sleep in the firm's van on the way back. I was knackered paying the bills. My wife came home late one night. Whose car, I asked? "My boyfriend's," she said. I was too numb, stressed out to feel anything.' He lost his house and daughter and went to bits. He goes slower now, more thoughtful but unhappy. 'I'm still looking how to start again.'

Walking near Vision Farm near Capel-y-ffin didn't help; stony, leaning trees, abandoned vehicles; a cow sat in the middle of the lane, mud-splattered and tired, and slowly pushed herself up and wandered to the fence of rusty corrugated iron. I wondered what they had seen here. An old lady in a blue cotton smock tightened with a belt led the way to The Monastery at Capel-y-ffin. She seemed out of the fifties with her rim of curled hair, the straw-plaited bag and a dumpy walk as if she had done this all her life. Her grave, chiselled features and so large a face startled me... It didn't take long to choose the place, a natural dell beside a stream, with trees to keep out the booming wind racing the cloud mist over our heads. Rob made the fire, carefully. 'This is what I always wanted to do.' He collected the twigs, placed the ring of stones and crouched over it, balanced on his long arms. He blew and fanned the flame. This is a special place, I say, the plentiful dry wood, the cleansing water, the protection. It's a good place for a dream. He asked for one, and in the morning he said he saw himself as he is now crying out his heart. I dreamed of the resentful child who punishes by witholding, the white mime face, the one who stays silent when he should speak out. In the morning we smoothed the stockade of branches (against marauding sheep) and left Nant Bwlach with the feeling that something had happened. But what? The wind rustled the long, flanking hairs on the mountain ponies; they gazed stoically at us. The mist, the mountain ridge by Hay Bluff, the gale – all three converged into my worst fantasy. The mist pumped the adrenalin through me. I clung to the cliff edge as if it were a safety line. At last the sun appeared radiating benevolent light and warmth on our faces, uncloaking the tiny black-lined squares, green fields of Wales. Step by step, through rolling clouds, the cairns signed the way to the reservoir. 'It clears my head,' says Rob... Below Bal Mawr are the marginal lands of big-boled alders and thorns, ruined hafods in a sea of golden bent grass. A grandparent's place. I loved this half-managed place between the sterile ranks of conifers below and the moorlands above. Life is harsh here, tadpoles in shrinking mountain puddles, dead lambs impaled on thorns and pecked clean from their fleeces. This beautiful land, the Vale of Ewyas, is full of ghosts. When I close my eyes I see the old people with their old ways, fenced in, ingrowing. At this moment I see the broad sweep of the Black Mountains but they are not black. They are golden, rusty and red. 'We walked that,' said Rob. We did. (April 29, 1994)

MAY CHANGES

Insect consciousness! Apollo walks by day, flowers are pollinated. The ghosts return as butterflies, mayflies and all the winged connectors. The dawn sings, the day dreams of staggering transformation – hundreds of woodlice congregate on gravel path on a moonlit night, immobile and fully open – St. Mark's fly hanging in the air above marshy grass, dangling its long legs – bluebells peep out through unfurling bracken – pappus winds of poplars and willows – cow parsley transforms waysides – mayflies swarm up and down by River Frome – ladybird larvae 'crocs' suddenly abundant and out hunting greenfly – wild carrot flowers (*Daucus carota*) attract hunting wasps, black ants, solitary bees and ruby-tailed wasp – yellow-staining patches on wayside are celandines – when dandelions go to seed, buttercups take over – six rusty picture-winged flies sunning on a fence post

– shining green beetle (*Oedemera nobilis*) basking in bramble blossom – pregnant grass snake sunning on santolina bush – elm leaves (*Ulmus procera*) covered with tiny green pimples – small grey-brown larvae munching hogweed – goblets of buttercups (*Ranunculus acris*) beside shorn black heads of wavy ribwort plantain – hoverflies see their reflections in the marsh marigold – twining hairy shoots of hops (*Humulus lupulus*) in hedgerows – flowers of red, yellow and white dead-nettles – cardinal beetle flies from my open hand – thick, red-curled leaves on peach trees – May bugs stirring under the turf – hawthorn petals everywhere.

HAND-SIZE INSIGNIFICANT GROUND

I feel brave lying awkwardly here looking at this outcrop of dry crumbly earth. An ash seedling borders one side, only six inches high, and around it are curling brown beech leaves blown in from the hedge. I like the sun shining through and warming my legs and edging everything with sharp shadows. I want to touch this earth but I will spoil it, send things scurrying away. Nothing is happening and it's fine. I am always saying to myself that if you sit long enough something will happen. A minute dot scurries along a leaf rib. Gone! The breeze, filtered by branches, rocks a beech leaf, the tapered sides are curled into the centre, the way departing wasps do it. An armoured troggie, the woodlice, appears nudging the leaf. He's a slate-blue armadillo. The breeze brings shadows to play over the earth, chewed, pocked, with off-white pebbles and the odd bit of red brick. I haven't done this for ages, just looking, waiting for nothing in particular.

When things are at an end, when they return to earth, the colour is taken out of them first; the leaves brighten with minerals for a moment, then fade, get washed out, twigs and grasses, too. The beech leaves become stony, likewise the shell and plant roots. Nothing is happening. I notice the stain of bird shit, a super-bleached white even cleaner than the daisy florets. It appears unnatural as it has no gradations, tints or tones; the colours of earth, plants and stones are never uniform. High above, some-where, starlings wheeze threading the notes into long strings with beads; the gaps count as silences. The rain has washed the soil from the tops of the clods into tiny scree beds; all the particles are as fine as pebbles. It is a beach. I imagine the best way of climbing up the

*worm casts where I can bivouac for the night. It's like a strange
formation from the Hoggar mountains in the Sahara. Ants dart
below the gaps in the ground. A sharp shadow appears, then a fly.
It crouches as the breeze rises, turning to sun its body and stretching its back legs one at a time. I shoo it from this page.*

*Inhospitable this baked earth, a knacker's yard of browns, off-white
and greys; stone dry it is, the roots dangle in the air. The brightest
colours are the protective sheaves of new beech leaves, almost
chestnut daggers. Nothing happens and I am content. I return to
the pebble shore, the chestnut dagger is a long-keeled boat, Viking
adventurers beached on an island shore. They have climbed the
easy southern slopes and are at the flat stone camp overlooking the
sea. They are short of water and are arguing whether they should
explore some of the cave systems. The shadows crossing the sun
settle their arguments. They will wait until the dawn. A large
droning creature prowls the cliffs. They drop to the ground. Let's
hope, one says, nothing happens. (*Upton Cheney, May 18, 1990)

FUSSELL'S EYRIE

*I could not find this trail in summer, only in the bleak lines of
winter is it bare enough to see my way. Snakes is what I think of
here, sunning themselves on hot rocks, peering thong-eyed from
crevices; a snap of twig and I turn sharply expecting to see the
broad, cocked head of a black bear. These outcrops, rugged by
twisted crab apple, are an animal place where I come to touch
ground again. It's a healing place. In my left hand I'm holding a
shrivelled apple flower, a starfish bent back on five arms with a
head of brown anthers. This tree is fertilised and the flowers are
dead. A troop of jackdaws arrive noisily on the greening oak, peck
the hearts from leaves and leave noisily as a group. Far below me I
see the red and yellow beak of a moorhen glide along the Mells
Stream. I come here for the silences, the gaps and views from the
rock. I come here to be alone.*

*This morning I worked at Critchell school with a dozen children
all under five, some unable to talk or coordinate their arms or legs,
or respond in any way when spoken to. They stared away
somewhere. The women who work with them are dedicated, strong
adults, always gentle and making an opportunity for contact from
the trivia of every moment; for the morning register, singing a song
to Darren: 'Darren, Darren, where are you?' And Darren taps*

147

his chest: 'Here I am, here I am, how do you do.' This gentleness is always strong, entering the spaces of the children, keeping the micro-boundaries and building self-esteem. I always come away more centred, calmer, as if the pain and turmoil of my life derives from a similar child of three or four unparented in me.

The butterflies, cabbage whites rise up and down through the holes in the tree canopy on an invisible ladder. I keep thinking an animal is approaching stealthily on four feet. I am nervous. I am unhappy in Frome, confused. My dream life has dried up... I think this is the hardest thing accepting myself as a writer. Perhaps my pattern is to live simply, creating a holine environment, and aiming my journies at people and cities... I have been asleep to all this abundance around me. How well camouflaged the drake mallard is beside the river; the broken colours, metallic green head, white collar and chocolate brown wings, mirror the muddy river banks, splashes of white water and leaf shine. I am the hawk and the prey is myself, how to be whole, active in life... In Frome I am hardening myself as I did in Paris, becoming more able to sustain myself without collapsing. There is too much of the past here, old girlfriends and work patterns, worn out friendships. I struggle with being an adult and keeping my inner family connected. I struggle full stop. I struggle with being alone, being settled or travelling. I struggle with uncertainty, knowing when to surrender, when not to budge an inch. I would like to think this struggle could change into acceptance, and I find more dignity in this process. (Mells, May 22, 1992)

ON WANTING TO BE BIG

I am sitting beside my omphalos stone, the wayside stone I am carving at the farm. Small birds sing after the thunderstorm and rains; a great pall of mist adorns the Cam valley, muffling the senses and only waiting for the sun to transform this so English day into a temperate tropical rainforest. This statement – on wanting to be big – appears distant from me and I am afraid I will approach it too analytically. The truth is I don't know how to start this and I'm full of cold. I like leaning on this stone, an inverted staddle stone; because it is dense and heavy my touch is light. I sense myself easily. I find it hard to focus on anything. I notice the lushness of the alder leaves and the angular mosaics of cow parsley, the uncut margins of Stag's bender. The stone is so solid I don't *even notice it, I take it for granted. It starts to match the substantial emptiness I feel when I am truly relaxed, at ease with myself. It is there whether I hold onto it or not. On wanting to be big is about forcing myself away from this solid rock. I do this when I am frightened, a fear that I brought into this world, that I am too small to be loved. This little man, a buffoon, wants to be loved for himself. My poor brain stumbles over these words. Who is it then that wants to be BIG? The dwarf in me, this exima figure, either a blessing or a disease; his spectacular wasting diseases, always in love, superman with a wraparound dick, always in exile, a refugee dreaming dreaming, his delicious malicious humour, profound sense of worthlessness, his unconditional love, common as shit... he shows my back, my instincts; not my face, not me. Then there is this snake thing, something coming into life on this stone, a natural sideways movement out of the earth... I am frightened of this energy as I can't control it. I can only lean on it lightly, find support with its tremendous natural stability. I can imagine my creator as an intimate lover who listens, looks into my eyes...*

Faces are important. An adventurous Israeli once told me that we can only love what we can understand. I do sometimes want to be big in people's eyes but what I really want is to be at home with myself, at home with myself with others without acts of self-violence. When I close my eyes and touch the floor with my head and the emptiness fills the corners of my inner senses, I talk about my hopes and fears, and sometimes I feel the cosmic divinity longs to hear these unique voices from Earth. (May 26, 1993)

A MODERN FABLE

I remembered Jose while cycling along straight pencil-lines under horizons of wheat and mustard in Lincolnshire. The repetition of goliath machines trailing wide spray bars, the absence of people, the sight of neatly-sprayed verges burdened me strangely. I thought I had stumbled into the 1950's. Jose appeared unbidden, a small-time farmer from Brazil. I had seen slides of his charming pictures, his son Sebastian milking the house cow, his hand-painted chicken house, his daughter feeding pigs with kitchen scraps – subsistence farming, maybe, but they owned the land, fed themselves and produced a small surplus. They had their dignity. The big world they heard on the radio, the exotic foods in the supermarkets, holidays by the sea. If they sometimes longed for diversion they were glad not to have the car exhausts or the crime. The radio told them about soya beans and the high market prices paid by the food processing industry to fatten animals across the ocean. It sounded like a good idea. The first year they grew a bit and sold the crop for more money than they had ever seen. They grew a bit more and that year bought bicycles for the children. They heard on the radio about the big-yielding soya strains, more expensive but the crop would pay for that. It did! These experts knew their stuff. He started thinking about buying a second-hand van. He put soya where he had grown his crop of subsistence maize. They had the cash to buy that from the market now. The problems appeared some years down that road – the super soya strains became more expensive to buy and they needed additional fertiliser and protection with sprays. It was a hard decision getting rid of the pig and the vegetable patch. But they had the money and more, he proudly told his friends, to visit the supermarket and buy Pacific pilchards or fancy lettuces from Texas. He could not have foreseen the steady fall in the world prices for soya. He grew soya on more and more of his land. By then he knew he was trapped. He had to buy more fertilisers, more sprays just to stay still – the real income steadily diminished. It was heart-breaking to sell land to a neighbouring farmer. The house cow was the last to go. They bought all their food from the markets now. The price of fertilisers and seed continued to rise. The following year he sold more land to the neighbouring farmer. Later they sold out completely. The small farms, the community, had vanished under the ocean of soya, now owned by a handful of farmers. Jose and his family moved to the city. They ended up living in a shanty town with thousands of other landless people. All he had left of his farm were his little pictures, exquisitely naive, as if seen with a child's eye. (Bath, Farmers' World Network, 1992/ Lincolnshire, May, 1995)

SURREAL EXPRESS

I left the Orient Express at Geneva at 3.30am one morning, closing the door on the hospitable Turkish peasants bound for drudge in Strasbourg, some in a state of obvious shock from sitting opposite bra-less French girls. This incident happened in the station's waiting room shortly afterwards. It is true in every respect and I cannot fathom it.

I joined the sleeping bodies laid flat on benches, some acting as props for others, the youngest lying on the floor in sleeping bags. I was exhausted. I tried to sleep but couldn't. A stout Frenchman snored in one corner, occasionally grunting or yawning or making irritating clicking noises with his tongue. Someone muttered 'quel cochon'. It made no difference. He rumbled there, a force in the corner. A faint breeze came into the room with a prosperous looking Arab. He sat next to the snoring man doing it as quietly as possible. Our cochon woke up and accused him of waking him up. The Arab apologized in an American accent. This started an argument between them about the Middle East, waking up one by one about half the passengers in transit; they listened, as there was an energy in the room stronger than their resentment. A third person entered this exchange, a smartly dressed Frenchman with a briefcase. He sat opposite the Arab. He said (for everyone to hear) that he did not like Arabs. 'Is that so, dick head,' said the Arab. The insults crossed the room steadily becoming louder. Everybody listened now. The Arab stood up and slowly paced a small circle around the room. He spat on the floor. Our cochon emerged from his corner. He walked threateningly towards him. Several people inched towards the exit door. At this point the Arab pulled out a plastic bag from his coat pocket. The cochon stopped and no-one moved. From that he produced a box of big cigars. He handed them round at four in the morning. The smartly dressed Frenchman walked out uttering oaths. The Arab left later. They never returned. The cochon went back to sleep snoring loudly. Others lay smoking cigars and wondering if they were in a dream. (Geneva, 1974)

PHILIPPE GAULIER

Why do I think of you? Were you the cochon in the Geneva waiting room? A dream led me to this man of the theatre, the night after I had decided not to go to his theatre school in Paris. He appeared squatting opposite me in a large room decorated with cheap floral wallpaper. He looked at me without speaking then raised his hand, making himself into a living sculpture. I responded in like manner and this repeated itself several times until cracks appeared in the wallpaper revealing blue skies and mountain peaks, a hitherto hidden landscape. On the strength

of this dream I went to study the art of buffoons for a month
with him, along with young people from twenty three other
countries. At forty, I was the oldest. I had absolutely no idea
what I was letting myself in for. Buffoons are the people with
deformities, no arms or legs etc and were made into outcasts by
the medieval church. If God is perfect then his creation must be
perfect; therefore that which is not perfect cannot be the work
of God; it must be the work of the devil. They always parodied
people with power and their weapon is the buffoon's own
pleasure. 'The buffoons stand at the centre of the argument
between God and the devil,' says Monsieur Gaulier. 'They don't
give a shit for your love or respect. They want to know the
truth, and knowledge is the dream of the devil – that's why Eve
wanted it.'

A strange person definitely, this man. I see his stick, long, gnarled at the top and fashioned into a curling horn. He beat the floor with it to make his voice heard, loudly when he disapproved and his big lugubrious eyes and glum sagging face reddened with real anger. The price of being a clown. 'C'est un plaisir pour frapper les Anglais,' is a favourite line. If the student is good, he nods 'pas mal; if very good 'un peu', and if wonderful, he smiles a little: 'Elle est content.' He is in his late forties, always with a hat, stetson or gigantic French beret, and he walks slowly or sits staring at the students without any expression. Our efforts to please he mocks. 'Your smiles are your first defence,' he tells me. To someone upset about singing a Russian nursery song, he says: 'You can find your tears or your pleasure or stay as you are.' Always he thanked us for accepting his ruthlessness. 'It is a tradition here that the professor kisses each of his students in his mind.'

It would be easy to deify you but that would be a way of not being here. Always you said: 'Don't show me the actor and your tricks. Show me you, your experience now. Trouvez votre plaisir.' We danced for you, we danced for ourselves, dressed in outrageous clothes as crippled dwarves with huge bottoms; vestal virgins; with gigantic cocks or tiny ones; homosexual priests, hysterical, lustful ones; every beautiful monstrosity we ·paraded in that underground hall in Paris. Down into the shit come up smelling like roses. 'Catholics make good buffoons,' he said. 'They have excellent imagination for perversity.' I loved the dwarf in me, the little man I keep silent, whose hands I have tied behind his back, whose legs are short and with his queer little face he peers out on the world, a world in which he has no part to play. He is pure enjoyment. It is vanity which makes me sweat, which puts false idols before myself. It is vanity which controls others. As a reward Philippe, like some old crone, would sometimes curse and list the actor's faults and she had to stand there and take it. The happiest picture of you is when your assistant could not control her laughter and you stared out of a leaden face, and each time she laughed until she cried you looked at us dumbfounded, showing us your clown. I left four days before the end. I could not take any more. I squirmed inside with embarrassment and accepted my failure as a discovery: I am not an actor. I salute the spirit of all those students, brave people in squats far away from home, washing up to finance courses and living a life of great uncertainty. (Paris, 1990)

DISTURBED GROUND

The whistle goes. The thousand hum drum chatter of children's voices vanishes into a vacuum. I'm eavesdropping beside this open ground at the base of a fanned gooseberry bush. I disturb the earth. I see the moving things, the temple of chewed earth, the scatter-fall walk of a wolf spider, moving shadows, invisible when they stop. The teacher scolds the children into forming a line. They obey instantly. 'DO YOU LISTEN?' she demands. How I hated schools, the life inside a net cage; I could see the world but not touch it. School was always an open prison. I stare at the earth, the hard dry lumps, a leaf stalk which switches up and down, and does it again, curving until the rear end suddenly springs forward and both ends touch. An uprising breeze water rustles the crab apples and quince trees, carrying the voice of a child crying across the gardens. This patch of soil is a restful confusion of green leaf, grass curl, stone face, spider abseiling to water avens, a damp haunt of celandine, a fast yellowing stain. Dandelion domes are taller than the flowers; the parachutes skim off in the breeze like hover-flies. A dog barks and I leap forward. I am part of this scruffy garden, this native bit...it is pioneer land, the first stage in a re-afforestation programme. Nature dreams, works day and night, to cultivate large spreading branches, the call of the jay, the soft padding of badgers; nature dreams of a procession of flowers, sunlight filtering through leaves. This disturbed ground is where it starts, open and ready to change. I sit here, one eye half-closed to screen the sunlight, thinking that I have not come a long way in my forty years. I am still squatting among grasses and flowers and insects I do not know the names of, listening to the crow's hard wheeze and telling flies to land on my fingers. My earliest memory is seeing a film of a child running through the long grass, along a path to some secret place, a garden, and it's a sunny day before me. Perhaps I have never grown up. Is this an illusion too, middle age, old age and the rest of it. The older I grow the more I feel the same. (Bath, May 1, 1990)

154

LUSH DAWN

I came out for the dawn chorus and here I am! For the past hour I have walked slowly up and down Tepee field, the lush grass squeaking against the hard cloddy earth. I came out at four o-clock with the thought: perhaps I should take a knife, it's dark and who knows? I haven't intentionally done this before. I chose to sit against the old apple tree, the surviving relic of the orchards at Dunsford Farm...with the blossom, the massive fluting trunk, the natural dome of friendly leaves. The dew chills my feet, cools behind my ears, the tip of my nose, the cave of my mouth. It is still dark. I hear the cockerel from across the valley, a strutting call louder than the machined murmurs of the printing works two miles away. Orange glow lights of street lamps blink in the low tide of the night; the sharp cold lights of single stars are in the tops of bare ash trees. There is so much I want to say. It's all happening! The half-sweet, half musty scents of cow parsley is carried by the nearly freezing air. The clusters of pentagonal flowers light up the grass just as the first single bird opens up the sky world. Goblets of buttercups are dull ochre and sleeping; they open a little after five, and the first bee trails above them following the first mosquito. I keep changing position to stop my toes digging into this cold ground. But it's the floating spheres of the dandelions which light up the dawn, a posse of them appear to float without moving. The explosive greetings of coot − or is it a cock pheasant? − resound from the depths of the canal. The little owl cuts the sky with sharp, electrical zips as if calling quickly through the teeth of a comb and playing it back fast. I like it. I like breathing this lush air charmed with songs and flowers.

The sexual fantasy arrives easily on the back of buttercups, warm and moist and slow, and she definitely has blue eyes. This chilly air soon dispels this...after the little owl comes the skipping tension, the wire of wings, and the solitary squawking of a duck crossing the batch (the disused coal tip) unseen; then another cockerel greets the first light in the east. A breeze appears, brushing away the clouds looming pastille pink. The song notes come singly at first, hissed out, warbled from the deep cover of hawthorn. I listen intently. A sharper melody answers back still with the big night spaces between them. I look along the Tepee Field; unnoticed, the dew-trails cross boundary land between these thoughts and what's outside. Often they are connected. And then it happens! I hear the dawn chorus as colours, in streaks, notes intertwining, always moving, so I can never say where one starts or finishes. As soon as I listen hard the sound travels, or I hear the background, glimpsing another range of hills. Then this thought appears: not the birds singing but the air breathing the birds. They sing loudest and longest at this time of pollination.

My poor feet! I keep moving. The cuckoo sings out of a base wind pipe, a lonely, sombre two tones below everything else. Lambs bleat after that, and last of all are a pair of crows hopelessly out of tune with the songsters. They alone are visible. My watch says 5.45am. This meadow grass is waking up, the buttercups opening, the tucked-in edges of cow parsley being slowly ironed out. It's cold. The clouds have closed all the gaps. No more bees except for another buff-tailed bumble. The small birds lurk as shadows in the thorns, flitting from cover to cover. I cannot identify them from their songs. What strikes me most is the delivery or pace, whether it is warbled, chattered or quickly repeated, the speed counting as tempo. At 6am the crows take over, the woodpecker drums. Small birds appear on the outside of bushes. The marauding midges arrive. This is my first dawn chorus. How many years ago did I say I would do this? (May 9, 1994)

KATHLEEN TREVELYAN

I never knew her well but in 1976 I honeymooned at Godshill in the New Forest where she lived in a log cabin and rented out six caravans. She was a woman who was carried by her dream to the end. She said that Britain would be saved from its darkest hour by small groups praying for its salvation. Every morning we sat in her sanctuary, a converted shed, for silence and words together. Once she asked us: 'How do we love each other? Not by looking at each other but ahead and to the work that is required.' (1978)

RED KITES

I saw my first red kite as a half-waking image on Dragon Hill outside Glastonbury. It fluttered low over a field, the rufous markings showing clearly over the golden heads of wheat, except in real life it was a field of maize so I knew that I was seeing it with the inner eye. I had a similar experience on the shore of the Elan Valley lake; at dusk a sharp-piercing cry jolted me from my reverie but I could see no bird, only one in my imagination, incredibly real and red. These two experiences weave fact with fantasy. It is significant that both these sightings occurred at times of inner turmoil, one at the convergence sundance camp (1986), the other on a psilocybin journey after my marriage break-up. Four days ago I walked into their homelands across the Cambrian mountains from Elan Valley to Strata Florida. I used a compass bearing to navigate the sea of golden bent grass of the uplands, a terrain of boggy tussocks, dry peat beds, and on that day only the blue sky was bigger. I had visited the Elan Valley many times before, each time venturing a little farther from the lake; to the remnant pine wood on the lower slopes, to the outcrops of milky quartz on the beach, then twice in three days I worked the medicine of mushrooms to unlock the grief welling in my broken heart, a path of bones and emptiness I had never known before. I walked around the shore following the razor lines cut into the gravel by rising water levels. I clambered up through the dwarf oakwoods to the rocky outcrops where a peregrine falcon landed ten feet from me; I fell backwards (onto grass), it plummeted forwards into two thousand feet of blue haze. Twice I had stood before the forgotten interior, the boggy savannah lands opening up a world I wanted to visit; and twice I stepped back as this trackless place threatened to overwhelm me as waves from a wild sea.

The red kite brought me back a third time... With a friend, Robert Burns, I stepped due west into an exhilarating morning, from tussock to tussock towards the mountains on the skyline. The only other things that moved were the guileless sheep, the snap rustle of lizards, the ponderous crawl of amethyst beetles, crows and buzzards; once I scooped water from a pool to drink and caught a tiny frog in my hand. At the eastern end of Claerwen reservoir a red kite flickered black in the shadows standing on swallow tails above the jumbled hills of Bryn Glas. There are no trees; the sheep have eaten the lot. Only this can explain the ominous sight of cracked river beds in May, tinder dry grasses – yet nearly four months of rain fell this winter. (Not far from here I looked up suddenly, while walking, and saw two greyhounds and a man in a rusty cloak and strange pointed shoes walking ahead of me. I blinked. They disappeared.)

By the giant cairn on the fortress cliffs above Strata Florida, I descended into Gondorlands: the intense green light of Cistercian farmlands glimpsed through the gorge of dizzy screes, the outlying islands of rocky promontories all shades of grey and black. John Sell Cotman, the 19th century watercolourist, would have loved it here. Gladly I walked into this light, sensing the antique spaciousness and peace of tall trees sheltered in the valleys; here the red kites played over the rocks as giant butterflies in a tropical glade. They worked the slopes in pairs, not shy of our presence, the unmistakable forked tails and slow, lazy wing beats making identification easy. The ruined abbey at Strata Florida is the haunt of Welsh princes, and notably, where that unique poet, Dafydd ap Gwilym is buried, a rosy light shining in the winterlands of 13th century Wales. I collected twenty yew berries from the commemorative yew tree. I made another connection with red kites. These birds long to travel from a distant shore into the foreground. They struggle for survival. It is a struggle of our times. They are forced in winter to haunt the rubbish dump at Tregaron and the hand-out of butcher's fat. This forgotten part of Wales, this forgotten part of ourselves, is twinned mysteriously with that which sees the farthest. Kites have good eyes.

The walk back underlined that discretion is the better part of valour, and — for good measure — the longest way round can be the quickest. It seemed easy on the map, returning by the mountain ridge on the far side of the reservoir. Foolishly, we ventured up a wild valley along a vanishing way-marked trail, side-stepping boglands and abandoning our compass bearing; for one terrible moment I stared into the elemental stronghold of a cold-flooded mountain lake, Llyn Gynan, a maze of mountains, prehistoric bogs and into the clenched teeth of a wind scattering mist into our faces. We ran howling back into the safety of the valley. I wanted the gods and goddesses, not the Titans. We struggled 25 miles the long way over Ffair Rhos mountain pass, hugging the reservoir shore, lingering in the bluebell woods at Elan. I stopped for several minutes looking at a hawthorn, almost completely uprooted and lying beached on the shore fifteen feet from the bank — yet the leaves covered every branch. I traced back three slender roots, amazingly enough for this tough tree to survive. (May 23, 1994)

HOLINE (III)

The wind is talking in the rafters of this barn. Outside, in the old wheel-house, the suckler cows are snortling and sometimes they

158

pummel the connecting door. I am grateful for their company. It's only 7pm and I'm alone in Kildale camping barn, in my sleeping bag with all my clothes on, and a little bar heater next to me. My breath is misting. I approach this page cautiously. I am into my third week of this British cycling journey swimming with impressions of people and landscapes. I listen to the little movements in my heart... In the daytime I cycle under glorious blue skies; in the night-time I descend into the tawdry workshop of my dreams. My intention to cycle around this island is a kind of pilgrimage of old friends, places special to me such as Iona, as well as a chance to visit some famous gardens of Britain. This surface, this intention, I thought holy, but my dreams tell another story...

I remember the wearying times, pedalling the straight roads between horizons of wheat and mustard. I hardly saw a wild flower for a long way into Lincolshire. I meet hardworking, decent people and they astound me with their cleanliness; their gardens perfectly manicured, every domestic orifice powdered and squirted with disinfectant, the air I breathed sanitised with deodorant. One woman spent the best part of three days killing all the flies in a youth hostel. This war against microbes, this obsession, troubles me. Through a large part of the drained fenlands I felt queasy and resentful. I wanted to see something in opposition to this order – travellers, weeds, flies, anything. In Lincolnshire everything seemed in the day-time.

I don't know how this next thing is connected, but at Lastingham in the North Yorkshire Moors I discovered the ancient crypt church of St. Mary's, the Saxon foundation of the monastery of St. Ced. I walked down the steps and sat in the half-light among the head-pieces of broken Saxon crosses, Viking burial stones and a pre-Reformation bier for carrying the dead. I danced in that darkness the steps to the four directions, making a kind of Celtic cross. I felt content with the piety and grittiness of that place, the juxtaposition of Celtic and Viking Christianity, down in the under-belly of that church. For though I was literally undergound that place luxuriated with a warm, reddish glow, neither day or night nor a mixture, something with these elements yet distinct. They made a holine, an admission of what is above with what is below, where the warring parts find their place, their peace in that. This holiness I experience as gratitude. The tawdry dreams are the shadow cast by an honourable intention, the necessary ground, a depth of awareness of *where the pitfalls lie. This pilgrimage, I understand now, is also a descent.* (Kildale, Yorkshire. May 16, 1995)

THE STEADINESS OF COWS

Peter Willis is a painter from Newlyn in Cornwall. Joanna, his wife, is a dancer working with professionals, beginners and people I used to call mentally handicapped. They work to performance level in front of the locals. 'They are all artists on the stage and suffer the same agonies and joys, and get gutted when things go wrong. No-one stays the same.' That gutsiness is in their lives, too, and mixed with piety for they are Russian Orthodox Christians. Above their bedroom door is a blow-up photograph of their daughter, Mary Seraphima, in the arms of her mother, minutes after her water birth. A golden light of dawn suffuses their beatific smiles. In every room are small icons of Russian saints, particularly St. Seraphim of Sarov, an eighteenth century hermit striking a counterpoint to modern chords with his home in the woods and trust of animals. Peter is in his mid-forties and struggling with providence and his painting. Joanna says the money will come. He remembers the hard times working as a lone farmer on 72 acres in west Cornwall. 'I didn't realise what I was doing to myself. I carried the worries around with me. They became heavier each year. I used to sit with the cows some evenings and feel their steadiness. That helped. My first marriage was a casualty of that time.' That farm belonged to Robert Fripp, the musician, and he remembers showing Elizabeth Bennet, the wife of the philosopher J.G. Bennet, around the land. 'There's so much to do,' he told her. 'I don't know where I'll get the energy from.' 'Look up,' she said and pointed to a hawthorn bursting with blossom. 'That's where the energy comes from.' (Newlyn, May 1, 1995)

HELIGAN

This lost garden of south Cornwall keeps returning. I had arrived before the crowds and walked in the company of slanting light among the Tasmanian tree ferns, the sunken pools, cascades of exotic rhododendrons, stately eucalyptus: a primeval palace in the relic old woods of Heligan. The magic is real. I forgot about time. The boarded raised path led me into its snaking world, magical because it belonged to itself and me –

for a moment. They call it *The Jungle*, and it is that if you compare it to the formal walks of the kitchen gardens, the walled beehives, melon house and pineapple pits, but something else kept emerging – the juxtaposition of the native trees and the Pacific ferns became a perfect metaphor for the cosmopolitan world view of the eighteenth century: the farthest view of the known world and all there in that remote, steamy valley. I kept thinking of the people who made the crystal grotto to glitter when lit by candle light – while the industrial revolution gathered steam around them. And the posse of gardeners, in childhood seclusion, who salted, weeded, watered and rolled miles of garden paths; a quarter of the workers are said to have died in the mud of Flanders. To think that this jungle path led to this slaughter. Then I thought of the peace grove at Inverewe gardens, the peace woodland at Robert Hart's forest garden on Wenlock Edge, the dream of peace in our world, remembered by gardeners. I walked out of *The Jungle* – a holine for a changing world – and the waves of visitors landed me firmly back into the twentieth century. (Mevagissy, May 5, 1995)

COW PARSLEY VERGE

Here I am as I said I would be, sitting with the cow parsley on the wayside. A car trundles by with the driver leaning on the wheel and staring at me. I have the clear, eerie impression that his air-conditioned room hinders some vital flow of energy. This breeze cools my cheeks and eyes, rocks the myriad satellites of cow parsley above which scurry and dangle the long-legged St. Mark's fly. Up the road and down the road, and both sides of this lane, shimmer this May picture of English rural paradise. This is the first time I have associated the fly with this flower. That's amazing! I only saw them when I stopped moving. How invisible insects are; I believe they connect up the worlds. The sunlight brushes each grass blade with silver; the flies appear to be fire-walking, darting sideways, sweeping back their legs and wing-like arms. They are evanescent next to this great ash tree; beside the cow parsley they are visitors dropping in to re-fuel. A flock of pigeons play follow-the-leader making my head turn as they turn. I like it here sprawled on this verge with the journal on my knee. I'm content. I want nothing. The wind puffles the white clouds across the sky. Another car speeds past the flies. I stare at the silver-edged grass blades bending and swaying, and I think of grass snakes; they keep coming into my life, alert, sun-throated and dwellers in long, damp grass.

I notice the bleached bird shit under the ash tree, the rusty margin of ash flowers. The brightest parsley flowers face the sun from the edge of the shade, the darkness adds depth to their brilliance. The ones all in the light are out of focus and anaemic. Of course! That's why St. Mark's fly appears with the cow parsley; they are lovers destined to meet each May. The road to Warminster swallows up more cars and drivers. I never know what to say; this white space is a trail swallowing up these words. I listen to the stone clash rattle of the silage mower...lose interest in the flies. I can't follow them long enough. The cow parsley flowers in the shade disappear in the same way, becoming blurred. I make another connection with snakes; the verges twist and so do the white flower lines following them.

With these empty, open places, I judge myself as inadequate, that I will fail to be myself, as if I can only be myself when I am full of some feeling, or action or girt big erection. I am embarrassed to have nothing to say, for my lover to touch my soft cock, touch me with tenderness... I stumbled upon a grass snake basking in the Wadbury Valley. I imagined that I tried to catch it but it slid away leaving one golden scale on the tips of my fingers. I rubbed it off but when I picked up my knife I noticed that my fingers and thumb were still golden; in fact every time I rubbed them my feet wanted to move. I hid them under the table but if I accidentally rubbed my finger and thumb I had to do this funny dance shuffling along the ground, sideways, going forwards and backwards... Naturally I pretended at first it was a game, and I was an idiot for that is better than being thought mad. Then another thing happened; every time I rubbed my fingers and my feet moved, I had to hum a certain tune. I could not stop myself. I remember the first time I rubbed my finger and thumb in a busy street; I danced and sang and everybody looked...and someone followed me. I like this fantasy. I recall a dream of walking through grass and stroking their tips and feeling strongly how I am connected to the life in the grass. We are so different and yet both need something from each other, a gift, an acknowledgment which would make this hard-to-see bond tangible. What can I give this cow parsley? I picture an animal trying to articulate a feeling; to be known by others is to be

162

loved by others. How hard to articulate to ourselves these evan-escent, powerful healing connections. Cars float by from both directions. I do not know these people or where they are going. The breeze rustles the white flowers along the road. I must go now but I shall carve you and your lover on my stone. (Lullington, May 7, 1993)

CONIFERS

I cycled north through Kielder Forest, mile upon mile of sombre crowds of conifers under an equally sombre sky. I was glad the foresters had left grassy strips on both sides of the road other-wise I would have felt submerged by the trees, and I would have cycled harder to escape that oppressive feeling. The rain stopped me and I sheltered in a dry corner of the forest. I noticed the trunk of a conifer, the crusty detail with lichens and wood ants; it would be cut down with the other factory farm trees and no-one would remember it. This thought touched me. I decided to dance for this tree, and I did. A passing cyclist stared and I refused to be shamed by my odd appearance. I returned to the road and straightaway the trees had changed, or I had changed. I felt they were on the inside now, on my side, and no longer strangers. (Kielder, Northumberland, May 23)

* * * *

There's a road from Braemar to Tomintoul where I had to push the bike up a long hill. Every time I looked back I could see over the shoulders of the mountains and the beautifully-random spaced pine trees, not planted me thinks but fenced off from sheep and deer and allowed naturally to regenerate. They liter-ally glowed in that evening light and I couldn't help thinking of the closed ranks of plantation conifers and the literal desolation of the land when they are bulldozed up. The same trees, but one a vision of paradise, the other hell. (Braemar, May 27, 1995)

MUD SLIDE WILDERNESS

I feel like a beginner in these ways, in this bowl of silence below a cliff wall, sandy and collapsed in steps; below me baked mud, red metallic streams and willow scrub fall sharply to the sea rolling the shore pebbles. I returned to this wild carrot (Daucus carota), the jewelled centre of this strange, marginal hideaway, a wilderness of

163

underdcliff. I am surrounded by churned mud, mud slide with felty coltsfoot leaves, bright green brushes of marestail. I came back to a flower picture of fast precision colours, a mound of little mounds on a cushion of fine cut leaves. They mock my attempts to name them. I am fascinated by the insect visitors: a pale red grasshopper treads warily around mobile black ants; there are tiny picture-winged flies, midges, small fat pollen beetles... A sharp, ragged ruff protects each flower head – there must be twenty five on this one plant – unfolding rose-pink at the edges yet oddly stiff and bristly. A crow glides along the sandy cliff-line and I suddenly realise that this place is timelessness, nothing of the modern era intrudes, no wires or sawn wood, just the millions-of-years-old perfection of dazzling ruby-tailed wasp alighting briefly out of the sky. Crows circle, land, hop down the mud for a closer look; one gargles water from the stream: children scream chords of happiness from the beach; other parallel worlds, as is this carrot in the crack of mud, or what the crow sees from the rock.

There is a lot of live and let live on this nectar factory; the scavenging ants pass by the flies; the ruby-tailed wasp is unconcerned, back-combing its feelers, washing its metallic green face. The lurid red and green markings suggest a sinister small print when it comes to paying the bill. These carrot flowers change at every stage: the ruffled knot, the carmine edges, the spreading umbel half a sphere, the spaced islands on a frost sea, the single pink one in the middle, the green backwaters of the seeding heads. I am amazed how insects literally drop in without any formalities. I marvel at their tracking systems. Ants prowl everywhere and I lose interest in them. The giant fertility of marram grass, eight-feet spears crossed with side-spurs, puts me in my place. I am a stranger in this mud-slide wilderness with pyramidal orchids on rafts of crumbling clay. I will leave this world, time told by waves, the gaps with children's voices, but something has crossed over, will stay with me... This is the first time I have sat beside a wild carrot and felt its benign influence suckering me with little pictures of perfection... I over-stayed my welcome. I retreated from a sudden appearing image, the adrenalin sliding my feet across wet mud. I didn't look back. I imagined or I saw (and it didn't matter which) a giant red-breasted insect lurking among the mud-moved boulders. It flitted before me. I panicked, the second time I have fled out of a wilderness. (Eype, May 28, 1990)

FOR ME

I stopped at Denholm near Hawick, a village on the Scottish borders, people going about Sunday, friendly to this traveller on a bicycle studying their village map. I read about John Murray, the lexicographer who worked on the Oxford English Dictionary, and John Leyden, the scholar poet, who died of fever in India. Both were self-taught men who left the bosom of that village – and one can imagine how isolated it must have been in the 19th century – and educated themselves at Edinburgh and other places. It wasn't until some miles later, through that bare-breasted land, that it occurred to me that out of all the many thousands of people born in that village the ones they remember are the scholar and the poet. Then I recalled two poems by John Leyden; 'An Address to an Indian Gold Coin', and 'Scenes from Infancy'; the titles touched me, kept tapping at some door. They are here at Abbey St. Bathans in this dry oakland, steep down to the river, tourists meandering by the edges. All this cycling, gripping the bars, pedalling hard and pushing, head down, speeding along and somehow I have gone too fast, too far too soon, too determinedly, and a part of me is left behind. I know that by my locked jaw and a sadness tapping some door in me. I feel better sitting with my back against this oak, letting the wood-rush take my weight, being supported like this. Now I want to collapse. And somehow the thought of Denholm's illustrious son, John Leyden, helps. Though nearly two hundred years must separate us, there is something in common at this moment. For I fear that I have left an infant part of me behind. This infant wants to be held, sung to. I'm not very good at it. When I let the ground take my weight the softness starts to grow again, the hard points in my eyes soften. I am more here now. Did Leyden write this poem for such a moment, himself far away in India? Want to connect himself to home, to the early part of his life? I am happy holding this moment and changing nothing. The tapping on the door has stopped. (Abbey St. Bathans, May 21, 1995)

MY DARK BROTHER, GLOWING

I always feel like a new-born baby with this writing, trying to coordinate the different flapping parts of me, my arms, feet and head, trying to make them move together, to make some sense. I smoke a cigarette to remind me to go at my own speed, to listen to myself. I chose this pallet outside Darren's bender in the Tepee Field. It's outside with hoverflies, buttercups, seeding dandelions, the dairy cow, Ziggy, suckling her own calf and an orphan. Home is where I see the world through one pair of eyes, where all of me is on the same side. The word keeps changing. Home used to be with my biological family, uncles and aunts and their children; they were my world... Then there were (and are) the creeping things in nature, at the bottom of ditches. They are home, too, separate but attached to this family home. I never associated journalism with home, that was something different. My marriage and children made another kind of home, a step towards independence yet, in essence, the same as my biological family. When that world shattered I fell back onto my childhood world of the wayside. I have revisited this wayside home at every big change in my life, as if to remind myself of what is always here, what does not change. This bender home of hazel and tarpaulin belongs here with the echoes of tree houses, dens, secret places. All my life I have been looking for a place to call home. Yet this place is as much inside me, more so than stones and mortar...

This dark brother I carved in this sculpture lying on the grass, a robed man supporting him by one arm, and both their free hands touch the arms of a young girl, the guiding big eyes of the inner man. She connects them both. It is this connection that I am looking for, this new sense of home. It is the place where I am at home with myself. I have walked into the sunlight, twenty paces in front of Darren's bender. It's tucked into the cover of hawthorns before a rusting corrugated shed. My dark brother could live there, a life on the wayside, living a life of soul, of natural things, the things that I love. I find something beautiful about its simplicity, its size for children, close to the earth, bird song, the endless patterns in the light made by flies, of hours dreaming themselves away, away from this man-made world of time, responsibilities of the upper world of adults. It is a half-lit world really, belonging more to the underworld, a fitting world for the dark brother. I cannot disown it. It is me, too. This work of bringing things onto the same side, through one pair of eyes, involves many journies back, opening up old floors of homes, finding lost keys, releasing buried ducks — and these journies are part of my home, my fulfilment. Home appears more about standing up for this world than living it.

166

The bender is a patched-up home, a home for the explorer, the committed, a home for the desperate or the romantic playing with rural idylls, such as dressing up as cowboys at the weekend. I will not find the answers in this way. My heart wants creation to satisfy its spirit. The gun explodes on the far side of the batch and I shake a little. I have no protection here. I am vulnerable as a child is without the protection of an adult... When I am separated from my dark brother I go backwards and forwards looking for myself, looking to a future where things will be better. I am forever living at the crossroads between two homes, between two lovers, between two ways of working... The trail arrives here and goes from here. I am on it! Its the cutting edge I want not the dead wood. (May 11, 1994)

THE MILLER'S TALE

The eight sails of Heckington windmill – unique in England – puzzled my ears long before they appeared winding and creaking in the sky, the sail-boards charmed with pennons of coloured fluttering flags. This monument to Victorian ingenuity had been restored to working order by local enthusiasts with the support of the council. Dignitaries, experts and supporters crowded the small yard on the official opening day; the villagers lined the street waiting for the majestic sails to comb the sky. They did not sing. They screeched, the miller told me. They complained a mile away. All that work and dedication doomed. Everyone, of course, had their theory. They tried all the adjustments but it made no difference. In the end they contacted a professor at a Welsh university. He rang back and told them he had the answer. It would be the end of the mill, they thought; modern technology has a price on its head. 'Tie string to the sails,' said the professor, 'only make sure it runs parallel.' They did. The problem vanished. (May 12, 1995)

THE KEY

This absurd incident means a lot to me. I had parked my bicycle at Ryton Gardens, the national organic demonstration garden, and was crouched fiddling with the lock. The key fell into a patch of long grass. Could I find it? I searched every inch without success. It had to be there. I searched again and again. I sat in front of my bicycle torn between despair and not wanting

167

to give up. A staff lady came over 'You lost something?' 'My key,' I said. 'It has to be here.' She kneeled and studied the ground. At that precise moment I saw the glitter of the key. 'Ah!' she exclaimed, sticking out her tongue. 'Determination. Never give up. I'm your lucky lady.' She sure is. Her plucky words warmed me every time I faltered on the long road around Britain. (Ryton, May 10, 1995)

RICHARD SECCOMBE

He asked me this: Where have the visionaries from the sixties gone? He didn't have the answer. I said that one of them is standing in front of me, the headmaster of Hartland Small School in north Devon. Typically, he bellowed out his laughter, then boyishly shrugged his shoulders. 'I suppose we all want to give something to the future, something that will last.' Alternative education is Richard's life work, struggling on shoe strings and working to influence main-stream thinking – modern primary school education owes a lot to such people. Richard cannot be pigeon-holed – an idealist and immensely practical with his vision, a lover of fast cars, an avid stamp collector, a Quaker. He is known and loved by thousands of children from his lifetime's work on the educational fringe. They are his family. He lives by himself a few doors down from the school, a small alternative to the fashion for large schools, large classes and commuter children. I could say so much about Richard, a fire-walker, never tiring until he drops from exhaustion; a complex man, not always easy to get along with but always a friend. I am reminded of those solitary white fritillaries in water meadows which, by contrast, light up their many purple-bloomed cousins. (Hartland, May 3, 1995)

* * * *

QUEST'S END – FOR SALE (sign outside a bungalow between Stoke and Hartland, Devon, May 3, 1995)

GREEN TOWNSHIPS

Craig Templar comes from Cape Town. I met him briefly at Bradwell Mill, a smallholding in North Devon. I mistook him for a traveller: the narrow face and stringy beard, hair tied back, and both wrists pleated with brass torcs. I thought he was

English until he gently stretched his vowels. England he found full of contradictions. 'There are all the answers for me here, especially with alternative technologies, but I am devastated to see the lack of trees.' His dream is to start a tree nursery in an African township. 'I'd like to live in a township but that's fifteen years down the road.' In the meantime he wants to introduce the greenwood skills to the African: coppicing, pole-lathes, steam bending, renewing old skills to empower people on a local scale. 'Wait a minute,' I said. 'That's what they're trying to do here' (Barnstaple, May 7, 1995)

TRAVELLER – JOHN B.

I knew you in the sixties. You are probably dead now. I remember you first walking back from the pub and seeing this old man with a suitcase standing in the orange sodium lamp-post glow and reading a newspaper, cricking your head to squint through your thick glasses. You probably had a cigarette in the corner of your mouth, making me think of Harry Lime. I can still see the moths flying around your head. I was sixteen. Perhaps I thought you were another eccentric like the old hunch-backed woman who pushed a pram with junk in it to the Saturday market and pushed it back again. She owned land that was worth millions of pounds to property speculators, but she refused to sell. I can't remember exactly how I came into your life, perhaps I had been out exploring the back lanes and had stumbled into your garden thinking that it was part of the wood. I may have wondered about the ivy growing up the drainpipes or the bamboos shooting up through the gravel drive. I thought the house was deserted for there were newspapers stacked up the inside of all the windows. I still had not made the connection that the old man under the lamp-post carried a suitcase of newspapers, the early editions of the nationals which the night train brought to our town.

I sneaked into your garden many times exploring, curious-eyed; I saw the stone sun-dial covered with ivy, the glasshouse heaving with brambles. In the garage I wondered about the Rolls Royce stacked on bricks and covered in cobwebs and ivy contoured on the chassis. I was intrigued by the meandering garden paths, Edwardian style, the ghosts of shrubberies and a swimming pool colourful with floating lilies. I had stumbled into a garden, between a wild place and a nature reserve. Looking back I see that it was a sort of haven, not only for plants and insects but for you.

I remember climbing to the top of a wildling birch tree, leaning over until it bent over and I fell, not to the ground but to another birch tree, and I did it again, travelling from one part of the wood to another. With my red scarf I felt like Rupert Bear. I was in a tree when I first saw you in your garden. This old man, in his fifties then, smiled with the butt of an embassy cigarette in his mouth (you always kept the silver foil in place in the cigarette packet). The well-born voice, soft and gentle, without any demands, surprised me. Was I not trespassing? Then I saw your camera and tripod, focussed on a flower. I could hardly believe that someone could stand still for minutes to photograph flowers and insects, the perfection of long-horn beetles dusted with pollen... You said that you let everything grow so the wild flowers would come. That was in 1966, a voice in the wilderness.

You amazed me with your memory. If I mentioned a war-time incident, say the Battle of Britain, you not only knew the number of missions but the names of the pilots and where they came from. If I mentioned a flower you knew its host insects, their Latin names and the names of their predators. I returned many times, bringing friends and you were always there photographing some small-legged beauty in a flower. You were my curiousity, half a gentleman, half a tramp; your clothes, though well-made, were always threadbare. Then one day I came in for tea. The front door was not locked but you had to push past the mound of unopened letters on the floor. I say floor but it was a carpet of letters pressed down like pages in a book. There were no walls, only stacks of newspapers with tunnels between them and tea chests piled on top of each other or the corner of a wardrobe poking out like some foreign object. I was awed by the chaos and your total acceptance of it. Tea was brewed on a paraffin stove and then you showed me your house. I could not believe it, a house made of newspapers, and only the bed appeared above the surface, and half of that was stacked with letters and books. On a bedside table was a brass plate with cigarette ash shaped into a cone a foot high. I thought it a work of art.

Then there were times I went to your house and you were not there. I poked my way through the rooms, rummaging under the newspapers, finding a drink's cabinet with bottles of wartime Dimple whisky, To His Majesty The King, unopened. I found books, wonderful old books with engravings of sailing ships, an early edition of Livingstone's journey to Africa. You were like darkest Africa to me though I did not know why at the time. Then I began to suspect that the house was indeed a tomb of some kind, and the papers a shroud that had been placed over something, or someone. I found darker books, books on torture, Marquis de Sade. I learnt that you had lived there with your aged mother, and that the house had been a smart Edwardian interior until her death, but that had been many years ago. The papers had preserved it, as it was then. Goodness knows what else was hidden in that house. I did in fact take some of the bottles of spirit and I regretted that. Some years later, after I married, I gave you a book of another tramp naturalist, W.H. Hudson, as a kind of compensation... You accepted that without blame, accepting both the foolishness and greediness of erring youth. You had not changed in fifteen years, only I, still unknowing, had grown more like you, yet not you.

Four nights ago, well into my forty third year and fifteen years since I last saw you, you appeared in a dream standing smoking a cigarette at the end of a frozen trail. I panicked and ran but you had seen me and I had seen you. I tried to lose all trace and scent of this contact, running through butcher's shops with the smell of blood on the ground, but it was too late the police had caught up with me. In dreams I was always running away from you. It was going to come out. Shame. That people will condemn me for once I shared a bed with you, not sex but tenderness, one lonely person to another, for at that time I believed that I was impotent and no earthly good for any woman. You were like a grandfather to me, accepting my unspoken confusion, listening, and far away from the sign-posted world. You glowed, both light and dark, like the smoke curling up from the end of your cigarette. Both a warning and an inspiration. There is in you something valuable and I only have an inkling of what it is. It's almost as if you are both a blessing and a disease. And I run away from this.

You were the first artist I met, yet you would never have called yourself that. You were a wild-life photographer, a sort of chronicler of the wayside, a native garden maker. You needed that haven in the sixties brave new world. In you I saw my first reflection and it frightened me. This wilderness is a place of uncertainty, I might easily lose my way, become a literal tramp or fall into some chasm of vulnerablity. This is the danger, yet without meeting it I will not find my way. This strange boy still wants to be listened to, to be held, to have a protector. I could not share these things with my father. You became like a spiritual father to me. I carried the shame of your tenderness for thirty years. Some years ago I heard that they had bulldozed your house. That you had only gone away.

With your blue eyes I see the world. In your arms I am carried. It's like that song, 'Stand By Me'.

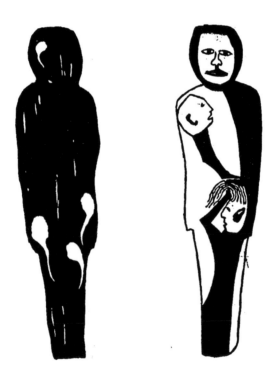

TREVELOG

What comes first is the picture of the single stand of alder at the far edge of the field, by the sharp line of bracken and the thick, lush grass of the bog with water peppermint. I had emerged from the coppiced alder, long overgrown, but this solitary alder with a field of meadow buttercups between us held me, made me aware of standing by the wood. I can still see the enormous boles of toppled elms along one side, bleached white against the grass, the cardinal beetle winging it from my open fingers. I can understand the contradiction that a few minutes in paradise, in timelessness, can keep me going all day.

What can I say? I should be a poet and distil the life juices into a small white space. I prefer to meander. Dear Nikko, four-year-old sage, strong as rock, hand in hand, through the long fine grass we went looking for grass snakes, stepping carefully over hundreds of marsh marigolds, luxuriating in this unimproved, forgotten corner. With Tom we turned over stones, pulled back black plastic, found sheep skulls, he asked questions and I answered them. Is it a slug? It's true, isn't it? There were lots more questions, all important at the time.

Woodcraft Folk presses many buttons, the time, every bit of it, organised, the wappenshaw inspections, the endless queues, the calls for seconds, the organised campsite fires. I awoke early one morning with the thought: this is how we live our lives, completely programmed from morning to night, or the opposite, lots and lots of time and never the time to get on with things. I could run away from this organised adult world into timelessness and I know that this is not my way. The hunting ground is where my buttons get pressed, it's where people meet. At times on the camp, my left leg went numb. I started disappearing – I returned when I stood up for something. 'What do the children want?' I said. Do you love me honey? Honey I love you but I just can't smile. That's what the little girls wanted.

The picture of Mark Angus as the dwarf with someone behind him, blindfolded and in a sack, feeding him custard with a spoon. I laughed until I cried, my little man in me happy, revelling with enjoyment. I am a holy fool when he is awake and looking out. This feeding with spoons is what we do to our children, feeding them co-operation, purity of mind, native Indian teachings of suppleness of hare, spirit of eagles – but the hunting ground of life, looking for meaning, work, love, the warrior spirit, the conflicts, the ability to keep boundaries are left out. Christianity does the same, emphasising loving others, being selfless, pure and we grow up feeling that we are full of holes, full of trash, full of stunted things that don't belong in this adult world. I have this wonderful dwarf in me, impotent but wishing he was a tiger. He is wicked, selfish, deeply loving, lustful, unworldly and knee deep in chaos and very wise. I am getting into my preacher mode. What I want to say is that despite all the organising manias, the love of children at the camp kept breaking through, taking my eyes away from the broken branches and seeing the sun shining behind them. (Woodcraft Camp, Trevelog, May 1991)

FORTINGALL

I came to this village in western Perthshire to see the ancient yew tree, reputed by botanical savants to be the oldest living vegetation in Europe. I came with a glowing feeling of expectation as if (and I was) bowing to the earth at this special place. A red squirrel – the first I had ever seen – bounded along the parapet of the bridge smurmuring under its breath with indignation and leaped onto the ubiquitous sycamore. Almost at once I sensed that I was in a place that had been loved for a very long time – for what other word can convey that steadiness, fullness and harmony between the river, mountain crags and pines; the cottages and farms appeared rooted to that spacious glen. The remnants of the yew are enclosed by a stone wall and iron railings next to the church. The antiquary Pennant measured their girth at 56 feet in the 18th century. I sat beneath the tree but could not settle. The brooding intensity of that place, the funereal ivy and the voices of other visitors catapulted me back over the railings. Then I noticed that the enclosure was also a graveyard of the Stewarts of Garth, clan chiefs of old. The head-piece of a Celtic cross peered over the top of a neighbouring wall. I liked that association but I could not say why. Inside the church (and the wave of mustiness) I discovered the 7th century hand-bell, with lustred and hoof-horned tones, and I easily imagined St. Ced, the founder, standing in his woollen robe by the yew (and it was ancient then) and ringing the Christian message of hope in this tree-singing glen. The building of his church next to the yew would have been an act of respect, for did not those old Irish Scots crown the kings, accept fealty from their lords under such trees? How else could a tree, reputed to be 5,000 years old, have survived?

I cycled down the rocky gates of Glen Lyon along the quiet mountain road to the Bridge of Balgie. The young leaves of the broad-leaved trees shimmered on the shoulders of the mountain. The youthful waters of Glen Lyon charged down the gorge. I cycled on air. It all made sense; the aligned megalithic stones in the fields, why the Celtic missionaries chose Fortingall to worship God, as others had done for thousands of years before them, and spanning this time a single old tree. They responded (I responded) to what our senses showed us: the landscape temple of Glen Lyon. I mused on this until I saw in the distance two figures sitting on a wall. They had their backs to the gorge. Both were women. I looked for the car or bicycles and didn't see them. I wondered who they were so far along a remote road. Then I saw they were completely dressed in white, and strangest of all, wore white crocheted hats tapering to a point. I waved as I passed. Neither moved or acknowledged me. They continued smiling. One appeared very beautiful, younger than the other. Both touched me with their tranquillity. I had the impression they were listening to the water. They were not there when I returned ten minutes later. No car had passed me. I could not imagine them walking down into that gorge or up into the mountains. Neither did I pass them on that road back to the village. The doubt came that night when I closed my eyes. Perhaps, it said, I had looked into the eyes of angels and they had smiled back at me. (Fortingall, May 27, 1995)

SUMMER

DOWN THE GARDEN PATH

I have always thought of potting sheds being outside the world, outside time, outside the whole business of making ends meet. The beauty of potting sheds is that they don't have to make sense. They are generally concealed, along with the compost heap, down the garden path and, though I have known some which resembled three-star accommodation with hot and cold water piped in, tea-makers and carpets, generally they are rattle traps, the destination of odds and ends and a paradise on earth for spiders. Already I can see the door, wooden and on a latch and warped by damp so that it doesn't shut properly. The mile-a-minute Russian vine (*Polygonum baldschuanicum*) is covering half the window (which doesn't open) and the damson tree screens another quarter. They should have been cut back months ago, but they are still there. Open the door and the web on the outside breaks but the spider, a fat diadem, makes a new one each time. It's dim inside even though it's daylight. The floor-boards squeak and some sixth sense guides the feet over the rotten section to the wooden platform by the narrow strip of staging. It's the warmest place to stand in the winter.

The reminders to prune the roses, prepare to do battle with slugs over the hostas, get more tea bags, are tacked to the elm cladding above the window. There's a new rotation plan for the vegetable garden, side by side with an ancient, curling card pinned there by the previous owner; 'Irish Peach' and 'Beauty of Bath' are the only two apple varieties still legible. The eyes have adjusted to the owl-light by now, and glints of dull, polished metal appear slowly beside the pile of oily rags. They belong to the wooden handles hung off the floor, each one supported by two wooden pins at hip height for safety. They all have histories but most were bought at the flea markets where such features as a tread on a spade (essential) and a turned ash handle on a rake can still be found.

This order contrasts dramatically with the rear of the shed which resembles Dante's *Inferno* on dustbin day. Everything that might be useful one day finally arrives here. It is the last stop before the garden fire or foundations for a new path: broom handles, hoover shafts, oil cans, old carpets, net curtains, hose-pipes, stakes, sou'westers, polystyrene casings and much more co-exist happily and are lorded over by unspeakably big spiders. Somehow, despite the chaos, nothing seems to get lost.

Walk farther round to the right and the staging begins. The clay and plastic pots are built into miniature Towers of Babel and they lean precariously over the mound of potting mixture, seed boxes and lollipop sticks for pricking out. Next is the special box, full of very useful things, especially files for sharpening hoes (it makes 200% difference) and the small wooden spade called a 'man'. This, or something like it, was used by the 19th century navvies when they worked on 12-man piece-rate contracts building canals and railways. They used this miniature spade to scrape the clay from the shovels as they worked – they reckoned it was worth the equivalent of a man's labour, hence the name.

At the far end of the staging is a kettle – yes, electricity has arrived here! There is a collection of waif and stray mugs and cups, three glass jars for sugar, dried milk and tea bags. Squeezed under the staging is a paraffin stove for really cold days and one wooden stool. There are few things to equal the pleasure of sitting down when one is tired. Back to the door; the loose mattock can go into the water butt to tighten up the head. It really is time to cut back the Russian vine and to get more tea bags – but still, there is no need to hurry. There is all the time in the world. (This first appeared in Somerset and Avon Life)

MARGARET TOWNEND

She described herself as a born gardener, a constructor, a builder with trees, flowers and earth. The genes ran in her family line – Sir Joseph Paxton, the designer of Crystal Palace, was her great great uncle. In her own words, she ran a spotless upper-class bread and breakfast establishment in Widcombe, conforming outwardly to her customers' needs, but secretly in her back garden she indulged her great passion, gardening; a place where plants could express themselves without interference or conforming to modern society. Over two thousand plants intermingled on one third of an acre. She knew every one of them and arranged them the way she liked: a series of constantly changing pictures.

'I like having beautiful things around me. Whenever I feel depressed I go out and buy another plant. I couldn't live without my garden. Like most people, my garden is my retreat but it is also my achievement. (She pauses). I had an allotment when I was nine at Barnes Common. We actually lived in a top-floor flat on Shepherd's Bush road. I had window boxes there. Every Sunday I would cultivate my allotment with the help of all the other gentlemen and I used to come home with carrots and flowers and God knows what else. It had to stop when I won a scholarship to a grammar school; but then I had a school garden for the whole time I was there. It was only about four feet wide and six feet long. I only grew flowers. That was my first garden. It became monotonous because I won the gardening prize every year.

'I suppose it goes back before then when we lived in a house in Cricklewood. That was during the war. Both my sister and I were sent to a convent to be out of London and it was a very high Anglican convent so on feast days you had flowers which were ripped to pieces with all the petals spilled in front of the procession. My mother sent some paeonies in a box which the Reverend Mother made me open. I can remember having a tantrum on the spot when they started pulling the petals off. I stood there screaming that they were killing my plant. I can't have been more than about five or six years then. My aunt bought me my first gardening book at the age of seven. I have still got it. The very first one is, 'Where the flowers come from'; the second, 'Where did your garden grow?' It cost the grand total of 8s 6d. I have now a library of about one hundred gardening books...

* * * *

'In 1964 this garden was derelict. The back was literally non-existent. There were about a dozen old fruit trees, an ancient lilac in the corner, absolutely enormous, and there was this bramble, the Himalayan Giant. It can grow twelve feet in one year and every time it hits the ground it roots again and then goes on growing. The garden really evolved rather than me sitting down and making a big plan of it. Next door lived old Mr Ottaway, the head gardener for Major Locke at Rainbow Wood. Mr Ottaway would always give me bits of advice or pop over cuttings and say 'Have you tried...' or 'Don't put that there dear, that would be too big.' And there was me looking at this cutting six inches long and thinking would it ever be too big. The front garden consists mainly of the cuttings he gave me... Each corner of the garden is a different picture and it changes each season. I consciously create pictures. There is a picture in one corner of the garden at one time, then the whole thing moves onto a different side and then it will come round to the original one... My garden is quadrupled planted; there are the evergreens and shrubs which everybody can see but underneath are masses of bulbs which I have overplanted with herbaceous, and I also plant a few annuals in the spots you can't do anything else with...

'My mother bought me this tree paeony fifteen years ago. I still have the bill. It cost £3.50 and in those days that was very very expensive. I tried for seven years to get past the leaf stage...once it was on the way out and I tried all sorts of things to revive it without success. So I dug it up, someone called me, and I left it out in the grass in November for a week and it got frosted and I still couldn't throw it away. So I picked up a spade, went round to the front garden and opened a bit of soil up, literally like you do for a cabbage, dropped it in and trod on it, chucked some peat over it and left it. Now I have this fantastic tree paeony... The flowers are dinner-plate size, of the softest softest yellow with the edges of the petals all ragged with a pink blush and a deep pink centre. The flowers are so enormous and heavy that every stem is held up with a bamboo.

* * *

'I don't use herbicides if I can help it. It sends the garden into imbalance as far as I can see. You can pull out most weeds if you don't want them. If I use herbicides on things – and the birds eat all kinds of seed – the birds will eat the herbicides and so will the bees. Nature is a balance and if you don't put back into the soil what you take out of it you end up with a dead piece of ground. So I make my own compost and only use organic fertilisers. I use sulphate of ammonia on the lawns but that's the only chemical, I think. This again comes from Mr Ottaway's influence. He was a very old gardener; he didn't like all these new-fangled things. He just didn't. Soapy water for the black spot and Jeye's fluid or coal dust; if you spread coal dust over the rose bed in the spring the sulphur in the coal dust would kill off the fungus spores. He used to allow Jeye's fluid but this is also based on coal-tar which is a natural thing. You have to put the organic stuff back into the garden because you have got to have your insects there, good and bad. You have got to have your bad ones to keep the good ones. I honestly have very few pests in the garden. I don't have any greenfly. I have masses of birds and thousands of ladybirds. The leatherjackets attract all the birds and they don't do that enormous amount of damage. The black-birds are very efficient at pulling them out. I don't use slug bait unless I have to, otherwise the slugs eat the bait and the toads eat the slugs... I use beer so the slugs go to the beer, don't ask me why, and if the toads eat the slugs all they do is get drunk. I like it natural and my whole garden is one of formal informality. The basic layout is formal with the terraces and trees in the focal spots. They are like the bones, the skeleton on which my flowering plants, the roses and shrubs hang, because without the solid mass of the evergreen the rest would just look a mess.

'I don't like hybrids in my garden. Once you start hybridising things they lose something. I don't really grow a rose which has no scent, even 'Iceberg' has a slight scent. Okay, I have a bit of the old mother earth in me. I like my plants to grow in their natural state. You can't really improve on nature...nature herself has weeded out all the wrong strains. And a lot of the hybrids are really very weak, especially the hybrid tea roses, so prone to blackspot. It will go, "Oooooh! Blackspot, I'm dying." One or two of my plants I talk to very sharply. "If you don't flower this year you're out..." But I will take cuttings off things if I think they are dying. I can't be ruthless. If something gets too big I feel like a murderess going out there and chopping it down. This winter nearly killed me. I really felt that I had lost some very dear old friends in the garden. My standard fuchsias, which I love and I have grown myself ...everyone of them in the greenhouse is a goner. It took me two months to summon up enough courage to get in there and sort them out. It was a gorgeous afternoon in May, I will never forget it. The sun was shining and I thought, don't be a silly bitch; so I got hold of the wheelbarrow, took it to the doors of the greenhouse and looked at this carnage and thought, right we'll start from one end and work on through and see what has happened. And funnily enough, I had left it so long there were some shoots coming from the bases of one or two plants.

* * * *

'I had an uncle and aunt who lived at Writtle just outside Chelmsford. I am very fond of my uncle Bill, a super man, absolutely gorgeous. The whole family knew I liked plants and he used to take me out and show me the wild orchids, primroses, violets and ferns. They had a small cottage garden and they had just planted a plum tree. In those days you could dig things up because not many people would dig things up from the woods, so he dug up these orchids, violets and primroses and they were planted around the plum tree. This was my garden. I had ferns there, too. It was all wild flowers, vetches and things like that. I still love primroses and I still love violets. How about that! I have white violets, pale blue violets, great big dark blowsy violets, but the magenta ones are very unusual. I love clematis and that stems from the time at Cricklewood; the house next door had two old ladies in it and they had this gorgeous clematis which would travel over the fence. I love clematis. I have 28 in the garden now.

'I love fuchsias and that associates with my great grandmother because during the war I was evacuated to my grandmother and she would take me to see my great grandmother. She had a house in Barry, and along the side of this house was a conservatory. I was always dressed up in my best with a big sash in my hair, and put into ringlets, and I was told to behave. After a walk along the sea-front my great grandmother would poke me in the back with her stick and say, 'Shoulders back, deportment child.' I would have a large knickerbocker glory and be marched back and grandmother and great grandmother would sit in the living room talking and I would be sent out to find grandpa. I would go through the conservatory to get into the garden. She had fuschias and I would pop all the fuschias. Do you know how to pop fuschias? And then I would join great grandpa in the shed where he was allowed to smoke. I have never thought of all these associations of plants. That really is strange. I do have a love for standard fuschias. And I love clematis. I hope to God I am not recreating my childhood! The rest of the gardening just grew. Actually my great great uncle is Sir Joseph Paxton, the man who designed Crystal Palace. He started out as the head gardener at Chatsworth... I love making gardens. My family say that I am a throwback. If I had to leave this garden all I should do would be to start another. I am a constructor I think, a builder. I have the most vivid imagination. I can look at a squat, nasty town garden and turn it into a leafy paradise in about three years.

'My talent is for seeing something and being able to produce my vision or my imagination into reality. For me it is not difficult... I used to make indoor gardens for people. I started with Uncle Bill with these primroses and moss and violets and stones and bowls and catkins – these were little indoor plate gardens. I'd love doing it, little houses, little Chinese pagodas. My gardens never had any nasties in them. They were always places of tranquillity and peace. I did one once about fairies coming out at night and binding up broken flower stems with cobwebs (giggles). The spiders were their little minions who would run up and down these flower stems, weaving webs to hold the flowers up, bees coming with their honey to stick the petals on. I must have been about nine. If I see a tree that has been broken by vandals I could really screw that vandal's neck, all those year's of growing and you have done this. That's why it broke my heart having to chop down the twelve foot pittosporum after this hard winter. I could only do it on sunny days. I couldn't do it on a dull day, it would be too much like a funeral. I feel that this year my garden is out of balance like a one-armed man, for I have lost this beautiful pittosporum...it takes so long to get that back.

* * * *

(She says that she is not well and could go into a state of shock and die overnight) 'I don't live in the past. I live in the future. What I have created if somebody else wants to enjoy that's fine by me. It's no longer mine. I now have to create something new, for me. I am not really sentimental, up to a point. But if anybody ever buys this house I will give them a glossary of the weeds and say leave everything else alone... I don't impose my will on my plants. I don't ask my plants to conform. My garden is the other side of me you could say. I spend all my life being hostess, being efficient, looking tidy, conforming to what my guests expect from a landlady who runs an upper-class guest house. So my garden is allowed to do its own thing. I don't really care what other people think. I have no wish to impose any human requirements, especially modern day society upon them. I keep things in gentle order, trimming them back but I never interfere. I want them to grow naturally, waiting to see what will happen. I love them to intermingle... (She touches a viburnum leaf) Now this is a he-plant, hard and irregular but this choisya and garryia are she's but don't ask me why. I have never thought. I suppose they have more delicate leaves. All the flowers are she's. I was brought up to expect men to be strong and solid (laughter). (July, 1982)

CONNECTED?

These two incidents make me laugh and I find them perverse. On the front page of the Somerset Standard is a picture of a traveller's vehicle. The young travellers want to be left in peace before they continue their journey away from mainstream society; their residential neighbours complain about noise, possible health risks, stray dogs and social disruption...

On the back page is a picture of a couple with their children. They are beaming from the cab of their mobile home and are about to travel the world after selling their house and giving up their jobs. The report quotes envious neighbours wishing that they had the courage to undertake such a journey.

The second incident is more subtle. One Sunday I cycled to The Talbot Inn, at Mells, and the moment I stepped onto the soft carpet of the lounge bar two things happened; several people stopped drinking and looked towards the floor or, more precisely, at my trousers tucked into my socks. Two minutes later a group of racer cyclists entered the bar with bulbous yellow helmets, floral lycra tights above hairy thighs and racing shirts more like mini-skirts. I watched them come in. No-one batted an eyelid. (1993)

ABSENT HEALING

Simbana, my sister, said this is true. A woman who heals at a distance was asked to put a certain man on her list. He had damaged a leg in a car accident. This she did and practised her absent healing. A month later, while driving in the Cotswolds, she saw a man hitch-hiking. Normally she never stopped but this time made an exception. Now a curious thing happened; the man looked carefully at her and said that he had seen her before but could not say where. She remembered that he had limped into the car and asked him about it. He had damaged his leg in a car accident. Out of curiosity she asked when, and he said about a month before. She asked him his name – the same man on her list! (July 12, 1976)

JUNE CHANGES

Expansion! The whole world slips and slides to keep up – wolf spider with long front legs guards silken tent teeming with young spiders – yellow underwing moth flashes yellow below bark-grey wings – children use conker thinnings as missiles – field maple leaves covered with small red galls; snout-nosed galls on wych elm – first red admiral sips nectar from escallonia bush in Bath – hemlock grows tall and lacery by first week, in flower by third – grizzled skipper wings it at South Stoke – tadpoles have four legs – first juvenile wasp forages among cotoneaster flowers – *Volucella pellucens*, a large pied hoverfly, on viper's bugloss (*Echium vulgare*) – small tortoiseshell larvae munch stinging nettles – hawker dragonfly (*Libellula depressa*) mate in tandems – thousands of small black pollen beetles on the rampage, heads down in flowers – garden spider webs starred with whitefly – moon-eye daisies, red poppies and yellow stonecrop brighten dry waysides – smell of flowers in the rain while walking in Tellisford Wood – bonfire clouds of pollen erupt from pine trees (*Pinus sylvestris*) – a wolf spider carries live young on her abdomen – as elder flowers fade, field maple wings redden – young fruits on blackthorn – St. Mark's fly in dead embrace on seeding cow parsley – baby grass snake is an animated shoelace on hot road.

WALKING BY THE CAM RIVER

I take up my pen reluctantly, partly drawn by the Englishness, the English walking together on a Sunday morning, partly fearful that recapturing the spontaneity of the morning will prove elusive. Brown coats and trousers, green jumpers, small, well-behaved children, pleasant smiles without conversation, and the grey, brooding sky – a typical start from a restored English village of Combe Hay, elegant, subdued, everything in its place. Watch out for the lion, I tell the little girl Sammy. You can see its yellow eyes glinting in the bushes or find the big paw marks in the mud by the stream. It's true I tell another child. 'Garbage', interjects my youngest son Michael, but he still plays the fantasy. It escaped from the travelling zoo visiting the school at South Stoke. The police searched all night but could not recapture it. 'It's probably not very hungry,' I say...

This is Range Rover country; several beetled past us, all men helping to cut the cricket pitch from the corner of a hay mead, striking a privileged note for most of this walk. I collected seeding grasses wondering about names, knowing only cocksfoot for sure. The commonest things are still unknown to me. I stood apart with most of the adults as the children paddled in the river. I resisted the temptation of doing what I wanted the children to do, to explore and turn over stones. This well-intentioned playing masks a controlling attitude. Combe Hay bridge, dinky and dating to the 17th century, carried us into the water meadow − and out of the blue-green grass scuttled thick, long moths, bark-grey wings until they flew flashing erratic yellows. A yellow underwing, Paul Somers said, and this is the first time I have made this connection. Mayflies, damsel flies performed their duties on flower stalks and trembling hands of little girls, nearly all by this time weighted down by enormous bunches of grasses and flowers. The shiny prints of alder leaves, many gall-pimple villages, bow down to the river with secluded ratty holes, fallen trees. 'An island,' says Susan Berkley, 'heaven for my child.' Ben, my son, sees a square shape protruding from the bank. 'Pirates,' he says and we understand instantly. The deer prints are in the mud. 'It's the lion!' says a boy. Sammy shrinks to her mother. 'It might be near.' Someone points out the forty or so speckled grey caterpillars munching nettle leaves, their progress marked with silken webs spotted with small tortoiseshell dung. A handsome, black-speckled-spider-eating-wasp eludes my insect book. I identify a spectacular frog hopper, red and black-banded (Cercopis vulnerata). It was there, in the same place, an hour later. Some people sit on the uncut slopes for picnic; suddenly I picture frogs in britches, out walking and hunting, and carrying off children tussled by their legs ready for the pot. I laugh at this absurdity and yet it endures. I walk with Paul. 'How long have you been interested in insects?' For as long as he could remember, collecting larvae of six-spotted burnet moths and keeping them in jars until they pupated and hatched. 'I knew more then when I was eleven than I do now.' I understand. 'They are curiously neglected,' he said. He carries his child on his shoulder. 'I had the freedom then to go off for a half day on my bicycle. They expected to see me again.' Times have changed, but perhaps there is more publicity. 'You've got to finish the story,' says Michael… 'So I was stuck to the ground. Pins and needles skated down my neck. Are you out hunting?' said the old man sitting in the tree. 'Stop there! Pizza time.' (June 24, 1990)

SWAN SONG

In the children's park at Swanage an ancient couple shuffled past the trampoline. 'You'll have to take your shoes off if you want to go there,' said the woman to her husband.
(June 28, 1995)

A DAY IN TELLISFORD WOOD

A strange day this, lovely for the work of milling green oak posts and batons from logs, and an emerging host of little connections, darting, disappearing at various speeds like the flies in the shafts of sunlight. Ken Day and myself, Greg Tucker from the vicarage at Chew Stoke, met for breakfast at Wood Cottage, late starting but it didn't matter. Greg is bristly and pony-tailed, his skin tired until he smiles, and then his forty five years rejuvenate as laughter lines: he has fallen in love – at his age, he says – with a Californian girl at the Universal Peace Dance camp in Dorset the week before. No alcohol, tobacco or drugs, he tells us in his almost fluty voice, just the energy of opening up to other people in the dances. Outside the high blue sky is stacked with billowing clouds; two kestrels appear in the oaks, love trailing it through the branches, one calling plaintively to the other. From rough cut oak trunks, we used the double chainsaw to mill out the oak posts. 'That's your oak,' says Ken, smiling under his straw hat, his cheeks flushing cherubically.

Greg and I shoulder the posts in a sling, slipping and sliding along the still wet woodland rides, past the male ferns, miniature cycads, and the arching heads of big woodland sedges. Greg says he is a painter as well as a wood person; he helped to start Tree Aid, with Ken and others, ten years ago, the charity funding community tree planting in the Sahel. I talked about writing and gardening, the uncertainty of it all... I felt like a donkey and a bird of paradise, one needing the other; too much earth and plodding and I lose my wings, too much air and I wonder who I am, where I am, what I'm doing. (Ken interjects that that dynamic can never be sorted out but it's our nature to attempt to do so.) Helen Adam, Ken's girlfriend and very pregnant, appeared with a thermos of tea and we sat in the clearing sipping from plastic cups and watching the free flight, trust and fall of red admiral butterflies, newly arrived from North Africa. One lands on Helen's forehead, opening and closing its wings. Absolutely amazing. 'I've never seen that in my

life before,' I say. 'It likes our third eye,' says Ken. It dances with
another red admiral then lands on Helen's hair. It's from the
Sahara. It's never seen people before.' It lands on Greg's forehead.
He tries hard to see the wings but cannot.

Greg and I hauled more wood in the afternoon and we kept
returning to this point: that it is when we stand in our uniqueness,
our uncertainty, our own faltering voice, that change is possible. 'I
remember,' said Greg, 'when I painted this picture, not a big one,
but a picture which I did for me; and whatever others thought
about it, it would make no difference to this feeling. It was then
that I accepted myself as a painter.' He kept pressing me on the
point of – what's the use of having a dream if you don't do
anything about it. I said dreams create obligations or they lie dormant in the soil. 'It's by owning what I see, by what I feel, what I
do, my physical actions, that I ground the divine in my life. This is
just as important as the dream and the eternal.' This is the point
he wanted to make, don't be frightened of embodying who I am.
Then came the clouds of ear-piercing wood dust. The red admiral
stayed perched at one end of the plank while we milled the other...
(June 24, 1993)

A NIGHT IN TELLISFORD WOOD

The wood skirts the black cattle field, and the specimen oak trees,
stag-headed and splendid, are the ones Ken Day photographed in
spring, summer, autumn and winter. On mid-summer's night,
warm and still and with stars shining in the gaps of the branches,
the trees are remote, another country. Each step Susan White and I
took over the cropped grass, hard, dry and crunchy, carried not only
our groundsheet, blankets and rucksack with brandy and tea, but
also the beginnings of a distant stirring unease. Would we find the
path in the corner of the field where it drops into six-foot bracken
or the badger trail cutting up the wooded slopes? The torchlight
bounced off the gloom, soft and diffused except where bushes threw
darker shadows across the path. Everywhere, after the big storm,
were fallen trees, some leaning on standing ones, and there were
great hunt-and-find caterpillar tracks driven at sharp angles across
the wood. I felt safer on the track the deer used cutting up the old
wood bank with a sharp, thirty feet slide to the stream below. At
the end of this ride, beside the straight-drawn beech, on a flat part,
we made camp. 'My hearing is stretched out like radar,' says

Suzie, sitting in bed and turning her head to catch sounds. For a moment the uneasiness evaporates; cars pootle in the midnight distance but here, in the middle of Tellisford Wood, the silence hangs along with the criss-crossing branches mazed around and above us, a strange buffer zone from the world outside.

The ground is hard,. I can't sleep and lie awake listening to the ever emerging background of stealthily broken twigs, the first snuffl-ings in the leaves... a sudden, pumping whistling noise rings sharply through the wood. It's a screech owl. We both sit up. Our hearing reaches out into the silence and picks out something bigger moving in the stream below. A creaking sound cuts through the still air, wood straining against wood, finding the resistance... CRASH! The silence thunders and our hearts well up. A tree has fallen down, not fifty feet away, and panic tingles every nerve end. Is it not Friday 13th today? Some unspeakable presence in the wood is looking for revenge after the storm. It's too dangerous to speak but the bicycle pump bird screeches, circling in the dark and sounding louder than before. I can't sleep now and I lie down looking for forgetfulness and thinking only one thought. It's not possible for two trees to fall down. Time flies, who knows where. Stars still shine in the high branches. 'Wake up,' says Suzie. I need no encouragement, her voice, anxious and whispering, directs me to the trees on the slopes above us. Tiny twinkling lights are moving along the branches, as if each one is being carried. I can't make them out properly. I stare and see black lines in the lights moving slowly and around each other. People with torches? Bandits? No, this is not happening. This is England. Immediately another thought arrives, the unspeakable presence has found our trail. 'Glow worms,' I say and I don't believe it. Nor does the bicycle pump bird, screeching again, pausing then screeching some-where above us now. 'What is it? And in the far distance come tinkling sounds, each one clear and distinct, clamouring the edges of the silence and the still, lustrous light. 'They're cow bells,' I say relieved.

'It's the moon,' says Suzie. 'She's calm and thoughtful.' Of course, I understand now. I can explain the twinkling lights but not the feeling that we have strayed too deep into this wood, at a vulner-able time soon after the storm, and only our innocent intentions placed us fifty feet away from a falling tree. (Tellisford Wood, Somerset, July 13, 1990)

TREGASTEL

The marquee appeared overnight next to a pantechnicon lorry
with CIRQUE DE FRANCE painted on it. I paid the ten franc
entrance fee to a bright-eyed teenage girl happy in a pink ballerina dress and shoes. I had no idea what to expect. A big man
with a satiny waistcoat and tight black trousers stepped into the
ring. He cracked his whip. Immediately half a dozen chickens
scrambled out of a box and circled around him somehow
synchronising their steps. He cracked his whip. They jumped
together. They did it every time. His sequin-spangled wife made
a goat stand on a box, then step onto a smaller box and so on
until it balanced on a biscuit tin. The ballerina pedalled a giant
ball in front of us; she pedalled standing, lying on her back, on
one leg. The two sons lifted extraordinary weights and balanced
tables on their noses and chins. I clapped forgetting any mis-
givings for this homespun entertainment. The man reappeared
with a mongoloid boy. I know people disapprove of this word
but I want you to see this boy. He walked awkwardly across the
stage. He climbed onto the cupped hands – and with a flick they
balanced hand to hand, first the right, then the left, then just
with their fingers, the boy at ease, a perfect balance between
them. They radiated joy. I realised then they were father and
son. The tears came unbidden, flooding my eyes, cheeks and
mouth. I couldn't stop crying. Afterwards I wandered among the
pink granite rocks of Tregestel beach, a wonderland of sculpture
at low tide, solitary leviathans, or balanced on top of each other
into rock cathedrals. These images are powerfully intertwined
ever since. (Tregastel, 1989)

THE AMERICAN

He sat on the bed with a cudgel in his hands. It had started out as a walking stick to replace the solid brass one he had posted back to Boston. He admitted it was more for self-protection. From what? He shrugged his shoulders and grinned shyly. Around him were signs of relentless organisation, a dozen piles of neatly stacked letters, clothes, pamphlets... 'I guess I'm scared.' The trip to Europe had gone wrong from the start; food poisoning on arrival in Dublin and four days in hospital. In Ireland he retraced the steps of Yeats and was followed by scroungers; that evening in Oban he had fled the pub when drunks crashed through the window. The English popular press he found unbelievable. He had left America to get away from that. For six months he had planned this European journey to reconnect with his roots: he knew the names of the Scottish kings, the clan chiefs and where they lived, how they dressed and much more. He astounded me. Back home his stuff was in a warehouse, 'boxes and boxes of books.' He said he moved every six months; that was normal. I advised him to dress down, to put away his green gabardine cloak, his gold pocket watch; change his brogues for trainers. 'Imagine the rubbish in the 18th century,' I said, 'the body odours, the clans of beggars, the infant mortality, the sewage in the streets. You can't just take a little bit.' He nodded his head ruefully. 'I guess it's all in here,' he said tapping his chest. We left it at that and surrendered to a night of budget accommodation. (Oban, June 10, 1995)

THE HIGH BANKS OF THE LUGAR

'If I hadn't met you, I wouldn't be here now,' says Donna Butterworth, a doctor of Irish and Italian descent from Lesotho in South Africa. Her husband, John Butterworth from Lancashire agrees, and that by choice they are pioneers in Ayrshire. I admire what they are doing, a partnership of four families growing and delivering organic vegetables direct to the locals. They call it community supported agriculture which puts roots back into local communities, connecting people with the land. At the beginning of the season the subscribers stump up money for a guaranteed number of vegetable boxes delivered each week during the year, sharing some of the hazard of the enterprise as well as the bounty. Their children, Jan, Alice and Francis speak with a Scottish accent. (What don't you knoo?' asks Jan. 'I bet you don't knoo the world turns on an axle.') Unexpectedly, the literary associations come: the big house at Auchinleck belonged to the Boswell family, the chronicler of Samuel Johnson (I marvel at the earliest fortified keep built on crags by the Dopple river); the bard, Robbie Burns, walked along the high banks of the Lugar, an allusion to the red sandstone gorge near their cottage. They show me the overgrown gardens of the old house, the exotic trees from around the world. I think about the ebb and flow of history, the movements of people. What is Scottish? What is English? Who are the white settlers? I call them British. (Auchinleck, June 12, 1995)

METER MAN

I escaped from the merciless sun into the second-hand book-shop. He sat in the cubby hole dressed drably in brown clothes and the gesture of a tie. His thick glasses, and the parted and the brushed-back hair kindled an impression out of the fifties. We bantered a little talk each time I came to his end of the row; how I accompanied my father on his bargain book trips in the sixties; he had met a man in Chesterfield who had read only one book in his life. He mentioned that he had started the youth hostel at Tobermory. Then you must know Mull well, I said. 'I have been inside every house on Mull and Iona. I had to read their meters.' I listened to his stories for an hour, standing under a cooler sky with faces fresh from his memory: the shepherdess who could wrestle any man to the floor; the two strips of concrete that made the road to Calgary, the Iona taxi with more holes than chassis between his feet, the ferry boat that lifted cars on and off by crane. I was amazed! 'How can you tolerate being cooped up?' He pointed to the books. 'I've always loved them. They're like windows on the world – and here I'm surrounded by them.' (Bakewell, June 20, 1995)

ANGEL

Sally works in Cumbria helping small craft traders market their products. She acts as agent, publicist, organises fairs and even works behind the stalls. This is what she likes best: she puts the candle-makers next to the people who make candle holders; the people who haven't a clue in presentation next to an expert, the

194

maker of small wooden objects beside a toy stall – then lets nature take its course. I liked that. (June 17, 1995)

WATER GARDEN

I choose without thinking to sit beside the cedar and at ground level to the pond. I am wondering what to say. This panic attack is eclipsed by the whirring fuselage of an unknown, not beautiful dragonfly with fat, washed blue abdomen and nondescript grey thorax and head... Out of nowhere arrives an amber and brown, smaller damsel fly and clasps the blue one; their wings clash at high speed as they make love in the air. Below, motionless on a leaf of creeping jenny, two azure slimlines, inspected by a third, do it stately and slow, abdomen tip to the back of neck it seems. I watch open mouthed as the washed blue with chocolate underparts rests on a rock; it turns its head sharply; there are tiny black bars on each wing tip. After this brief tangle of the sexes, the smaller waspy coloured one (the female) hovers a few inches above the water speedwell and keeps flicking her abdomen into the water. The larger one eyes her protectively, warding off a bumblebee, and as soon as the tail flicking ceases the aerial combat recommences, the pair vanishing on right-angle lines, wings crossing like swords.

I have never seen this dragonfly mating game before. I have never looked. I felt frightened, not by their power but by its unpredictable nature. Several times I ducked to avoid the velocity of their courtship... Chris, the genial electrician, walks in and confirms the slim ones are damsel flies, the fat ones hawker dragonflies. I gaze closely at one, stealing the ground, inch by inch, to see the deep amber head, the heaving abdomen curiously flattened with tiny blobs of black, white and blue on the margins. I say. 'Can you hear me?' and it flight rustles inches from my ear. 'They hear the sound vibrations,' says Chris, walking away to find the water pump. 'He'll count this as a victory,' he adds laughing.

I am amazed with water how things arrive unannounced. Its power to attract is enormous. Its presence appears to allow things to happen; how else did the grass snake appear only after the pond had been made. The same with the toad, the dragonflies, the pond skaters, the duck, the water-boatmen. This power of attraction has a feminine quality, a moon waxing and waning. I have often dreamed of my water garden, with an oak tree growing beside it, a rock steaming in the middle...and the water streams out of it in a

195

long straight line, a canal across the dry land... I am envious of the nuptial flights of the damsel flies; what a charming way to pass the sunny hours. The pond skaters keep their distance, except when two suddenly tumble over each other in a fit of passion; the rings of desire ripple beyond them, then they're back to the slow drift across the pond. The baby pond-skaters scatter as specks of dust.

Often when I am in the garden, I catch or inwardly glimpse Priapus, the Greek gardening god, and I can feel my, or this sexual energy, swell my parts, bringing fleeting images of desire into my walking self. They pass through me but sometimes these sexual feelings, almost coming off the flowers and their moving counterparts, the insects, can be so demanding, that I go to a quiet corner of the garden and release them. I understand why Priapus had big genitals! There is sexual energy all around me, especially in this fine skin of soil, the abundant metabolism. of micro-organisms, six tons to every fertile acre.

A water garden is a great receiver, a kind of emptiness which gets dramatically filled with fleeting lives, and reflects all these things. How strange that an inch of water can show you a distant star and be a world for a whirligig beetle. The water shows the slightest movement of the wind, every twitch of the pond-skater's feet; out of it come aerial things, dragonflies, drone flies, frogs. The water garden will be at the heart of my garden, a magnet calling everything else. (June 28,.1991)

GRASS SNAKE

I approach as a leaf in the wind, inching my way forward, toe by toe to kneel beside this silver santolina bush. The sun warms my back, perspiring me, calming me. A magpie shakes its rattle bag. The snake moves slowly, the olive green teardrops, the black apostrophes I notice. I hardly dare move. It is as thick as my wrist and must be two feet long. I stifle the impulse to grab and hold it firmly. This thing of possessing is deeply ingrained. The grass snake tapers beautifully, shiny and scaled to miniature perfection. I am drawn to this snake, the second I have seen in ten days. It leaves its tail exposed, the longer part of its body is hidden in the bush. I sense other ripples, trusting stirring energies in me, non-rational but changing the outcome of things. (Upton Cheney, May 22, 1990)

HOLINE (IV)

I arrived at the caravan in cotton sheets of rain concealing the waters of Loch Na Keal (The Loch of the Cells of the Missionaries) and the 1,000 foot cliffs of the Gribbun on the opposite shore; wet, despite waterproofs, well tired and one of my fingers throbbing from an old rose wound. I had come to this caravan on a rocky slope belonging to Lagan-Ulva Farm to rest after five week's cycling. I don't know what I expected to find but it wasn't peace of mind; the companions of this British journey crowded into that thread-bare caravan. Who were they? They were there at the beginning leaving Penzance with the gift of the tin Celtic cross around my neck. In the daylight hours I called this journey a pilgrimage; in the night-time I descended into the shitpit. Oh boy! What did I see? My hair cut from the front and back leaving a tuft; the horny dreams oozing sex and blow jobs, then impotence, tiny cocks, the horrors of homophobia, delicate young girls who became bearded men, or I'm fondling grandmothers and other inappropriate images. I can hardly believe it! Then spider woman appears spinning her webs. I tell her I want her to be my ally and not my representative. I make little sense of this.

The rain cleared and I indentified Eorsa, the small island in the sea-loch lying like a beached turtle, then farther out, the low headlands of Inch Kenneth, home to the disciple of St. Columba – all within sight of the great rock of Iona, Dun I. I have always loved these Celtic saints (I think everyone was called a saint then); completely crazy really, risking their lives in coracles, probably carrying portable altars and hand-bells, facing rain in corbelled cells without heating. Some chose Loch Na Keal, no doubt awed by the volcanic beauty of Ben More, the plentiful shellfish, fresh water, sheltered wooded bays; the oystercatchers must have chorused their prayers, the salmon leaped out of the water. They made a home for God in the arms of Nature herself. I stepped out of the caravan and the first thing I saw was a clean sanitary towel and tissue paper. I instantly recalled the red car I had pushed past in the rain, the two bodies, the man naked to his waist, the woman in the old-fashioned headscarf caressing his chest. They did not see me.

I wound my way down through the boggy pastures to the tumbled basaltic boulders on the shore. I stood opposite Eorsa and it appeared to me that I stood between this holy island (now of goats) and this furtive lover's scene, and that's exactly how I have been feeling throughout this journey, my perverse Catholic imagination shadowing my day. I could not flee from me without encountering the other. The Cells of the Missionaries came into clearer focus. How do they enchant me? Their renunciation – the white martyrdom – the breaking of ties is extremely romantic yet this isolation I feel now reveals the brutal reality. That holy island drifted farther away from the mainland. I danced my simple dance to the four directions, the one I have danced for ten years, acknowledging the great stages of life, infancy, childhood, adulthood and old age and finding in that a pattern for the day. At the end I remain standing in the middle not identified with these directions, but just me. On that wild shore I stretched out my arms like the old saints did and felt better for doing so. I had not changed anything but I stood in the centre of my world like the fixed centre in the Celtic cross and saw it through my eyes with its oppositions and contradictions. I didn't want to change it. I think most of my life I have gone too far, not known how to hold this centre ground. From the mainland, Eorsa, Inch Kenneth, Iona appeared calm and detached. It's not these islands I want to live on – that would be a tragic escape – but to find a place in me which illuminates the whole, as this island sees the entire coastline. (Loch Na Keal, June 4, 1995)

FIVE AGOROT

Each morning the sun rose over the Dead Sea, a shining white ball shimmering the waters pink from the Jordanian mountains; each day the rock-lands along the western shore became towering solar heaters, all the way from Jericho to Qumran and En Gedi. By the outflow of the Nahal Arugot, a stream issuing from the Wilderness of Zin (one of the last wild places in Israel), the marmots are up by dawn raiding the date palms belonging to this isolated kibbutz. I watched these furry rodents as I walked up the canyon to the first waterfall hidden behind luxuriant bamboos. Small green-banded snakes and huge butterflies live there, and I marvel at the memory of jumping fifteen feet into seven feet of crystal water and pushing off from the shelly bottom. Then I floated on my back, counting the rock terraces stacked hundreds of feet above me, the highest ones quartered by bright sunlight or a gliding scavenger griffin, or mountain ibex jumping between boulders. Along some terraces straight lines were cut into the rock, the channels excavated by the

Essenes two thousand years ago to divert precious water to their crops. Once I rolled away a stone and saw a skeleton lying sideways in a small cave; grave robbers had chopped off several fingers. I wanted to stay longer in this paradise. I wanted this experience to last forever but even here there were bills to pay. I would be dazzled by Smyrna kingfishers and catch myself thinking about money. Then I had an idea.

The boss wasted no time. He interviewed me while showering; 200 shekels and an extra 50 if my work was okay. Long before the tourist coaches from Jerusalem honked their way up the dust trail to Masada, I had scoured, polished and scrubbed the food mixers, giant pots and pans before a single dirty plate came my way. I had peeled and chopped cucumbers, green and red peppers and aubergines by the crate. They came to the Masada restaurant in waves, corresponding to the coaches, and everyone was hot, dusty and very, very thirsty. Twice daily, to meet kosher standards, we washed down the kitchen, sponging dust from surfaces and polishing them, mopping floors and polishing them, fast-speed figures in a fast-food world. Masada, the rock fortress of the last Jewish zealots, could have been on another planet. We ate our meals on the hoof for the boss kept a commanding position by the swinging door between the restaurant and the kitchen. Once, after the last coach had gone, a lone mouse appeared from behind a cooker and the boss saw it. He grabbed two knives, one for each hand, and cursed that mangy infidel with Hebraic oaths. The cooks grabbed pots and ladles; the dishwashers armed themselves with brooms and they chased that mouse from fridge to freezer, pushed them aside, emptied a walk-in cupboard before finally cornering the mouse. It ran between a pair of legs and headed desperately up the Snake Pass.

I collapsed at the end of my first twelve-hour day. I had earned two days in paradise.

The following morning it seemed that I had known that kitchen a lifetime. I saw my fellow inmates more clearly; the Hungarian chef who called us gentlemen and disappeared every half an hour to sip his 'beetroot' juice; the reformed kibbutznik saving for a bulldozer and freedom; the hard-working North African jews who accept their lot as if they are second class citizens. Only the English travellers saving to go to India complained but they had little to lose. Another kibbutznik, Svi – 'See as many sunrises as you can' – said it was an educational experience of capitalism. He had been Commander-in-Chief of the front line by the Dead Sea. A Jewish Englishman called everyone Beloved and in turn was called a friend of God. We shared a common religion of money, dreams and freedom. Already the Smyrna kingfisher appeared more iridescent. The rest of that week I can only recall drinking cheap banana wine in the evening, watching 'Hercules and the Barbarians,' a special showing for the workers. After dark the restaurant was guarded by an old man with a sub-machine gun. Svi says he is always asleep by midnight.

There is a moral to this story: the three brothers who ran this restaurant had an ancient father with enough brain cells left to work the cashier's till. At the end of the day, when he should have gone, he stayed in his seat looking at the huge waste paper bin and then back at the till. 'There is something missing,' he said, and he stared at the bin. Very slowly, and with a look of infinite determination, he removed each wrapper until he emptied the bin. He plucked from the bottom a five agorot piece, the equivalent of a penny. He held it between his fingers until a smile of gratitude transformed his face.

It took the crack Roman battalion several months to breach the siege at Masada. I escaped in less than a week. (En Gedi, 1973)

WHAT!

Anne Lauder is an intrepid Swiss cyclist. She is extreme. She will not travel by car; she is a child physiotherapist and has to deal with the consequences of motor accidents. I met her when she planned to cycle over the snowy peaks of the Andes. How many mountains? I asked. '99,' she said laughing. Earlier that day she had asked for an ice cream. '99?' asked the man. 'No no, only one,' she answered. (Bath, 1995)

TRAINS

It is fitting that Dave Shearwood spotted his future home from the train window. That this tall, lean and bearded man carries the mark of his trade, a stooping shoulder from years of precision engineering. His workshop is painted in the cream and chocolate brown of the old Great Western Railway. He remembers his early encounters with steam locomotives, the hissing air pumps, the big wheels turning, enamelled paintwork, the elaborate timetables dividing the hours. Almost without realising it this inspired a love of wheels turning within wheels, the genius of moving parts. Later he studied production engineering. The wheels became clock wheels, the paintwork clock faces. They tick away on every wall of his house; some work by weights, some he winds, some are digital; cuckoos and crows and trumpet blowers serenade the passing hours; little ships rock on the sea; grandfather time reaps the seconds. His latest custom-built clock is a woman with outstretched arms as signals; they rise to mark the minutes then fall simultaneously on the hour. He shows me the hand-made clock case. Did I think it fair value? Cheap for genius, I thought. (Carleton-in-Craven, June 18, 1995)

JOHN HUCKETT

He eludes me, this man. I can't write about him without misrepresenting him, making him appear too romantic or too bluntly earthy. I picture him in his oily blue dungarees, his knuckled fingers under the bonnets of vans, dismantling transmission shafts of tractors, or the solitary shadow in the caravan beguiling the night-time with his Scottish and Irish piping. He lives on the axis of Bristol and the Applecross peninsular, and when he's not working or music-making, he's sailing or thinking about it. He says that he has returned to his beatnik roots now that he is in his fifties – finding wild food, living on little money and being independent as possible. He gave up his engineering – he couldn't see the sense in a career – and tied his worldly possessions onto a delivery bicycle and cycled to St. Ives in the late fifties. He trained as a classical musician, worked as a farmer, then became a sailor. He is an original but you could pass by this man with his grey-curled beard and matching locks. I don't know him that well, but this I do remember: once, I glimpsed his eyes, and the normally grey lights were transformed by the angle of sunlight into a brilliant sky blue. Only for a second, but a glimpse, sometimes, is long enough. (Applecross, June 2, 1995)

LAND RIGHTS

To visit the Greenwood Trust at Coalbrookdale is to enter the realm of a powerful paradox. Here, in the upper Severn valley, is the cradle of the industrial revolution – Coalport, Ironbridge, the furnaces of Bedlam, the Babylon of nearby Telford – and into this world came the rural landless, outmanoeuvered by the Enclosure Acts and hungry for work. The Greenwood Trust works in the opposite direction: appealing largely to a restless city dweller wanting to find roots in the country. (I'm exaggerating). I thought of the travellers, how many of them are the bright ones once trapped in the cities, and now searching for a rural base. I think they are the friends of farmers, given time. They remind me of the dustbowl Okies in Steinbeck's books and how they were feared and harried by the land-owning classes. How they were misunderstood to distance settled people from their legitimate needs. Gerwyn Lewis at the Trust is aware of this predicament, and the Trust's initiative to set up a Woodland College with a NVQ qualification could provide a bridge for these people trying to change their lives. I hope so. Whichever way you look at it, homelessness is a crime. The Trust aims to give people skills developed when technology had to be sustainable, when life was hard and people had to use their brains to make it easier. Anyone who has seen some contemporary greenwood shelters and furniture will realise that they belong to the 21st century – elegant, flexible, sustainable, accessible.

* * * *

Mike Pearson is the friendly charcoal burner at the Greenwood Trust. With Soot, his dog, he has landed on his feet after a former life as a road engineer. He told me this story: Once, in the eighties, he worked in the Sultanate of Oman. He arrived in a drought and stayed with a friend who had the idea of selling sun-shields to the locals. His friend bought a job lot of 1,500 black umbrellas, the type used by London city commuters. He positioned himself opposite the grand bazaar. The locals laughed as they darted in and out of the cavernous entrance in their flowing gowns. Some even threw him coins as if he were a begger. Those laughed loudest. He stood there every day for a week without selling a single umbrella. He used local children without success. Nobody wanted them. He resigned himself to one more day. On that morning a cloud appeared in the sky. People pointed to it, especially when it turned black and the first drops of rain hit that parched land. Now they would want an umbrella. Not likely. The locals danced in it letting the rain splash their faces. By lunchtime the rain fell lightly, and in the afternoon it became torrential. His friend sheltered under his umbrella certain his hour had come. The locals huddled in the cavernous entrance of the bazaar enjoying the spectacle. No-one bought an umbrella. The rain kept falling and by a quirk of design – the bazaar was built along a dry wadi – the floodwater flowed into the bazaar. It wasn't long before the sceptic tanks overflowed, and when the turds floated out of the bazaar the Arabs dashed into the storm. His friend and helpers sold 1,000 umbrellas in two hours. (Coalbrookdale, June 21, 1995)

KYAN'S GARDEN

The plum leaves rattle over my head, a mega-sneeze follows from under the mulberry tree where Mr Kyan is painting his revolving tennis pavilion. I love this so English garden, fruitfulness with disorder, a vegetable garden enclosed on one side by a hedge of espalier apples, on the other by the green oak pergola I assembled like a big stick insect two years ago. The vegetables are overgrown, one of the quince trees carries no crop, the plum I didn't prune is the only one bearing fruit, and I could go on and on naming things; the soft fruit garden in the sunken rockery, the walled bonfire garden, the gravel walkways of lavender and roses... Mr Kyan is followed everywhere by two enormous labradors, both male; one called Tigger faithfully carries his cap in case he should need it. The old man is hard of hearing and shouts to make up for it. His appearance reflects the garden, comfortably off and in a genteel state of collapse; his green raincoat is liberally plastered with bicycle repair kit; his glasses stay together because of the stickytape. He normally is expressionless, a mask of an ageing face, then suddenly laughter opens his eyes, mouth and cheeks. I smile, noticing the swifts behind him, black dots under the storm clouds. The air is still. The rain drops menacingly one by one. The 'Beauty of Bath' leans on a crutch: the spreading branches are full of fist-size fruit. I keep closing this book as a sudden wind scurries around me. The light fades, almost dusk. I feel poignant sitting here on this cold frame, the sombre sleeping clouds lit brightly at the edges tease memories from me, the dusk fires at the first Glastonbury Dance camp, being outside with the elements, the big sky... At the end of the day's gardening I am relaxed with myself.

Today I worked a little with Linda Cresswell, a counsellor and a gardener. This is the first time this year, and we mixed tea with gossip about relationships. Not a lot to pass on and it's always enough. I will scrump some windfall cherries before I go, the red sour ones quench thirst like lemons and grapefruit. Apples, plums and cherries I scrumped as a child and I'm still doing it. I've lost my way with this writing; it is disorderly, rather ramshackle and lacks finesse. Kyan's garden always appears on the edge of chaos, yet a glance at the espalier apples, the rows of vegetables shows that this is only half true. The chaos passes through the garden and ends up in the compost heap. I should mention Mrs Kyan, indomitable and catholic, absolutely no nonsense or pretension; she has had eight false hips and still travels to New Zealand to see one of her daughters who lives on an island with her crippled husband. She potters around the rows of redcurrants and raspberries tied up by me on the wall besides the children's playground, and she freezes the lot. I am part of this family when I am here, the doors are open, my boundaries are clear; a sophisticated alarm system seals off other parts of the house. She loves her roses and lavender bushes by the pergola and often walks up and down there. Let it be recorded that this double-span green oak construction marks the high spot in my gardening work. I am proud of it. In two years it has coloured silver grey, distorted a little and cracked, and looks at least twenty years old. If I were never to come back, I will always remember this cold frame where I sun myself and drink Kyan's home brew, where the poplar leaves rattle, the plums fatten − and I can watch the swifts, dark bows speeding under the sky. (June 27, 1990)

A PLACE OF FLOWERS

I find it almost impossible to start. I am so delightfully unfocussed and wanting to be mesmerised by the swirling plant shadows on this page and the picture of slender, waving grasses, the chuck of magpies, or the solitary pathways of meadow browns. I came here alone wanting to name the flowers on this original face of chalk grassland, wanting to reach back again into the timeless world of flowers, wanting to not do anything in particular. I fell asleep on this bed of common milkwort, bird's-foot trefoil, common and pyramidal orchids, and the coloured lights printed by the pine needles danced before my closed eyes. I slept. I don't know long and it did not matter. I woke up and noted with pleasure that there was no sign of the twentieth century, only the broad-leaved lime *skirting both sides of the combe, while below, islands of maple, privet and pine intruded into this remnant of antique grassland. This uncultivated land, native for sure, is a site of special scientific interest, in sharp contrast to the surrounding monoculture of cereals and 'improved' grassland. Here is an enormous variety of plant and insect life. I came here alone and yet another is present, my flower lady, the woman I met on the wayside at Tellisford; she pointed to the cruciform flowers of crosswort; she told me the names of flowers. I remembered her grinning brown eyes, her natural intelligence and honesty. I undressed her here and sank my lovejoy into her welcoming reception, the sinuous quaking grass and knottyheads of salad burnet stroking her friendly thighs. This fantasy passed and I remembered that on the other side of Cleeve Woods I had toiled against inertia, in the sun and baked hard clay, making the inner rim of a water garden, and every hour the clock gained seemed longer than the one before. I fell asleep again letting the grasses support me as if they were my mother. I wake up. I keep noticing the waving grasses, the way they are with the wind, bending, shaking, always returning under this intense blue, curly-tailed sky. They are everywhere; the flowers are holes.*

Women appear with smiling faces. I take off their clothes and the grasses wave around us. This timeless world has no boundaries, one, two women is what I want here, the delicious secret of sex, sunshine on the earth. She showed me places like this, places of my childhood, where we wandered down the timeless ways naming the species of the natural world. On the other side of this hill is time, a world of work, objectives, clarity, a cultivated world as the cereal fields are to this protected grassland. I want to make some sense of this polarity. The things that matter to me belong to both worlds. Here I come for inspiration, without many thoughts, the smallest things content me; on the other side of the hill I realise my dreams. Here sex is promiscuous, sensual without commitment; on the other side of the hill I have commitment, focus, a partner, an address in the world. This place of flowers is off the back lanes, far from a main road. It reminds me of childhood and I feel sad about that, as if it is only an escape without value in the real world. Perhaps that is why our relationship never worked in the long term. The world of childhood is full of demons and unfinished business. I come to Cleeve Woods as a visitor, not to live here. I think it was the hardest thing letting go of you; we could not have grown in each other's shade, each other's neediness. I need the sun to be independent.

What do I find here? Solitariness, diversity, hinterland, sexual energy, heart, insects and these words. It is the writer and garden maker who is nourished by these journeys, who can give shape, expression to the things that I find on the wayside. If I lived in this world of flowers I would succumb to glamour; I would try to put a spell upon this world and fail. Sex would become undifferentiated. I do not want that. Childhood can be a very conservative place, as the species belonging to this grassland are very traditional. I do not want to recreate it. I come here to learn from what is original.

The word that I would like best to describe me is a traveller, one who makes journeys. This is travelling for me, to squat before a dozen pyramidal orchids, thick stems clasped by leaves, the plants keeling over by the weight of intense red-rose flowers, the size of a baby's fist. I lose my way when I mistake the journey, the places, these orchids I visit as my home. I do not live here. My home is the place where the traveller lives. At this moment, it's this page. My house in Frome, so perfect in its dimensions, in its antique ways, is beyond my means. I'm gambling selling it. I want a home where I can realise my two dreams, writing and garden making. Not long ago I went in a dream to the non-polluted source of my Holy Maker in all her guises, a place of clear springs underground yet full of light, to a shrine where all through the ages devotees had placed their offerings, carved their statues. Surrounded by giant statues from all traditions, the medallion I chose showed two blue madonnas; this is what I want in my life, not two lovers out there but to realise the two dreams in my heart.

'Nothing left to repeat, only love and more love.'

(Cleeve Wood, Wellow, June 23, 1994)

VISIT TO THE HERONRY

The prospect of seeing a heronry had brought me to the edge of a pine wood off a back road between Dumfries and Dalbeattie. They nested on a dozen of the tallest pines, I had been told, only one hundred yards from the road. But where? Any tracks had surrendered to the smothering shade of rhododendrons. I listened to myself breathe. I was excited. I stooped under branches, liberated wood dust, crawled over mossy blankets, followed a column of wood ants to a grassy clearing with a welcoming beacon of light and a fern. The sweat clung and dribbled into my eyes. I listened for clues of beaks clacking and watched the blue spaces above me for gliding wings. From the shadows came mosquitoes, droves of owl-like silhouettes humming on a thousand needle points. They were hungry. I stumbled deeper into the wood, stepping on swellings of puff balls, cracking bone-dry twigs, wiping mosquitoes from my arms. Twice I stopped, twice I vowed to go back, the third time I admitted that I was lost. I sat down with the sinking feeling that I was the only person alive in the world. Far away something clacked, sharp and purposeful, and I saw a heron flap its wings in reverse to make a perfect landing high in the tree tops. The dipping sun brought down golden light into the pines. I saw a shadow that would not lie down, too straight for a branch, and upright. I saw another. One spoke, another answered, clacking its beaks. Then the thin black line turned, hunched and stared at the miniature bundles of heron. More clatterings rang out from the nearby treetops. Slowly, it dawned on me that I was in the middle of the heronry. (Dalbeattie, 1975)

BIRD MAN

'Don't ever grow old,' he said. 'That's not fair,' I retorted. The old man sitting in the youth hostel shrugged his shoulders and carried on tipping out his breakfast from small plastic bags. Yesterday had not been a good day. He had visited cliffs on Mull of Kintyre but had only spotted a few cormorants and a pair of eiders. 'There was nothing in the sea for them to feed on.' He had seen a wheatear, yet he remembers those ash-lined birds flying up from his feet there twenty years ago. He grumbled a lot. 'The pensions here are on a par with those in Portugal. I can't afford to eat out anymore.' Youth hostels had changed, he said emphatically: the well-equipped kitchens, most people in cars, the lack of chores. He couldn't believe that in his youth he had cycled hundreds of miles on a bike without gears. 'We had no choice then.' He had been an only child on a farm in rural Norfolk and made companions of the small songbirds. He watched them for hours, the goldcrests plucking seeds from thistles, swallows sipping water from the river. 'The numbers are down dramatically. It's hard to keep my enthusiasm up now.' I mentioned pesticides. He nodded his head. 'I have my own theory. All last winter the songbirds came to my table but by March they had gone. Where did they go? I looked out of my window one day and into the eyes of a bloody big sparrowhawk. That's where they went.' (Minnigaff YHA, June 13, 1995)

STARLINGS

The tree dominated the water meadow meandering with the backwater of the Thames near Hinton Waldrist. At first the starlings dribbled into the tree, dropping out of the sky to fill the leafy spaces. More and more landed attracted by the crescendo of clacking and cackle. Little clouds of birds became dark streaks and vanished into it. The landlord of The Blue Boar Inn stepped outside to see what the fuss was about. The tree visibly darkened before his eyes. The windscale pipings and mutterings drew out the neighbours from Holly Tree Cottage. Amazement sealed our mouths. Three crows flew into the tree and immediately silenced the starlings. The tree spat out the crows and the noise erupted again boiling fit to break the branches. All the pub regulars stood outside along with the neighbours and two passing motorists. We gaped. Then a cloud of starlings motored high in the sky and kept on flying towards the Downs. Silence struck the tree. It tingled on my arms and skated down the inside of my legs. The tree exploded into a large dark circle. It held its shape for a moment, just a moment, then rained starlings far into the sky. (August 25, 1978)

ROSS LINKS

I wanted to write Lindisfarne, to hang these words on the coattails of history, to be linked to the saints Aidan and Cuthbert working on this sandy isle rising above the salt marshes. I resisted it. I fear I have too little to say, too much of personal moods as murky as the tidal flats between Lindisfarne island and Ross Links, a surreal sweep of sand dunes lying opposite the Northumbrian coast. A continuous silver line follows the blue sea, interrupted only by the level headlands of the Farne islands and the slowly flashing lighthouse beacon... It's surreal, made that way, by the arch romantic castles of Bamburgh and Lindisfarne, rocky full stops at each end of the bay. This uncultivated place, Ross Links, appears to be connected to Holy island but it's illusion; intense blue waters at high tide block the way between the two red stone obelisks, the 19th century navigational aid said to be visible 25 miles out at sea. The low-lying nature of the sand dunes encourages big skies. This strange mixture of castle pomp, drawing attention to itself, the invisibility of sand, is here already on this page, the high points of history ecclesiastical or strategic — tantalisingly close and yet inaccessible. I feel this cleavage in myself and can hardly express it...

Distances are illusory on the sand; Bamburgh Castle stayed the same size after walking towards it for nearly two hours. The marram gass capped the interior of Ross Links as completely as a cloud covers the moon; the stunted thorn trees were dead or dying, only half flowering from the dry summers. Two dead seals were beached at high water mark, their insides mummified into horse-hair stuffing for a mattress. The winds had plucked dry the rabbits littering the beach; many lay in the hollow of the dunes with the survivor ragworts and creeping thistle. An intense surge of negativity had accompanied me into these dunes; my load was too heavy, my partner did not understand me, resentment oozed from every orifice. I did not see the make believe beauty of sea pink, millions of paper blooms painting acres of the mud flats. The red obelisks appeared freakish and sombre, a little menacing; later they transformed into minarets. I glimpsed, surreally, a union of a Christian princess and a lion-hearted Islamic prince.

I can hardly recapture the day and night on the dunes, so much is tacky with my rubbish. This feeling is landlocked in me sometimes, that time is precious and that only my uncertain effort can make headway against this inertia. I stuck black slates into the mud so they would cast a shadow.

The strands of fantasy which tease the pages of the Lindisfarne Gospel belong to an earlier tradition. I like the fact that the great days of Holy island were in the long ago before any of the visible ruins, that some church of timber and mud-daub housed the Anglo-Celtic visionaries scribing away at their books, not mass produced but one at a time. Increasingly I go with this coming and going tide in my life to go slowly with writing, and this creates problems. Perhaps things should not last forever; it's not these ruins but their lives which matter. 'It's in the things which are always changing that the eternal lives.' I usually call this my rubbish, the pieces which don't fit (The ancient plants on Lindisfare are not the trees — the sycamores are introductions

– but the ephemeral wallfowers.) When I am holding little Elfie, my three-month-old daughter, I slow down and do everything at her speed. I take things in, the pearly tread of moss, the cool inbreath on the tongue, the freedom of turning my head, the big eyes that see everything...

I came away from Ross Links with pictures of stubborn saints, hard grafters, gloomily ascetic I suspect, yet clinging to a dream, a Christian dream of individuality. I feel linked, not to the clichéd Celtic scrollwork, or the ascetism, or the recluse in off-beat lands, but the spirit which sees through my eyes and acts in this world with love. And if love is our way of being connected, then it must start with ourselves. The muddy slacks surround Holy Island; I see it best from Ross Links. (June 12, 1994)

NIGHT-SONG

I remembered the blind woman while walking around the cloisters of Iona Abbey. She had been helped off the ferry – not much more than an open boat then – and used a white stick to sense her way up through the village, a fragile figure claiming her independence and our respect. Two nights later at the Abbey, late and everyone had gone to bed, I heard an effortless, pure voice lighting up the dark corridors. I listened entranced, the more so as the words were Gaelic. I listened with my eyes shut. I knew it was her. Without realising it, she had taken me into her world. (Iona, 1975)

FOR YOU

The old man walked back with me from the restaurant bar on Iona, the summer night still and luminous over Erraid. He had talked of many things, and I had listened, for he was a fount of all things Scottish. And do you know the corncrake? he asked. No. They are rare, only 300 birds in all of Britain and most of those on wild shores. A secretive bird which runs and calls, calls and runs, and you never know where it is skulking. There are a pair on Iona, he said but who knows where. We walked in silence towards Sandeels Bay. The old man touched my arm. 'Listen,' he said. I heard a ratchetty key being wound up fast. It stopped. It did it again. 'A corncrake singing...specially for you.' (Iona, June 6, 1995)

HOLINE (V)

This grass bank supports me. I'm glad of that. I can smell the foetid, penetrating odour of fox. Perhaps she sat here too, eyeing up the white-shielded coots so close yet far away on their mats of pondweed. Every so often a stone slops into these clear still waters except it is a trout leaping for the damselflies. I wanted to be beside water for I feel far away from this element on my solitary cycle journey. I am like the tree root I see shinning down the rocky gorge face in search of water. Maybe the fox, blue-eyed and tufty and full of tasty beetles, liked the coolness and airplay of courting midges. A coot slides under and comes up with an explosive note. The baby coots twizzle in its absence perturbed by the bubbles. If I close my eyes the song notes of small birds are traces of coloured light out of blue shadows. I am none the wiser for this journey along the quiet roads of Britain yet something is changing. It will elude me if I try to hold it. I must meander. I keep noticing the rock face, a strong edge to these waters, a boundary in fact... I start to see the faces, the kind people who took me in, nearly everyone struggling with their integrity and wondering how to pay the bills. This fox would know, I'm sure. I certainly feel more commitment to what I'm already doing. Sometimes it takes a journey away to realise that.

I glimpse important things about myself. I live on the cultural borderlands and they are the centre ground of my life. This Celtic world of change, the borderlands of mist, neither cloud nor rain, or dawn and twilight, neither day nor night — they appeal to this instinct in me. Yet something disturbs this, makes me question the personal axis of my life, this hidden secretive person. Sitting here now, far from that world of the chainsaw I hear up the Lathkill valley. There is something foxy about him. I am, as if a child in its den, peering out on the material world, out of timelessness and natural magic. (A dog barges in. 'Sorry to disturb you,' says a man. That's it exactly.) This is my hermitage, this state of mind. For years I have tried to live it out there, and in that upper world I have been both a child and a wise man, and in ways I cannot follow I have used this magic to charm and seduce, as if reaching at people's hearts from behind. At Inch Kenneth I saw that child dreaming of his Celtic hermitage where the small birds alight by his feet and his magic words materialise in his hand. I felt such purity, sincerity and trust. How could I question these noble impulses or square them with my earth-bound desires? Then on the boat to

Lochranza I glimpsed this powerful seduction while standing beside a man and a woman. First, I saw faults in him, his stiff jaws, tired eyes, pot belly, and then I easily imagined his jealous, clinging nature. I switched to the poor woman having to put up with that, and how she must long for tenderness, charms, a gentle touch. Of course, she saw these qualities in me, my availability... In a flash I saw myself destroying the man in me, giving away the real things, the changes, to hold onto this purity, this innocence not subject to time; this charm. The woman, at that moment, became an ordinary woman. I had freed her. This unrealistic sexuality astounds me.

I have always found it hard to accept my face, my stiff jaws when I'm shy or lost inside, my height in bare feet, the lines under my eyes, the shit I dispel. This facing up to things is what I'm trying to get at. I feel empowered when I value my awkwardness, this tender touch, gaps and silences. I become real to myself and others. Slowly on this journey I realise I want to change the axis in my life; not put the hermitage first with the old man and the purity of a child, but the birth of a man with his faults, his changes, facing a woman. The child in me wants to be all good but has an imagination for evil beyond belief. I want to step back into this middle ground. I feel like a buffoon, really. (Lathkill, Over Haddon, June 20, 1995)

JULY CHANGES

All reds, purples and yellows. Time lasts forever paddling the murmur of balmy days. Everything is on the outside, the opposite of January. The first rust appears in the fine fretting rains, the first grasses seed – starlings drop mashed cherry stones down chimneys – hazelnuts and sloe plums are fingertip size – six-spotted burnet moths mate on yellow spikes of agrimony; soldier and sailor beetles on cow parsley (*Anthriscus sylvestris*) – hundreds of tiny red mites spin on hot flagstones – the lower leaves of hemlock shrivel brown – the flesh fly (*Sarcophaga carnaria*) sunbathes on showy flowers – butterflies blown into roadside gutters along main roads – a bumblebee scrabbles to reach flowers against a florist's window – garden ants carry dead to graveyard – leaf bugs smell acrid and pungent – tiny frogs make big leaps in undergrowth – first silage cut and insects disappear – fiery ribbons of rosebay willowherb on waysides – marble-white butterfly on common spotted orchid; meadow browns and small coppers climb the sides of hedgerows – hummingbird hawkmoth inspects hybrid petunias – a swarm of hoverflies (*Syrphus ribesii*) on Potentilla fruticosa – flying ants, wingless ones, prowl the streets of Bath – children playing at twilight flit like hawkmoths – common skippers flying in tandem, cutting edges in the wind – the lowest stinging nettle leaves hang like yellow flags – ten cabbage white butterflies nose-down in cow turd.

BRAMBLES

My attention is floating like these clouds, high vaporous clouds in this burning sun. I walk backwards and forwards looking for somewhere to settle, by an ash tree, by a thistle, now firmly on this wooden seat beside a billowing wall of flowering brambles. It is alive with insects, a sky of sharp metallic pitches, sharpening everything that I see. I have no idea where to begin. I follow the movement, the bronzed eyes of copper butterflies searching for something, perhaps each other. The tribal totems of hoverflies elude me but not their flights fascinating with infinite precision, sideways, fast forwards, landing instantly on pollen platforms. Their legs are as fine and springy as the anthers; almost in delight their abdomens quiver like tails. They lick themselves carefully smoothing the probiscus between their forelegs. The tiny black-streamed hoverflies glide in the spaces among the flower buds, each opening a little fist, five fingers of outer sepals clasping the folded pink blossom. I start to see details: solitary petals stuck in spider webs, rufous faceted eyes of flies, limp yellow flags of nettle leaves, the moss of fertilised anthers, collapsed into medusa heads of writhing snakes. The sailing flags of early summer now hang at half mast; rust spots disfigure every bramble leaf; the meadow browns are frayed at the edges; the cleavers droop as they fruit. The flowering brambles must be the high point of summer, nectar for insects, as the ivy is in the autumn. Everything is on the outside; it's almost as if I don't exist. *This profusion is dream-like, a million surfaces yet not one is a mirror. Triangular leaf hoppers crawl purposefully up broken grass stems; they crawl equally purposefully back. The small coppers keep fluttering past the underworld of brittle plant stems, hollow cow parsley...the omnipresent sounds slip in and out as the flies do, rocket trails of grasshoppers, single notes of birds, detached voices, shimmer of ash leaves, a distant beach; the harvestman spider treads quickly, stealthily in the lowest grasses. This world of detail is an ocean. I could disappear without a trace.*

A red-eyed fly leans forwards onto its forelegs, pulling itself up to examine its rear parts. A small copper feeds on a blossom, an autumn leaf made into a work of art with jewel-like precision. The hoverflies are the kites and kestrels here, their targets the newly opened flowers. I have walked past this wayside world all my life. Here, sensing is enough. I am happy and perplexed by this not-knowing. I touch a bramble leaf, prickle my finger against their downhill lancers; this sense along with smell comes last. The interior of this bramble bush is the dark side of the moon; I can hardly penetrate the thornish shadows. A torrent of cow shit splatters the hard ground above me. It's Willow, the grandmother Jersey cow due for the chop in the next few days. This economic end to all her days of giving cattle, milk, cheese, yoghurt is a cruel necessity. I sit back in this chair and gaze at this insect life; not one will escape the frost. This bramble marks the high time of their brief lives. I suddenly notice the invisible mist of spider webs bending, gliding, glistening with each gush of breeze, straddling every flowering branch. They pass out of my sight. My mind is only with what I see at the moment. There is nothing else. I feel strong like an infant; little Aelfrieda, my four-month-old daughter looks at the world this way, total attention with what she sees and touches. The toy falls from her hand, she looks at her knee; turn her over she is happy with the patch of carpet. This quality of attention, its purity, has great integrity. Yet babies are vulnerable and need the shelter of someone more knowing to hold them upright in this world. I am sitting gently with myself, this moment of innocence. The face value of things is enough. (Dunsford Farm, July 25, 1994)

MY GARDEN

Ann Loder was in her eighties in 1990, a small, sprightly woman with very blue eyes set in a face which looked like a paper bag that someone had crumpled before smoothing the edges. I met her through the glowing pink tips of the 'Albertine' rose buds which cover the railings of her town cottage – surreal besides the faceless concrete of high-rise blocks on three sides. Her garden faces north and measures 15 by 12 feet. She talked about her garden in a way that reflected herself: original, unobtrusive, full of details.

'As soon as you get a bit of cold weather the birds go for the berries. That's the birds' hideout there: they get in in the morning and they wait for me to feed them. All sorts... sparrows, starlings, blackbirds, thrushes. I get water wagtails as well from the river, and the blue tits and the green tits – they always come to empty the nuts. Those are the grapes. When it's cold and dry the birds come down for water and moisture so I put out the grapes that have gone off, and they will pick them all off and leave me the stems. They'll leave me the cherry stones and cherry stems, and if I cut an apple in half they'll eat all the apple inside and leave me the skin to pick up. It is unbelievable when you come to see it.

'I can't say I have got a favourite flower. They are all flowers to me and I think as much of one as I do another. I have always been like that. Right from a child I used to go out flowering. I lived in Wiltshire, Corsham and Lacock way. You could pick them in those days; we used to bring home violets, primroses, anemones and celandines and put them in vases. At Easter time when we were children we used to go out on Good Friday with a big clothe's basket lined with moss which we filled with bunches of primroses to decorate the churches.

'Cowslips will grow on a poor soil; they don't need a good soil. We never made wines but our school governess used to make a cowslip ointment which she used on the children when they had chilblains. It must have worked. She used to take us out when it was cowslip time and pick all the petals to make the ointment. I have never heard of it since. In the old days herbs were used a lot for cures. Back in the First World War we used to go out and pick the different herbage like ground ivy, and then it was strung up in bunches to dry before being sent onto the soldiers. They tied them in bunches and hung them on a line to dry naturally, before being boxed.

'I never use sprays. I think too many sprays are used. In older days we used to save the cigarette ends and any tobacco dust and we used to put it in water and spray the roses with that. A lot of sprays are killing off the bees and you want the bees to pollinate the flowers. I don't know why they are using all these sprays I'm sure. What is it? It is money, isn't it, all the time. I had a little bit of fertiliser given me but most of it on that garden is horse manure. I swear by the old fashioned stuff.

'A lot of people come along here and look at the garden because it is unusual. I don't regiment anything. I just put things in as I think, put it in here, stick it in there. I like to see plants growing naturally. That's what I call a cottage garden. If I see anything I like I bring it home and plant it. I don't have fixed plans. That seeded itself, the white alyssum, it was around those tubs. That campanula seeded itself... I have known gardens all my life. It will be a sorry day for me if I wasn't around my flowers, I think.

'I like gardening and I can content myself with it. Now if you get anybody who does gardening and likes it – not people that don't like it, and do it just for the sake of doing it – but if they like it they can lose themselves for hours and hours in a garden. They might not do a lot but they can lose themselves! When I feel I want a bit of fresh air, I come out and pull up a few weeds. I spend more time out here when I change the garden. I don't think I could ever live without flowers. If I didn't have a garden I would have to go out and buy flowers.

'I don't bother about insects. I just let them go on. If they eat one of my primroses I let them eat it. I shan't touch it. The greenfly is everywhere, isn't it? I don't mind a few holes. The birds come here such a lot, they pick up the slugs. They come down here and pick all the flies off the roses. I watch them picking them off. They do the work, I don't... I don't like things looking too tidy. See the winter crocus coming up through mind-your-own-business? It grows like a weed here and yet they charge the earth for it in the shop. That's Queen's Lace, not Lady's Mantle, from the wife of a gardener at Westonbirt.

'I don't cut any of the flowers here, only when they are dead. They last longer outside and I can look out on them. Not only that, it is something for other people to look at. Because there is so much bricks and mortar about and I thinks to myself, ' Well there are a lot of people that admire a few flowers.' There are such a lot of cars here. This could look like a slum if I didn't plant it. I could have a car here. A lot of them, they don't care a hang. They leave all their rubbish about. They get in a car and go for a ride and that's all they think about. When they go into the country, they go along quickly. They don't see anything... Well, my dear, I think I'll have to call it a day.'

(This first appeared in the magazine, *Growth Point*)

HARE IN THE WOOD

A Welsh dancer called Drew said that some friends were driving in one of the huge conifer forests in central Wales, going round and round looking for a way out. They had taken so many lefts and rights that the sudden winter night had overtaken them. They stopped before yet another junction utterly lost. But this one was different. In the headlights sat a hare in the middle of the road. They bleeped their horn. It stared at them and then lolloped off down the left fork. They went that way, too, and were astonished that the hare kept running in front of them. They followed it slowly to another junction where the hare bounded off to the right. They turned left as this road was bigger and looked likely to lead them out of the forest. A mile later the track ended at a locked gate. They returned to the previous junction. To their amazement they saw the hare sitting in the middle of the road. They bleeped their horn again. It bounded off to the right and they had no choice but to follow it. This narrower road led them to an unexpected exit from the forest. (The Unicorn Well-Being Camp, Grimsby, 1991)

VIEW FROM THE HEN HOUSE

A huddle of chok choks – chickens – perch silently on the wooden platform above the makeshift ladder and before the door to their house. One chooks, they all duck twisting necks to peer at the sky, vastly blue and empty. Others tread carefully on the hard, dry ground patterned with scrawny feathers, half white and fluffy, half downy. The worm casts are rock solid. Bumblebees search for nectar in the red clover trampled into a neat arc around the hen houses; they are wooden boxes on wheels with a sloping roof to keep the rain out. If I close my eyes I hear grasses being tweaked, grain being scattered, a sporadic intoning of single notes, and above that a steady strident conversation of hens sounding out this warm summer's day. Other hens hug the shade under the house or stand within its shadow. In fact they are pullets, youngsters without coxcombs, the combed red flag balanced on their head with matching ear flaps.

I wanted to come here and sit with the chickens. Usually I tread down the perimeter electric fence and walk from house to house with my buckets and take eggs from the four narrow laying boxes nailed to the outside. The laying hens look at me as if I am a ghost. My shadow falls upon them, and they may submit fanning their feathers against the ground. I can pick them easily, holding their wings firm under my arm. Only their eyes move, becoming bigger, yellower Now I do none of these things. I sit next to the wooden tripod supporting the water bucket, slung low.

The chickens let the tyres and planks support them, crouching over themselves, one against the other, immobile as melons. They stare beak first at the clover or shutter their eyes with pale lids. They crash motionless out of the sun as if they are debris cast by a high tide. One loner picks its way balanced on ivory trefoil claws; its legs are neatly shaved, snake like with scales. It stretches and cranes its neck to follow a bumblebee. I drop a stone. Most of them look my way, each one a hooked silhouette from beak tip to toe. Their feathers are folded perfectly one across the other. Suddenly half the group dive their heads and scamper into the clover; their tail feathers move like sails above the rosy brown flowers. I feel empty and lethargic as these chickens. The sky is too big, the sun too warm. Other chickens scamper from side to side, heads held high, eyes round and bright with interest; yet once in my shadow they collapse abjectly. When one runs, they all run; when one ducks, they all duck. I am here alone; they are here together. A chasm separates us. We have nothing really to say to each other. It's hard to believe we both started our journey from the same place, out of eggs...

I wish I could say something to these chickens to gladden or intrigue them beyond the cares of gravity drip food. I sing 'Jerusalem' to them. They do not run away. Some chortle, some bury themselves deeper into the burrow of their bodies; one or two step carefully forward, turning their heads warily as if listening.

Now I go into the inner sanctum, the hen house. The mound of pecked straw receives me, the humid cloud of dust, fermenting chicken shit greets me. They drop from their perches, clucking and clanking the feeders as if they are happier doing something. The chickens quiz me with the brown halves of their eyes. Step by step they come closer, craning their heads, listening, standing on one leg ready for a swift retreat. Looking out through the door, the sky is smaller, the world shrunk by the planks into a home; the white lines show the cracks, the cobwebs at every corner. I sing 'Jerusalem' again. As one they stretch their necks and physically ruffle every feather, shaking their heads as if trying to get rid of flies or disbelief. Yes, I am here. I get bored of singing, and so do they. My legs ache. I tire of this cramped perch. I cannot tempt one to come closer. I am a stranger in a strange world. (Dunsford Farm, July 2, 1994)

THE TURKISH FARM

Between Gazipasha and Anamur a pine tree spreads its shade across a road hemmed in by the Taurus peaks and three hundred feet above rocky inlets of fine white sand without footprints. The truck had dropped us there, a Dutchman from Leiden, myself and Carol Berry from Reading. The two Turkish men and their five sons stopped long enough to share a stick of honey, crystallised on the outside yet soft in the middle, a homely metaphor for the Turkish male. The hazy figure of a woman and a boy emerged from the baking wadi. She was unveiled and dressed in traditional shawl and pleated skirt and in her arms carried two water melons. Her son held two buzzing cicadas in the cup of one hand. She fondled the water melons talking loud and fast, stopping only to smile and show her gleaming white teeth or touch her tanned leather face. Her black hair rolled across her back when she gesticulated. She accepted six lira and produced a knife from the fold of her skirt, expertly slicing off the tops then cut the melons into four; she scooped out the red flesh with flicks of her wrist and chopped that neatly into segments. She wobbled back into the heat haze. Not long afterwards another convoy of army lorries passed us, the commandeered coaches packed with soldiers bringing a greyness into that emerald coastline. An army manoeuvre, I thought. The sandy beach beckoned; the path stumbled by spiny scrub and hotplate limestone into the deep shade of a banana plantation. A Turkish youth stepped out in trendy western clothes – he pointed out his sleeve pocket with pride. Would we like to stay at his family farm? Why not?

The dogs barked their welcome, the black-haired goat slanted its eyes. A sister jumped up from the carpet and tied a yellow shawl around her head. The sea below us lapped a shoreline of bananas. Cold water from a metal jug was poured onto our hands and a slice of orange melon given to each of us. A pregnant woman squatted by the fire making unleavened bread, rolling out the dough with a stick and lightly browning both sides on a hot metal pan before flicking it into a bowl. She did this for an hour. Mustapha behaved as if he were the king of the household literally throwing things around, terrorising gnats and playing over and over again his 45rpm Turkish singles. He became a mouse when his elder brothers arrived. Hands were shaken, explanations given, and they laughed when I said my name in Turkish. Mustapha's elder brother, a primary school-teacher at Van, practised English from his school textbook: 'I fell for him at first sight.' We laughed. The old man appeared for the evening meal and sat beside the hurricane lamp gazing at us. His presence commanded everyone. Three of his fingers were missing from the second joint. An accident, I asked. He cut them for 40 lira each. Why? To raise money for his pilgrimage to Mecca.

The men talked, the woman stayed as silent as female cicadas. The old man mocked our politeness. He urged us to scoop from the bowl of macaroni with tomato sauce, take big helpings of squash vegetable stew and tomato salad, or from the bread stacked into a square pyramid in front of us. I told the teacher that his father looked well for his age. On hearing this in Turkish he leaped out of his seat and beat his chest vigorously. Just after sunset the evening onshore breeze sparked up the embers and the daughters chased them around the verandah. As they laughed the pots rattled on the stove. The old man said goodnight and warned us not to sleep on the roof. In mime he rocked himself gently then suddenly lost his balance and pretended to fall. We shook his hands but when it came to Carol's turn he rose up and fanned his fingers mockingly. His family laughed: 'He is a devout Muslim,' the teacher said.

Inside, the carved wooden panelling kept out the heat; in one corner stood the family safe and above that a picture of Mecca and a love token in the shape of an anchor with the portraits of the eldest son and his wife; on the opposite wall a .22 rifle held centre stage. We squatted on colourful mattresses, the women sitting behind us. Did we like cards? They played it with gusto, all howling with laughter at the trump moves. Later they spread two carpets on the verandah and brought in mattresses, pillows and covers. They sat in the chairs around us. They shook their heads. They insisted we sleep in their own beds. I remember twelve faces watching me until I fell asleep.

Their preparations came to nothing; the hot night air, hungry mosquitoes and croaky frogs in the irrigation channels all worked their mischief. Before dawn, I noticed they were busy; the pregnant woman harnessing the donkey, Mustapha pumping up water into a row of jugs. He led us leaping down the terraces, criss-crossing the intricate water channels, side-stepping the trailing melons and touching the deep purple flowers of bananas and their finger-sized fruit. I peeled the brown skins from freshly picked sweet almond kernals. I had never done that before. Breakfast was a tray of tea, pungent goat cheese, pieces of flat bread dipped in strong aromatic honey. The two brothers were pessimistic about hitch-hiking to Anamur. Yok, yok, they nodded gravely, and plodded back along the trail past the blinkered horse trudging round and round to thrash grain from the straw.

The lorry convoys had multiplied in the night, a grim carnival of soldiers, anti-aircraft guns, military jeeps, ambulances, and helicopters menacing the blue sky. Fear and caution swelled in me. A bus took us to Anamur with glimpses of camouflaged troops digging trenches in woods or sitting by the road as if they had nowhere to go. At the pastry shop in Anamur the man's face dripped with beads of sweat. He chewed his cigarette with tension. The Turks are prized soldiers, he told us – the Anatolian climate breeds stubbornness and patience. The Greek he dismissed with an obscene gesture. He spoke fast in Turkish saying everything smiling, Staring straight past me. Kibris Kibris Kibris. Cartoons in his newspaper depicted heroic Turkish. Everyone over the age of seven would fight until the last man. I had no idea there had been a coup in Cyprus, that the Turks were preparing for war... The British he kept in a special category. 'Everywhere they go they leave a disease.' He returned to the bar where he worked as a tout. 'You want good pastries, postcards...' (Goreme, July 20, 1974)

INSPIRATION STATION

Andy Kurl considers his three years' travelling in India an apprenticeship in life skills. Somewhere there he met a maker of model steam boats powered by water and candle-flame. He remembered his childhood dream of working a water mill and he decided on the spot that he would realise it. He had no money. He worked for years (and still does) demonstrating and selling the little steam boats at British fairs and used the ordnance survey maps to track down over 230 derelict mills. A farmer eventually sold him Blennerhesset watermill in Cumbria. On shoe-strings, he is restoring it with his girlfriend Sid. They want to make it into an alternative energy centre. It's almost next door to Sellafield with its new visitors' centre; Andy plugs in his TV on open days to the little windmill. The children are always amazed. He's always disappointed that he can't get them away from the programmes. He's hoping to meet the Duke of Edinburgh or Prince Charles, that they'll be interested in his work. Sid calls the mill an inspiration station for volunteers and visitors, that everyone can make a difference: (July 19, 1995)

TAKSIM BLUES

Instanbul was louder, dirtier, the drivers more reckless, the daily life more strange and bustling than I had imagined. I marvelled at the performance artists in the spice bazaar, the way one old man bagged the onions, threw it over the heads of shoppers to be caught by the cash register man as if it were a bunch of flowers, who then threw it back to the first man (over the heads of the shoppers) who gave it to the customer. In The Pudding Shop, halfway house to India, I met, by chance, Clive Gooden-ough from Reading, and he waxed about the radiant energy in stones and our thumb nails. I sat on the steps of the Galatea Bridge, the floating pontoon across the Bosphorous, and watched the myriad water sellers, beggars, shoe-shine boys, sellers of deep fried mussels, sprat hustlers, grilled sandwich makers and tourists, a gigantic anthill of humanity and there were always more and more until I discovered that if I sat long enough in the same place, they were the same water sellers, the same sprat hustlers coming round and round again.

Instanbul is embarrassing to recall for this reason. My parents had given me the address of an archaeologist who would show me the sights. My mother said that ball-point pens are worth their weight in gold in Turkey and make a good present. The professor lived in Taksim, an upmarket residential area (which should have alerted me), and invited my friend and I to lunch. For two weeks we had hardly changed our clothes, sleeping on trains and in flea pits through Yugoslavia and Bulgaria. First of all we arrived an hour late for lunch, having lost our way in the traffic. A uniformed lift attendant sped us to the right floor. Our elegant hostess opened the door, just far enough to glimpse the long line of immaculately dressed uncles, aunts, cousins, nieces awaiting the English visitors. Several had presents in their hands. My dirty shoes, frayed jacket and worse came sharply into focus. We were introduced one by one. They spoke perfect English. We spoke no Turkish. We were given the seats of honour by the two long tables, end to end, and spread with exotic national dishes. The ordeal had only just begun. For three hours we ploughed through this culinary extravagance, with a choice of wines for every course. I can no longer see their faces but remember their impeccable manners. We said goodbye to each one in turn and, at the door, I handed the professor a cardboard box with five biros. She, with magnificent dignity, accepted them as if they were made of gold. You can't always trust your mother! (Instanbul, 1973)

JOHN BLACKSTOCK – AN ENGLISH FLOWER GARDEN

The English flower garden of Major Blackstock – splashes of double pink poppies, sweet william, mixed pansies, columbines on the hanging slopes of Widcombe – somehow matched the man, restrained yet passionate about his love of nature, a military man with neatness drilled into him yet anarchic in his love of flowing, exuberant colour. He loved his roses to be in a line but everything else could mingle. This neat man, slight with fine bone features edged with laughter lines, was once a gunner in the elite Royal Horse Artillery. He looked at his garden as thoughtfully as he looked at his own life and the world around him, angrily about pollution and concerned with the rights of spiders.

* * * *

'When I came here it was a mess – all concrete and slugs – and I wanted it to look neat and tidy. I am a bit of a perfectionist and that's probably why I have asthma. The Canterbury Bells here are doubles and probably not the originals but aren't they beautiful flowers? They remind me of H.E. Bates in *Uncle Silas*. I got rid of the concrete down to the end and put the right side down to grass. Then I decided to have steps leading down to the lawn, a Georgian sort of thing. We made a border on one side and a smaller one on the north-facing side. Bit by bit it grew. It is not a lawn, it is grass. In my married army days I would get a batman to come along with the regimental mowing machine and keep it low hahahahaha. I sowed the seeds, one for me, one for the birds. To me it is an ordinary garden because I see it every day. I suppose it is an English flower garden, flowers for the English climate. What better flowers are there than cottage garden ones? English roses, delphiniums, Michaelmas daisies. I love roses, I love flower borders. I call that a syringa but the number of people who argue with me and say that is a Philadelphus... Quite a lot of flowers are not bought; they are borrowed, begged or stolen. My wife's friends give her seeds and she will come along, sprinkle them and up they come. These geraniums I got from a National Trust house. I said to the gardener let me have a cutting or two and he did. Deep calling to deep.'

He stands beside 14 pots of cuttings. 'I think gardeners are a little bit kleptomaniacs hahahahah. It is amoral after all, nobody misses it. If one of my roses is growing over a wall and somebody takes a bit, I don't mind a fig. I only do to others what I would do to myself. This is not an arum lily. I have forgotten what it is but isn't that beautiful? I don't know the name of it but does it matter? I am an instinctive sort of gardener but there's nothing wrong with that.

'As a general rule I don't use insecticides. I like to see the ladybirds having a bash. If it's not too bad I leave it or put soapy water on them and that seems to work. I like weeds, too. At the moment I am undecided about rosebay willowherb whether it is a weed or flower. I think it is a flower. I call these Woodbines, probably because I am a snob. I leave the stinging nettles by the 'Albertine' because I want butterflies to come. I don't like butterflies in a case. I like to see them flying. I don't even like killing the cabbage whites so I am not growing cabbages at the moment. I have plenty of peacocks and admirals and I know I have seen a Large Blue – everybody tells me it is extinct. It might be, there again it may have been the only one. There are no blackfly on that rose but a week ago it was packed with greenfly. The badgers were up last night; you can see the holes in the grass. I do the lawn beautifully; it looks perfect. The next morning I go down there and there are at least thirty holes. I fill in every one. If you've got your grass cut short you can see where they put their snouts...

* * * *

'I was a soldier because I was eighteen at the outbreak of war. I am in my sixties now. In that war the whole atmosphere was different. You know we got quite patriotic with the Falklands, well imagine forty years ago when we are not so cynical as we are now – and the kids are very cynical nowadays. I was really fighting for King and Country and we believed this. Now a lot of kids say 'load of rubbish', don't they? I landed on D-Day in Normandy, I fought in Africa in the western deserts and so on and I know that I have brought down fire on German infrantrymen and I probably killed some. It's a ridiculous thing to be proud of now but during the war we prided ourselves that we could bring down fire and destroy anything within a two-mile range. Now this sounds a little dramatic but the older I get the more I regret that sort of thing. I suppose that it comes out that I would not harm anything now. I stopped mowing the other day because there was a damned great black beetle walking in front of the mower, so I had to stop, pick it up and put it to one side. I could never fight in a war again feeling as I do now, but when you are eighteen and your generation is due...

'When I look out of the sitting room window I like to see the grass down there neat and tidy, rather the same with my soldiers they have to form their kits in the right order...it is a facet of my character I suppose. But don't ask me who I am. I don't know. I don't think I was taught that; the Army taught me neatness and tidiness. I threaten the plants sometimes hahahaha. If I like the colour I plant it. I enjoy the garden but I am always surprised

visitors, especially older women, seem to really enjoy it.
As it reminds them of their gardens when they were children. I was brought up on a farm, hayfields, shire horses and so on but there was no time for gardening. See this lily-of-the-valley. I don't know how it got there. I am sure birds do a lot more than we think. I empty my pocket as I go indoors...now look a damned big cucumber hahahahaha.

'Whenever I am asked to do something I like to do it properly. This is another aspect, I suppose, why I developed asthma. I am too intense. When soldiering I used to have the best troop, the best guns and the best of everything you know. Now my garden, even though it is casual, it has to look good. I like my roses in a line but on the other hand I still like my smaller flowers to mingle with each other. I like to have a honeysuckle mixed up with rambling roses. I am not a good gardener. I just like to fill up the spaces and then sit and watch, if you like, the beauty of it. I have cured my asthma. I used to be allergic to roses. The doctor said I shouldn't grow them so I only had eighteen. A lot of people suffer from respiratory conditions because of the modern world. If we were to have every single item that is in the air at the moment, and we had them coloured red for anything that was detrimental to your breathing, and the other stuff green, we would all be walking on stilts to try and get above the red. How can we stop it? We are in this merry-go-round, aren't we?... It's the old story of upsetting the balance of nature. If you spray and kill aphids you kill ladybirds; if you spray aphids again on roses a bee comes along and it kills the bee... This starts with farmers. No matter what they say, hypocritically they are are in it for the money. If he can grow wheat and get a bigger tonnage with spraying, he will spray. If you boil it down it is all greed. You have got to be a very very good human being and not to spray and upset the balance.

* * * *

'All I know is that the older I get the softer I get. I don't like to kill anything, and I mean anything. The other day we spent twenty minutes with a bee which was caught upstairs in a window-pane. I had to go all the way downstairs and get the big stepladder, climb up to it, open the window and try and get the bee out. And then there was the cocoon which mysteriously appeared on the kitchen ceiling and, like a lot of asthmatics, I am a bit of a perfectionist. If I see a white cotton or specks on a carpet I feel I have got to pick up up, or I restrain myself from doing so on purpose to try and beat it. I saw this cocoon and felt – Oh it's on my white ceiling – but I left it there. When the spring came, we we were keeping an eye on it, it came out and stretched its wings, a peacock butterfly. We took it outside and away it flew. That rather pleased me to think that I had left it there. It was the first time I had witnessed it except for on television.

'I am no longer as busy in other things as I used to be... When I was a soldier I was extremely busy and now I have got all day. I have plenty of work, painting and gardening but I have got more time to observe. I knew these things existed before but it didn't concern me. I regret that now to a degree but I still have plenty of time to look. I would not say that I was very hard before but I would not have any compunction about killing flies automatically and spraying cabbages if I was growing them. Now there is so much wrong with the world that I feel, that in my small way, I can stop a part of it from going wrong. I always feel resentful when I drive towards Keynsham and I see those tremendous chimneys of the cement works and they are belching out muck. I feel that it should be stopped, after all we don't need cement. Will the world come to an end if we haven't got cement? There are other ways of making bricks, from clay... I made a mistake when I came here. There was a clematis growing up the front wall, old-fashioned and very pretty flowers. Well, with my mania for neatness and tidiness, I cleared the whole thing out. Then somebody said that it was really beautiful and it must have taken years to grow that size. I regret that immensely...

* * * *

'I seldom draw these curtains. I clean them but not too often for I have moths and everything else coming towards the light and I get in each corner of the windows various spiders. Now is that cruel, the moths come along and the spider catches them. I leave the spiders there for a period but when it gets too much I clean out the lot. Animals only kill something when they want to eat; a lioness may only kill once a day but the rest of the day the zebras will feed within yards of it. And they know it's safe... Maybe it's my own fear of death. Everything has got one thing and that's life. I am completely agnostic. You have got one thing and that is right at this moment that we are talking; we can see, I can look out of the window see churches and trees; it is the one thing that we have got and when that's gone that's the end of living. I think that makes me live more passionately, because this is so temporary. This particular world has been in existence for millions and millions of years, and we are going to be on it for not even a snap of a finger. Why waste it? Why kill other people? They have only got the one thing. Life and this moment. I like reading about the past. I am not too struck on the future; from what I see it is going to be very dismal...

'For myself I would liked to have lived one hundred years ago, providing I was healthy and could have been a farmer. I would like now to have horses in my stable. Can you imagine going round Bath on a horse and shopping? (He gazes out of the window). This is a very pleasant place to live but one third of the world is starving. We can feed the world now because of our distribution; they bring lettuces from Texas. But if we carry on the way we are going the only plants and animals on this planet will be the ones we eat. When I sell this house and have another garden, I will sit down and organise it properly. I reckon that at least one quarter will be at least completely wild. And I shall be interested to see what will happen. There is a buddleia in the front over the garage. That's not mine, I could have cut it down but I let it go and we counted 54 butterflies the other day, one mass of butterflies, meadow browns, painted ladies, peacocks and red admirals and one or two marbled whites. But I didn't see a Large Blue hahahaha.

'I like nature. If I get the time I shall do what I saw a young woman do on the box – I watch all the nature programmes – she used to sit for hours very quietly with food on her outstretched hands and she has the birds so tame they come and settle on her. That to my view is an excellent thing. I have had a robin on my foot. That's as far as I have got. Most animals are frightened of us. A badger, centuries ago, was not a nocturnal beast and surely a fox wasn't nocturnal. I can remember haymaking with horses and carts and I am only sixty. One of the most gentle creatures out is a shire horse, you would never see a vicious one. They are coming back because some farmers are finding them cheaper. What better sight is there than a pair of horses pulling a plough.

I wont see it in my lifetime. I enjoyed soldiering, the pomp and ceremony of it, the comradeship, all the little things which go with a military life. There wasn't much time to think of horses, though I was in a horse regiment, the Royal Horse Artillery. We would consider ourselves as good as any cavalry...

When we go down to Suffolk it is in my mind to have a pony trap. I think now that whenever I start my car I often think, well a bit more pollution. The thought is there. We are now becoming quite vegetarian. I listen to the farming programme in the morning and they say the price of hindquarters is so and so – you know it is a very disgusting thought when you really put it down basically – the hindquarters of some animal has cost so and so and you are going to eat it...it is, it is a wicked world.' (June/August 1982)

DADDY

You came into my dreams last night looking like a sergeant major, bold, imposing and strong, and I was scared of you. I wanted to hide. Then I saw you pale, tired, retiring to your bed, hiding with a blanket over you, and I wanted to step forward and find out how you were. When I woke up, I thought that's how I have lived most of my life, either too big or too small. Then I remembered the dream of you limping along the road, and meeting you sitting by the wayside. You told me that I was such an ordinary child, and you were surprised to see me there. I had to go on. I turned right and left you behind. I woke up crying and with a vivid picture of seeing into your eyes. Then other pictures came, the dream of the baby appearing at the very beginning with a tiny cock; my favourite last time with you, our walk from The Malt Shovel at Upper Lambourn, to the Uffington White Horse. (As I write this an exquisite chalk blue butterfly appears, the one I saw feeding happily on dog turds). Did I disappoint you? Not become the brilliant academic child, a path you bravely walked. You came a long way from the pernicious poverty of old London, using the lifeline of education and your natural industriousness. I don't think you realise the price that you paid to achieve this.

I dreamed that I had emerged after the earth changes, and I met my father-in-law, the Major. He handed me my natural son, and I knew then, without being told, that my legitimate father had been fiddled out of his rightful inheritance. I am attracted by this setting

*the balances straight. It makes my journey appear as part of your
journey. It gives a meaning to this shadow world of wayside
images; the lost pale youth, the invisible insects and childhood,
limping people, tiny omnipotent powers, and all their sins and
glories.*

*I'm sad that I never knew you better, that I didn't hear any stories
about your struggles; that the loyal, hard-working, humane person
that you are, also loved, doubted and dreamed. I heard you cry
once and I thought that the sky had fallen down, or at least
someone had been murdered. The strange thing is that I am closer
to you in my forty second year – over fifteen years since you died –
than I have ever been. Our histories have much in common but I
am not you. If you were still alive, I think you would disapprove
of my erratic life. I am on my own now, breaking new ground for
better or for worse. Going my own way means my life is full of
uncertainty. (Two youths see my writing this as if I belong to
another planet. One had to put me down: 'lying around and doing
nothing all day.') I felt angry and sad that I missed the opportunity
to stand up for myself. I went limp, felt intimidated and said
nothing. This is what I want to change. This journey we are all
making together. (Stowford Mill, July 31, 1992)*

* * * *

. My father loved his books. He collected them through the fifties
and sixties, taking me on his foraging trips into Bristol, Oxford,
Reading and London. He planned to retire to an antiquarian
bookshop. When he died all his books were put into a room and
this doubled as a spare bedroom. Now one night, his grandson,
Peter Beatty, slept there amusing himself with a puzzle where
you shake little metal balls into little holes. He couldn't do it.
That night he dreamed of his grandfather coming into the
room, exactly as he remembered him from photographs, and
walking slowly past the bookshelves. He stopped by Peter's bed.
In the morning Peter woke up and found that the little balls of
his puzzle were in all the little holes. (January 2, 1997)

MULL AND BEN ON A BICYCLE

*He said his name was Richard, a very English name was it not?
He appeared beside me in the clutter and bag ladies at Glasgow
Bus Station during an interminable wait for the night coach,*

taking us away from a tour of Mull and Iona. He looked like a tramp with a funny cotton hat, more like a cap, pulled over his grey hair and almost reaching his beard. His breath smelt of alcohol. But his eyes were clear blue and his smile crossed his face in a wave, creasing his cheeks with an inscrutable contentment. I can't remember much of what he said, a lot about the lunatics in city centres; one had hit him without provocation five times in the face. His philosophy mixed easily with a strangely soft Glaswegian accent: it's good to mix; each to his own; Scottish first, British second, all interesting but none of it remarkable. I noticed his clothes were clean and he did not smell. He asked me to guess his work: a bartender, a singer, a tailor, a priest. He shook his head each time, obviously pleased. 'But it passes the time, does it not?'. Then, out of the blue, he asked: 'What does Viking mean?... Fearless,' he answered, 'you'll remember that.' Of course I did, and I wondered how he had fathomed my interest. We talked for an hour on this and that, and I never saw him go. He vanished when I went to get some coffee. Absurdly, I am left with the picture of the broonie, the bearded old man in Scottish traveller tales who appears and vanishes unnoticed, returns good deeds for courtesy, punishes wrongdoings; part-priest, part myth, part tramp, part nobody.

Fearless is a word I think of a lot with Ben, my eldest son. We cycled around Mull together, within sight of the sea and the islands of Ulva, Iona, Staffa; winding below the cliffs by Ben More, up and down roads graded for horse and cart, sometimes singing my heart out with contentment. Shoulder to shoulder we cycled together, with few words but they were usually enough, letting silence and the girt green hills we passed do most of the talking... Viking is a word which has changed its meaning, speaking more about fearlessness, adventuring with integrity, making detours. I wish this for myself, especially for Ben crossing this threshold of boy to young man. The bond between father and son is precious but it is a bond that needs to be cut to free us both. I am very conscious that Ben is steering his way out of my life. And yet this crossing over, Ben looking for more self reliance, more authority, mirrors the qualities that I need at forty four. I could never tell Ben this, for it would need too many words to express; by example now, not more words and lectures, but the embodiment, the action in the world. Ben would not be interested in this abstract talk; the bicycle journey is everything. I sense that we limit each other when we are

together, and it is special at the same time. I am always Ben's dad,
and he's always my son. I am always taking responsibility and
Ben witnesses this, closely. This can be instructive – sleeping at the
Bay-at-the-Back-of-the-Ocean on Iona, his fears danced before my
eyes. Does the tide reach here? What about the animals? Who'se
that person? He learnt that he did not need to be bullied by them.
He discovered that a sleeping bag is essential inside a silage bag!
With Ben, I feel older, much older, and this I do not like. Curi-
ously, I am more myself when I am not with my children. Perhaps
I'm running out of things to say. I can see the two figures, gliding,
singing to the long white sands of Calgary Bay, up the straining
hill road beyond Dervaig. The bicycle imprints these memories. I'm
glad I've introduced Iona to Ben. In this I feel I have fulfilled a
yearning to share some of my own secret life with my children. I
showed Ben the small tombstone of Michael Forsyth, my first
gardening teacher. We collected citrine and carnelian from the Bay
of the Coracle, and hid while the wind raced rain over the top of
the sheltering stones. It did not matter that we got soaked, the
stones were safely in our pockets. Now Ben is part of Iona. This
ink has scratched this page and I say goodbye to this bicycle tour. I
say goodbye to the boy Ben. I will not meet him this way again.
For Richard, the wino̅ broonie of Glasgow, I will burn some sage.
(July 13, 1994)

JURASSIC STONE (IV) – IVOR RUDKIN

He worked the adjoining allotment at the bottom of Victoria
Park, Bath; a kindly old man, silver haired and sturdy, still with
blue eyes and a skin soft as his voice. I can picture him pulling
out a dock root and suddenly falling backwards and lying there
laughing on his back. He must have been in his mid-seventies. A
passionate gardener – he used to place potatoes one hundred feet
below ground and notice how the roots and shoots always went
in the right directions whichever way he turned them – he died
not long after I recorded these words, a way of life that is
scarcely believable.

'My name is Ivor Rudkin and I started in the quarry near
enough when I was 17. A bloke asked me if I wanted to work at
the face, the money was a lot better and so I went. It was
actually a stone mine; you go down a shaft about one hundred
feet below ground, and at the time I was working the face was

about a mile from the shaft. It was a sloping shaft. I always remember the old horse boxes had larger wheels at the back and smaller wheels at the front so the horse was more or less on the same level. What's strange about the stone is that it seems it was placed there underground for man to come along and quarry it. There is one bed, which was the ceiling that you worked in under, had the cracks – we used to call them cricks – running the opposite way to the rest of the beds of stone. You couldn't go in under any of the other stone beds, they would just naturally fall down because the joints were so wide and going the wrong way. But the ceiling beds had the cricks running just the right way so they keyed themselves if the ceiling tended to get weak or hollow or anything. It was uncanny when you think of it.

'The workings in the quarry were ten to fifteen feet deep and twenty feet across, wide enough for a crane or picks to swing in. Putting up a crane was quite a complicated job, yet these chaps had it off to a fine art. They never made the slightest mistake. They had no levels, no plumb lines, absolutely nothing but their eyes; and then you realise that they worked in the poorest light that you can imagine. You don't know what darkness is until you are underground. You can put your finger up to your eye and you can't see it. The first job of the day was to fill your lamps. When I started in the quarry the only light which was used was an old treacle tin in which you punched a hole in the lid, put a cycle tube valve in this hole and put a little bit of wick, one end in the tin which you filled with benzolene. That was your light, everyone carried one of these and there were always a few gallons of benz hanging around...

'In the quarry it was all piece work. These men pecked out the jad – that was the first bed cut, a narrow opening under the ceiling. It would take weeks to cut one jad out; it would be about fifteen or eighteen feet long and five feet deep and to see these men swinging these pecks was a real work of art. How they got to that pitch I'll never know. They were as expert with their pecks as blokes were with their stockwhips. As they swung these pecks into the narrow gap they turned the peck down for the first blow, up for the second blow and then they would hit one in the middle and that would bring a lump of stone out. They could more less pitch it where they wanted to by just a twist of their wrist. It wasn't something you could teach anybody. One amusing team, two brothers, were ideal for the job pecking. One was left-handed and the other was right-handed. The first knowledge I had of these two blokes was a series of two grunts Uh Ah Uh Ah. They both had separate grunts. They worked in tandem, as one bloke was swinging his peck in the other bloke was clear, and he knew that by the grunt. Otherwise it could be dangerous. They never missed.

'You could see the stone beds quite plainly marked. The beds were true and level. Perfect. (Though some beds could be like the waves of the sea) The sawyers put in wedges and steel chips and the method of driving them in was something they had learnt over the years. They never hit the wedge with a series of fast blows. It was always slow blows. They hit a blow, then wait, hit another, then wait, and the idea was that the slower the blow the more likely it would tear back to where they wanted it... The saws they used varied from five foot, the shortest, to eight foot. The boss always pitched the saw where he wanted and then he'd pass it onto the sawyer and say there your are, that's your work for today... He would be in there sawing all day just to cut one cut. They would cut a wedge piece out, three feet at the front tapering to two feet at the back on the first bed. People that came from outside to see and to try discovered that there was a knack in it, that they could push the saw in and out about twice and then they would stop. It was just a question of a lift at the right place. The method used was to have a little tin with a hole punched in the bottom with a matchstick in that. This was placed in a strategic position in the saw cut so the saw dust came out as slurry; you were pitching into dead rock at the face and the saw would pull the slurry out as you worked it.

'To go down into solid rock is worse than cutting it on the face. You would pitch a saw and it was a question of having the craft to know when you got to the bottom of a bed. Only a real expert could feel it...he would pull the saw up and down all day long with two hands on the single stick. You would keep on pushing this saw down and eventually you bring it back until it was nearly upright and then you would put a wedge at the back and then you would pull it up and down upright. That would take you two days to cut one cut of six feet, then another two days on the other side – it would take eight days to get one stone out, say about five tons. You would put the lewis in then, drive wedges down the sides and tear it off the bed. Sometimes you had gone through the bed and then you were cutting something for nothing.

'...Then there was the gaffer, he was more or less the bloke in charge. He employed me as a sawyer and chopper. Part of the chopper's duties was to put the lewis in to move the stone. These are three pins in a dove shape, the two outer ones are splayed at the foot and the middle one moved down and drives the outer two out to form a dovetail in the stone. For a big lewis you can lift five or six tons. After you pulled a stone out with a crane, your first job was to tap it with a pebble which denoted whether there were any cracks. Some of these cracks were so devilish they could not be seen with the naked eye; all you knew is that when you tapped it it sounded like a cracked cup. These fellahs would tap it and listen, tap it and listen until they found out near enough where the crack was and they would trace over the top with a peck and eventually you would see one piece break away and you would know that was the crack. Then you would have to trace the crack from one side of the stone to the other and then cut down through... But the first thing you did when you pulled the stone out was to mark it with a little scriber. You scribed the stone from bed to bed, because in Bath stone it is essential that you don't get any stone going in face-bedded for frost destroys it easily. During the summer months the stone was brought straight up to the top and stacked and that would weather and be sufficiently seasoned. It is similar to the seasoning of timber. If you brought it up in the winter months it would just crack. There was another underground dumping place for winter stone and then it would be hauled to the surface the following spring.

'The stone was remarkably healthy. You could have cuts and really deep wounds and you recovered quite quickly. They never turned poisonous. You could get a nasty cut from an axe, especially swinging it into calcite: you couldn't see it from the clay. The common remedy was to get the slurry out of the saw cut, a wet poultice, and dab it on. It was beneficial like spider's cobwebs. You healed very quickly. It was a hard life but more or less you accepted it in those days. Everything was hard. People talk of the good old days but they only remember some of the good times. Basically they were slogging days. The majority of blokes when they got outside and saw how easy it was to earn a living never went back. You would need wild horses to drag most of them back. The chap who came from *The Times* said he had never seen anything quite so outlandish, so prehistoric...he said it was the nearest thing he had seen to slavery. He tried it. He said to lift the axe to chop the stone was a feat in itself. In the winter months you go down about 7am just as the sun is rising and come up about 4.30 just as the sun is setting. More or less it was like a prison sentence to anyone who liked living. You wouldn't see the daylight from one end of the week to the next. It made you appreciate nature. You realised what you were missing. There were no unions in those days; if you didn't like it, pack it in. You either sweated or got cold. You stripped to the waist. You might have a muffler around your neck and the common dress was yorks around your knees, a leather strap more or less to keep your trousers out of the slurry. You had one half an hour break. You never took any hot drinks, it was always cold tea. No milk, just strong tea and sugar. By the time you had finished you were so cold you had to start working again. Actually it was fairly warm down there but after sweating and sitting down you began to get the shivers. We were plagued with rats; there were dry pegs into wall, usually pillars, to hang the food satchels.

'In those days you were only interested in the money. You realised afterwards that you could have found out more about things but you didn't, you just let it slip. If you did have the time you were too tired. They just carved the stone out but knew very little about it. Nobody ever talked about such things: you talked about women, football... They didn't even know that it was a sea-bed. It seems a long long way away now. You know, I am not one of those blokes where it all seems as if it was yesterday. You don't think that you have ever been through such times. It happened to somebody else. But it did. When I started working for the railway I had to cut my pace down to about a half not to make a bad name for myself. I feel a bit like a coelacanth now. I really feel ancient sometimes...you do, you do. You were all in the same boat; if you do something for them they would do something for you. I can't describe it. It was a feeling.' (Bath. 1986)

LEG OF NEW ZEALAND LAMB

In 1979, a New Zealand couple, Keith and Anne, shared my house in Fyfield, Oxfordshire. They worked in mental health community care with a premium on telling the truth. One evening Anne prepared a leg of lamb for the oven; she cut off the knuckle and put it to one side in the tray. Why did you do that, I asked? There was plenty of room for the knuckle without cutting it off. She looked puzzled, then laughed. My mother always does that, she said. She cuts the knuckle first and puts it to one side. A week later she wrote to her mother in New Zealand and mentioned the incident. Two weeks later her mother wrote back and said that she herself always cut the knuckle off the leg of lamb before putting it into the oven. A month passed and Anne received another letter from New Zealand, again from her mother. She had spoken to Anne's grandmother, now living in a nursing home. The grandmother said that she cut the knuckle off the leg of lamb and put it to one side in the tray. She had done this all her life. She had been one of the pioneers of New Zealand and lived, in those far off days, in a timber shack. Their oven then was an old biscuit tin and the only way they could cook their leg of lamb was to cut off the knuckle so that it would fit inside.(Fyfield, Oxfordshire, 1980)

RARATONGA BAY

I met Colin Hansen when he was in his seventies, suffering from rheumatism and living in Bath. His garden exuded luxuriance, an almost tropical feeling of everything supporting each other. I followed this tall, dignified, slightly stooping man along the path while he named even the smallest plants. At every change of level he had placed two or three rocks and planted foxgloves with different types of ferns... I commented on this, and at first he looked puzzled and then said that he liked that combination, those plants with rocks made him feel at home. He had created that feature in many of his gardens. Then his mouth drooped and he exclaimed: 'Of course. That's where it was.' He described with much feeling and waving of hands how as a boy in New Zealand he had once stumbled into Raratonga Bay, an elemental Eden. 'We had walked round the coast and risked getting caught

237

by the tide. We were just kids, and suddenly there it was, an outcropping of limestone almost like altars, and on every ledge were ferns and huge foxgloves. It was so beautiful...' (1984)

AUGUST CHANGES

Bottom-line days. Plants stop growing and everything hangs in the balance. The first taste of chaos – June's perfection comes apart at the seams – hornets (*Vespa crabro*) sip sap from oak wound and hunt flies on window by night – rich yellow browns of ploughman's spikenard grow with vervain and weld on old railway track – thousands of picture-wing flies mass on creeping field thistle – new bright ladybirds – ivy flower buds emerging – wayside grasses gold on top, flushed green at base – pale new growths of oak lammas leaves – pappus snow of rosebay willowherb and thistledown – daddy-longlegs appear with first musty smell of Autumn – the seed heads of *Centaurea nigra* are night stars on the ground – wasps, wasps everywhere – *Deschampsia caespitosa* arches its elegant flowers on woodland paths – twirling silver heads of whirligig beetles on water, slinking shadows of wolf spiders on land – early autumn signs: black rooks scavenging gleaming wheat stubble; first beech leaves in wind; leaning hemlock skeletons; strawy grass heads; rusty dock spikes; berrying reds of elder with yellow glittering leaves – cinnabar moth caterpillars on ragwort (*Senecio jacobaea*) – trails of harvested grain on roads.

AUGUST CHAOS

Reluctantly I take up this pen preferring not to venture into this quagmire of unrest and dissatisfaction. The grey-bellied clouds are reefs in the sky with tiny holes of blue; some clouds are lined with sunlight. I have nothing to say and no way of saying it. I am losing touch with what's happening. Everything is outside: the children are laughing in the next cottage, the grasshoppers chirp in the kaffir's lily, the pigeons hum their woody omens of contentment, the magpies shake their rattle bags, while all around are fleeting notes of small birds. The dews come with the end of August making it cold and damp underfoot first thing in the morning. I am in the dock for mixing my drinks. This 'sick' is an appropriate exclamation mark for August, a month of coming and going, a month of coming apart at the seams. I am fighting August, wanting to sharpen my boundaries and senses when the world outside is slowly dis-integrating; it's a month of dis-ease, the bogeys come rising to the surface. The sadness comes too, the melancholy, the tattered perfection of a holly-blue butterfly. I look carefully at the fine white outlines broken along the edges. Is it time to let go into something new? I don't know. I judge myself too harshly.

This is not a time for decisions. I will try finding my enjoyment for the next hour and report back: I enjoyed singing the doo wah doos of Buddy Holly and the Everley Brothers. I enjoyed my little man buffoon and his outrageous sexual fantasies with donkers as big as drainpipes and accommodating maidens on silky pillows. Impotigo is my jester's name. He certainly knows how to enjoy himself. When I keep my boundaries I keep in touch with people. I heal myself. Giving criticism, giving anger is a way of sharing. My clenched jaws is a way of withdrawing and rubbishing my feelings of shyness, sadness or resentment; then I become a titchy sharp-toothed rodent, critical and agitated.

August is a month of dirty dogs. The perfection cultivated since spring hangs, nods, leans, is rusted along the edges, yet I'm struck, too, by the beauty at every stage of this process. I find on the wayside the shining silver crowns of Centaurea nigra where the seeds once lodged. They are scattered on the ground. When the seeds are ripe, the old growth collapses. I need to remember that.
(Upton Cheney /Bath /Dinas, August 1991)

THE PRICKLY BUSH

Flash summer rains, great slate blue clouds, Cley Hill an island of sunlight, water sparkling all the edges, drama in the air – these are aspects of this August day. Drama and chaos and change at the price of breaking my heart. The words will not do justice to the honesty, thorn-daggered resentment and confrontation between me and my lover. The long road of half-truths, half-partings concealing neediness, in love, love, had its spell broken this past week. I have always been tormented by the terrible confusion of being loved and loving you, and the knowledge that our love never seemed practical. In some ways (though you were many other things) you were an older sister to me, beloved protector of my childhood, helping me across the initiation into the world, my first day at primary school. 'Oh Anne, never leave me.' I can still feel my clinging and despair now, and the safety I felt holding your hand. And that moment when you came back – after you had left – and said it would not have worked. Did that moment end the spell, the prickly bush of

239

need and despair and longing for four years? Sometimes I felt that the more I opened my heart to you the more sorrow I found, and the more I needed your love to cure this pain. This gave you the upper hand. I never had the strength to let you go. I always wanted to go back to you and escape. It would never have worked. My adult honours this, my child cries for I feel I have betrayed you, broken a love bond, torn myself away dripping with blood; at last we are separate. After I watched you walk away I cried in the high, whining voice of a four-year-old. Saying goodbye is a messy business. How did I get caught in that prickly bush? By omitting to share my struggle, my neediness, using silence and half-truths to seduce you, by my fear of emotional boundaries. Betrayal appears to be the force which breaks clinging on, the wind which scatters the grey, clanking clouds.

'And it's Oh! the Prickily bush/ It grieves my heart full sore And if ever I get away from that bush/ I'll never get caught anymore.' (August 26, 1992)

LOVERS (IN CHANGING TIMES)

Sometimes I notice a strange flower and in that moment my eyes are no longer mine but they are big, brown and intelligent, the eyes of my flower mentor lady. I see the flower because of her eyes; they illuminate mine. I remember your gift of love. It is there always, this giving. Then there are her questioning eyes, the search for freedom, bringing something new into this world. You were the first teacher in my life. Without your eyes what would I see? In that mess did we liberate each other? There is this giving and receiving, the pain of letting go, loss in full measure and betrayal, too. Ruthless teachers! Your playful eyes played with the catholic fetters of sexual guilt; your sensuous hands pulled me out of the abyss, touched me, reclaimed my body when I felt untouchable. You saved my life. I loved you. Did this contact open the aperture of broken hearts? I think so. But not in the way you wanted. Only pain and anger came out in the end. I discovered my cowardly charm, my avoidance of boundaries. I am not proud of that. I discovered the cutting edge between friendship and sex. I want to forgive myself for this mess, the pain that I inflicted, the pain I suffered. Is love to be measured by time? A good relationship lasts forever? Lovers are not bought or kept in cages, or to fill some personal emptiness. For what? I learnt to show my joy and pain, for by these signs is known a path of love. (1995)

JOHN DOWNIE

This is an effort getting up from the seat, willing myself to launch across another unknown page. The fear of failing holds me back, the challenge of being myself upsets this inertia. I stop by the Malus 'John Downie,' a cultivated crab apple. I am intrigued on different levels; the simplicity of this small, two-year-old tree, the brightly coloured fruits already ripened and lying on the drab brown earth; 'John Downie' as a dream metaphor for the Avalonian crab apple, half-sweet and half-bitter, beckoning me to travel down a road peculiar to the spirit in me... It must be one of the earliest crabs to ripen; at the beginning of August I tasted its opaque and translucent flesh, instantly returning me to thoughts of well-made cider with incisive gravel undertows. I like the way this tree grows, the leader bends with the weight of fruit, releasing shoots lower down to multiply at the crown, and, in their turn, to fruit, bend and release more tip seekers and so, by degrees, create that characteristic rounded dome shape. 'Beauty of Bath' is similar, ripening at the same early season, with smooth dark green leaves and luscious fruitfulness... Abundance in a word and in this lifetime. The fruits are like the sun, solar berries, yellow core flushing orange and vivid reds. The skins are firm and waxy, the dark green leaves cool and contain the fruits hanging close to the stem, usually in bunches of three. The bark, I notice, is dull and smooth with many light brown horizontal lines... As a boy I collected bags of fruit from a 'John Downie' next to The Old Leathern Bottle at Barkham; my mother made them into jelly, still one of my favourites. I love these bright, joyful colours of fruit against the dry, drained clumps of soil...the bird of paradise on a donkey's back. 'John Downie' is native way, sharp and sweet and fruitful; a cultivated way, the solar king returned to earth. (Upton Cheney, August 28, 1990)

BIRKENAU KID

I wanted to write about the piglets. Each morning I bring my infant daughter and we sit next to the bars of their pen, sit saying nothing and content to absorb the spectacle of a dozen piglets nosing the straw litter. Their flat, delicate snouts sensitive to soap on my finger happily dip into their own turds mixed with veggie

241

debris from the farmhouse. I wanted to write about this devouring I see, their sweet pink flesh, the huddle of little bodies, one body; it is foolish to separate them. Yet on my way to their stone byre I thought of the Birkenau kid, a haunting image from television last winter; a survivor from that Nazi concentration camp. Beside the skeletons propped on feet beside him, I saw an unbelievable expression of gratitude lighten that youth's face; he gazed into the camera, into my heart and is still here now. At the time I howled. I don't know why. I bring him here beside the contented breath of the old sow; she lies on her bed of shitty straw resigned to the probings of her fattest piglet. The word acceptance comes straightaway. She accepts everything and grows plump and pink and healthy. Her rows of tits suckle her infants, another Artemis, another goddess; fecundity from the lowliest place. Her piglets are marbles in a bowl, a pink satellite separate yet close to the mother. Elfie my daughter sits motionless on my knee intent with curiosity. It touches me this deep acceptance. The weight of the sow's body oozes up water from the litter. I notice that her cunt and arsehole are side by side making a wrinkled face when relaxed. I think of the German volunteers at the farm, young people two generations away from the Holocaust, and how last winter, the 50th anniversary of the liberation of the death camps, I sometimes felt that subterranean tide of grief. From nowhere it ebbed and flowed over me, and I could not comprehend it. The abiding image is this Birkenau kid and the beatitude of total acceptance. A victory, of a kind.

The sunlight fixes the pixie translucent ears and the snowy hairs gliding down their long backs. When one sleeps they all sleep; when one suckles they all suckle, nosing up and down on the same beat. They are free to step through the metal bars and roam the farmyard and hedgerows. They are sly with their eyes and always thinking with their turnaround ears. They make me laugh. Some will clear out old crops, a few sows will breed, and there is only one stud boar. The others are destined to be fattened in the pens and to be called porkers and good bacon pigs. Almost at once a squeal is magnified into a chorus which sails over a baseline of honoured grunts. The old sow descends to earth in slow motion and the piglets reassemble into a necklace around her, in to a pink crescent moon. A chicken and wasp seize this moment to prowl the corners of the byre.

I've never been able to talk to the German volunteers about this history. The subject is a chasm. Yet that tide that touches me must *touch us all. Perhaps there are no more words to talk about it. It is trivialised away. (We don't talk about that at the table,' said one of the English girls laughing.) I deliberately gaze into the face of the Birkenau kid, and each time, perversely, I remember a spirit of beauty, of creation at work in me. I cannot understand how they can be so close together... Gradually, the Birkenau kid changed. He fleshed out and instead of the cotton slip he wore baggy trousers and a tee-shirt. I imagined that he had been allowed to live as they had needed someone to pull out the bodies from the gas ovens. They are said to have made a pyramid as they climbed on top of each other to reach a ventilation shaft in the ceiling. He had wanted to live in spite of this betrayal. He held onto this dream. The baseball cap just appeared but it suited him along with the wry smile. I made him part of my family; just like the pig posse asleep now, every part is touching another. The crafty hen spirals her neck and listens. Elfie still sits motionless on my knees. Sometimes I carry her on my shoulders, holding both her hands so that they make another pair of eyes. With her big eyes I am on the spot. The Birkenau kid carried his hope through that nightmare. I want to carry my dream out into the world.* (Dunsford Farm, 1995)

600,000 CLUB

I signed in at the youth hostel. 'Come far?' asks the warden. 'Around Britain,' I say proudly. '2,250 miles.' The warden scratches his chin. 'We had a chap sign in three days ago...must have been in his eighties. Number six in the 600,000 club. Said he had logged up three quarters of a million miles in his life.' (Monmouth, June 25, 1995)

THE END

Also available:

THE LITTLE BIG STEP   (AWAY)

'Can damaged plants grow? Well, can they?'
Down in the garden all is not roses. The children start off with
their own gardens, but soon jealousies, strange friendships and
gang rivalries rub raw their past lives, exposing the rifts between
them. This bleak and poetic novel gets under the skin of
damaged children – a flawed mirror for our adult selves – and
allows the flowers to grow in the cracks. The drama unfolds
relentlessly to its midsummer nemesis.
Essential reading for learning from nature.
Illustrated by Val George.

£4.99   150 pages   ISBN 0 9530330 0 7

THE CHRONICLES OF THE WHITE HORSE   (FINDHORN)

The extraordinary mole sleuth of the underworld takes on a new
apprentice – and more than he bargained for – in this British
mystery thriller. For children of all ages.
Shortlisted for *The Guardian*'s Commonwealth Literature Award for
children. 'An unusual, attractive and original talent.' (Guardian)
Illustrated by Caroline Waterlow.

£4.99   155 pages   ISBN 0 905249 57 7

CHILDREN'S GARDENING   (HORTICULTURAL THERAPY)

A month-by-month practical guide exploring the educational and
therapeutic potential of gardening. Designed for children and their
helpers, it's bursting with fool-proof ideas, insight commentaries and
is humorously illustrated by Val George. Ring binder and laminated
covers for durability. 2nd edition.

£4.99   ISBN 0 9521074 0 6

Order direct from Away Publications, P.O. Box 2173, Bath BA2
3YN. (Orders over £15 post free. Otherwise add 55p [per volume]
inland / £1 Europe / £1.50 elsewhere.)

A W A Y
publications